SOCIAL
WORK
PRACTICE
for
SOCIAL
JUSTICE

SOCIAL WORK PRACTICE *for* SOCIAL JUSTICE

From Cultural Competence to Anti-Oppression

A Guide for Students

Second Edition

Betty Garcia   Dorothy Van Soest

Alexandria, Virginia

Library of Congress Control Number: 2021946178

ISBNs: 978-0-87293-210-4 (paperback); 978-0-87293-212-8 (Kindle); 978-0-87293-211-1 (ePub)

Printed in the United States of America on acid-free paper that meets the American National Standards Institute Z39-48 standard.

CSWE Press
1701 Duke Street, Suite 200
Alexandria, VA 22314-3457
www.cswe.org

September 2023 Printing

CLASSROOM EXERCISES

Contents

ASSIGNMENT EXERCISES

FIGURES

CHARTS

TABLE

PART I

Foundation and Conceptual Framework

CHAPTER 1

An Introduction

Diversity and social justice have been established as defining issues for the social work profession. According to the National Association of Social Workers (2017), promoting social justice is an essential goal of practice, especially with regard to those who are oppressed. According to the Council on Social Work Education (2015), social workers must learn how diversity and difference shape the human experience and how to advance human rights and social, economic, and environmental justice for every person regardless of identity.

Despite agreement that social justice is a core value, ethical principle, and goal, agreement on a definition of social justice is a challenge that has not been achieved or resolved in the profession. Our goal in writing this book is to clarify substantive elements of what social justice and oppression mean. We hope to make socially just and culturally competent practice more concrete, possible, and relevant across all concentrations and practice areas. As pioneer social work educator Helen Harris Perlman (1976) said, "a value such as social justice has small worth except as it is moved, or is moveable, from believing to doing, from verbal affirmation into action" (p. 381).

What Is This Book About?

This book is based on the definition of culturally competent social work practice as engagement in effective interventions that are grounded in a commitment to promote social and economic justice with diverse clients.

In other words, cultural diversity and social justice are inextricably linked—one cannot be practiced in isolation from the other. In unison, they embody a core social work value, which, in practice has the ultimate goal of transforming "unjust and oppressive social, economic, and political institutions into just and non-oppressive alternatives" (Gil, 1998, p. 1).

Developing cultural competence is a daunting task and must be considered a lifelong journey. The many definitions of cultural competence include sensitivity, self-awareness, knowledge of culturally diverse groups, awareness of within-group differences, and specific clinical skills that include helping responses such as therapeutic alliances and interventions at different levels of practice (Sue & Sue, 2013). Essential to all avenues to cultural competence is cultural humility—a practice that includes acknowledgment of not knowing, self-awareness, openness to learning about diverse cultures, a willingness to learn from mistakes while developing skills in working with others whose culture is different from your own, and so forth.

In this book we move from cultural competence to anti-oppression social work practice. Our main premise is that cultural competence, in addition to understanding and effective interaction with people across cultures, requires an understanding of how difference and labeling people as the "other" is used to reproduce structural inequities. Although the terms *anti-oppressive practice* and *anti-oppression practice* are used often interchangeably, we favor anti-oppression because it signifies that the work we do to change systems and the world is inextricably connected with the work we do to change ourselves. In other words, dismantling oppression is bigger than a practice; it is not a status but an ongoing, never-ending personal process of learning, changing, and growing. Anti-oppression practice requires learning about and comprehending what oppression is and how it works, as well as its patterns, dynamics, and consequences. This involves learning about how oppressive systems discriminate and harm targeted groups based on their social identities and what oppression looks like at all levels of intervention, in all practice arenas, and in one's own life.

The scope of this book does not include social work practice interventions and skills or learning about diverse cultures per se. It is not a social justice practice text. Rather, it is intended to serve as a supplement to such texts as assigned in practice courses or diversity/oppression courses. Here, we focus on identifying and understanding the ways in which diverse groups are oppressed and the crucial role of social workers in overcoming structural inequity based on diversity. Under the umbrella of diversity, we include all groups that are targeted by oppressive systems, all those who are regarded as "other" or different from the "norm"—including Black, Indigenous, Latinx, other people of color, female, people with disabilities, noncisgendered, nonheterosexual, non-English-speaking or U.S. born, and non-Christian. The focus of this book is on the dynamics of denial of and exclusion from power and advantage.

The language we use either invites in or excludes people from conversations. It either confers or withholds power and advantage in community participation. Thus, in this text, we opt to use the term *Latinx* with an understanding that it is currently controversial and there is active discussion about the inception of this term. We do so with a commitment to be inclusive, to affirm all voices, and to support movement of those on the margins to the center. Although this choice of term does not reflect our individual preferences, it is based on the rationale articulated by Kivel. In addition, we opt to capitalize *Black* and use lowercase *white*, in line with the current racism literature. The choice is based on our view that capitalizing *white* represents a political statement regarding dominance.

> I strive for respectful and inclusive language. That's why I use the gender inclusive third-person pronoun "they" instead of "he" or "she." It is also why I use the term Latinx, an alternative to Latino, Latina, and Latin@. Used by scholars, activists, and an increasing number of journalists, Latinx aims to move beyond gender binaries and is inclusive of the intersecting identities of Latin American descendants. (Kivel, 2017, p. xxx)

Based on the same rationale, we use the terms *Black* and *African American* interchangeably and capitalize *Black* as a way to confer respect and power to people with a shared political identity, shaped by colonialism and slavery. It is important to understand that language matters and the debate over racial vocabulary is evolving amid a growing recognition across society of the need to tackle racism in all its manifestations.

To move from cultural competence to anti-oppression practice requires an understanding of the role of power, privilege, and advantage in the way society is structured. In this book we intentionally begin with centering on racism as the core system of oppression for several reasons. The United States was founded as a nation with a deep-seated belief in white supremacy that is woven into the very fabric of American culture, society, and laws. White supremacy has proven itself to be intractable over and over again, both historically and in the present. Racism, therefore, provides the framework for understanding and working toward the elimination of other systems of oppression such as sexism, heterosexism, cisgenderism, ableism, classism, ageism, anti-Semitism, and anti-Islamism.

This book will challenge you to have conversations about cultural diversity and social and economic justice that can sometimes be quite difficult. However, based on our experience, we believe that your thinking will be stimulated and that you will be rewarded with significant insights about our institutions and the world in which we live. You will gain skills that you can bring into your practice. Our goal is to support you in your journey from cultural competence to anti-oppression practice, and we believe that self-reflection, self-awareness, and sharing with others can make your learning not only meaningful but also transformative.

Who Are We?

While the skills of self-reflection and self-awareness are important in social work education in general, they are particularly critical in the process of moving from cultural competence to anti-oppression practice for social justice. Many of the exercises in this book are aimed at eliciting personal reflections and thought-provoking examinations about who you are; your unique, diverse self with all of your identities and your positionality in relation to privilege and systems of oppression; and the implicit, subjective attitudes and biases that you have inherited. We find that, just as self-reflection is essential, so too is sharing with others what you learn about yourself. As partners with you on this lifelong journey, we share here a bit about ourselves.

Betty Garcia. I am a second-generation Latinx/Mexican American/ mestiza, with an Indigenous maternal grandmother and family phenotype that reflects the broad range of mestizo presentations and Euro origins. I grew up in an atmosphere where much attention was paid to the range and valuation of skin colors. My maternal and paternal family origins are from a part of Mexico that is known historically for its white settlers. I grew up in the east part of Los Angeles County; my father grew up as a migrant farm worker and didn't complete junior high school; and my mother didn't finish high school. My father's employment as a union steel worker secured a steady income and health services; my mother began working before I was 5 years old and worked until her health made it impossible for her to continue. My neighborhood was multicultural (i.e., Mexican American and white), low income, and middle class; my father commuted to work for decades with an African American co-worker whose daughter was my classmate. We were raised to "be proud to be Mexican American," and family values included working hard and speaking the truth. Intergenerational and contextual dynamics played out in ways that created hurdles for my siblings to manage as we moved on to our new lives. Through it all, we always had toys for Christmas and new clothes for both Christmas and Easter; school became my refuge and I got recognition in various ways. I was impressed when my mother was almost arrested for interfering with an arrest of American Indian youths, who she thought were Mexican American. I have memories of marginal status related to summer visits to family farmworkers in California's central valley worker camps and an uncle with a troubled life who died homeless. I also learned that some homes in my hometown "don't sell to Mexicans." In high school, the sociopolitical context and discrimination seemed remote to me. However, I grew up learning about the Holocaust and was stunned by Emmet Till's brutal death, seeing U.S. military on LA freeways during the Watts riots, and Ruben Salazar's violent death in the 70's. As an acculturated Chicana, I was involved with MAYA (Mexican American Youth Association) in high school and later with MEChA (Moviemiental Estudiantil Chicano de Aztlan) in undergraduate school. My move to San Diego to get my master of social work (MSW) degree was transformative. The year I graduated with my MSW, Martin Luther King, Jr., and Robert Kennedy were assassinated. My field instructor, in a clinical setting, took the students to a city diversity forum where we observed the intense responses from different San Diego communities to Dr. King's death (e.g., La Jolla); this was empowering. They wanted to know what was going to be done! My experiences as a clinician at the University of California, San Diego, further transformed my political views of the world due to the 1973 events in Chile and campus activism that had a global and class-based analysis; my learning about what can divide movements or create solidarity was eye opening. Those years included working with Mexican immigrant workers who worked in the San Diego fields. Along with doing clinical work, I received a National Institute of Mental Health (NIMH) grant to research Latinx dropouts in higher education, and I was involved in program development, teaching, and publishing. During that time, I began decades of international travel, first to all parts of Latin America, and these experiences inspired me to pursue my PhD in Boston, move on to teaching, and continue my writing.

Dorothy Van Soest. I grew up as part of a white working-class family in a small midwestern community. My father, who never graduated from high school, was a grocer, and my mother a homemaker with 1 year of junior college. Family life revolved around the church, Sunday mornings and evenings, Wednesday evenings, youth group on Fridays, and prayers and Bible reading before meals. My young mind took in but didn't understand the church's distorted moral narratives, such as how Black people were slaves and servants who had to obey their masters because of something called the curse of Ham and that slavery was common among the Israelites; how the Jews killed Jesus; and how the husband is the head of the wife as Christ is the head of the church, and that meant that wives should submit to their husbands and that women were to be silent and submissive in all things. Did the good-hearted church people consciously intend to teach me those things? Maybe so, maybe not. How many of those oppressive beliefs did I absorb? A lot, I'm sure. Purging them from my unconscious has been and will continue to be a lifelong endeavor. The purging process probably started with my rebellious nature, but it took off when I left my small-town bubble for college in Chicago. It was in the 1960s at the height of the Civil Rights and anti–Vietnam War movements, and I was young and impressionable. When Martin Luther King, Jr., and his family moved into a rundown building in Chicago to oppose housing segregation, I volunteered in some of those programs. I attended movement meetings where, like a skinny wide-eyed sponge, I soaked in ideas I'd never been exposed to before about how antipoverty efforts are a matter of racial and economic justice. But it wasn't until I graduated from college and began teaching, first in Chicago and then the Bronx, that I learned from people directly impacted by systemic racism about how evil it really is. My second career, in social work, began on an American Indian reservation, where my understanding of racial oppression deepened through the many mistakes I made, the times my white guilt kept me from listening and collaborating, the times my anger at injustice took precedence and clouded my thinking. After years of direct practice, I moved into teaching social work at the university level, where I focused on teaching and doing research about diversity, peace, and social justice issues. It wasn't until my mid-40s, after going through a divorce, that I came out to myself, and then to others, as a lesbian. That was when I became personally aware of the sinister and deeply harmful effects of internalized oppression. My unconscious had so deeply absorbed heterosexist ideology that I had no clue about who I was. And so, with an acute sense of humility as a lesbian, cisgender woman with white privilege, I continue to unearth the many ways I am both privileged and impacted by oppressive systems and to use my privilege as an ally and accomplice in the struggle to create racial and social justice.

REFLECTION/JOURNALING EXERCISE 1.1

Who Am I?

Take a few minutes to start your journal by responding to writing prompts such as the following:

- I am ...

- I was born ...

- My family was ...

- I grew up in ...

- When I think about engaging with this book, I ...

What Is in This Book? How Is It Structured?

We have organized this text into three parts, each one building on the other in a progressive way. In each chapter you will be encouraged to reflect on your personal beliefs and engage in critical thinking through various exercises.

In Part I we focus on foundational concepts and theories and provide a conceptual framework for moving from cultural competence to anti-oppression practice for social justice.

Chapter 1 introduces you to our main premise, to us as authors, and to the contents of the book.

Chapter 2 explores diverse views about what is just and about beliefs about what fairness individuals can or should be able to expect in life and on what basis. We present and raise probing and essential questions about how three prescriptive philosophical social justice theories have traditionally functioned to rationalize oppression. Two normative perspectives are then presented as consistent with our basic premise of anti-oppression practice: the racial contract that integrates diversity and oppression with social justice and the human rights perspective that builds on and broadens the racial contract to emphasize universal solutions.

Chapter 3 discusses two major obstacles on the journey to moving from cultural competence to anti-oppression practice: (1) difficulties when talking openly and honestly about diversity and social justice issues and (2) the current highly polarized and divisive political and social realities. We present a conceptual framework that focuses on the centrality of race and racism, the impact of socioeconomic class, and the complexities of diversity due to the intersectionality of multiple dimensions such as and not limited to color, gender, gender identity and expression, sexual orientation, ability and disability, class, culture, ethnicity, age, religion, and immigration status. Acknowledgment of our unearned privileges and a willingness to be confronted and to consider change (i.e., to address the inequality) makes it possible for us to become allies and accomplices to those disadvantaged by whatever systems advantage us.

In Part II we examine relevant concepts, definitions, and processes that promote effective social work practice characterized by cultural competence and social justice. Two concepts—oppression and intersectionality—explore how you may experience both target status and privilege depending on your different identities. The goal is to use our interconnected struggles to push for and activate coalition building and unity, to counteract the "us vs. them" and "divide and conquer" divisions in our efforts to dismantle oppressive systems, and to work toward revisioning our future.

Chapter 4 presents key concepts and definitions that provide theoretical grounding for your further understanding of the complex elements of oppression. Systemic poverty is used to illustrate the commonality of all oppressive systems, followed by a discussion of the interventions that are aimed at creating socially just alternatives.

Chapter 5 explores your social and racial identity development—using Black, white, and multiracial/biracial psychological models—as a way to think about your personal development through an anti-oppression practice lens.

Part III is an integration of your "take-aways" from the book as applied in the service of action, both in your professional practice and in your life beyond the workplace.

Chapter 6 presents two case studies that identify issues of power and privilege; oppressive systems at work in the case situations; and the use of interventions based on empowerment, cultural competence, and antiracist or anti-oppression practice approaches. Discussion centers on moving from *case* to *cause*; in other words, from assessment in practice with individuals and families to assessment of the structural inequities that negatively affect clients to interventions aimed at combating those injustices and ending societal or structural oppression.

Chapter 7 explores your commitment to social justice as a lifelong process that requires sorting through your responsibilities to professional ethics and practice, to society, and to self. We end the chapter and the book on a note of optimism by providing ideas about how to find hope in the face of the challenges of our day.

How to Use the Exercises in This Book

The exercises in each chapter provide opportunities for you to learn in three different ways: through personal reflection and self-awareness, through discussion and sharing with others, and through written assignments.

Reflection/journaling exercises invite you to reflect on your beliefs, values, life experiences, and behaviors. We encourage you to keep a journal to record your responses to the questions asked in each exercise. If your journal is connected in any way with your grade for a course, you will need to get clarity about any confidentiality concerns you have. To learn most from the reflection exercises, we encourage you to do *freewriting*, which means shutting down your inner censor and writing down your thoughts as they arise without evaluating them or worrying about the words you use. Here are some freewriting techniques you might find useful.

- *Write without stopping.* Either by hand or on a computer, write for a set amount of time (usually 10–15 minutes). It doesn't matter how fast or how slowly you write—just keep the writing fluid without correcting typos or reading what you've already written. Let the words come out without judging or evaluating them. They are for your eyes only. Remind yourself that you are in charge and can keep your freewriting strictly private.

- *Keep your writing fluid.* Relax your control and allow yourself to write whatever you want. If you get stuck and can't think about what to write next, you can repeat the last word or type nonsense until an idea pops into your mind. You might ask questions about what happened—what am I experiencing right now? where did my mind go?—and see what thoughts come. Usually, posing questions without searching for answers will trigger ideas.

- *Focused freewriting.* Each exercise in this book poses questions or provides you with self-reflection prompts about a particular topic. If you get distracted from the topic or your mind goes blank, it can be helpful to pause and ask yourself why that is and write about that. This is a gentle way of getting back on topic.

- *Loop writing.* This is a way to deepen your thinking about an issue. After doing focused freewriting for 5–10 minutes, go back and read what you wrote, and mark up anything that strikes you as surprising, interesting, or confusing. Then choose one of the marked-up passages as a topic or prompt for the next round of directed freewriting. Repeat this process as many times as it generates or unearths new thinking or insights.

Classroom exercises ask you to engage in discussion and/or personal sharing in a small group or in the class as a whole. Questions are posed to stimulate dialogue, identify different perspectives, and facilitate one another's learning. Conversations about issues of cultural diversity and social justice can be difficult. They require, in principle, the support that comes from hearing others' voices. When you have a learning atmosphere in which people are able to share their voices and stories, honest talks about difficult topics feel possible. Three kinds of group actions can help make it happen:

I. Establish agreement that everyone will honor the following four things to facilitate group interaction:

   1. *To stay engaged:* to remain present and socially and intellectually involved.

2. *To experience discomfort:* to not define a safe space as one free of tension, disagreement, or even frustration, but to "instead accept your discomfort and find ways to express it."

3. *To speak one's truth:* to be honest about one's thoughts and feelings and not speak for anyone else.

4. *To accept a lack of closure:* to not expect a conversation to "fix" the problem or resolve a situation or difference of interpretation or opinion. To hang out in uncertainty and not rush to quick solutions or agreements.

II. Establish ground rules for discussions. Here are six for you to consider:

1. Listen actively—respect others when they are talking.

2. Speak from your own experience instead of generalizing (i.e., use "I" instead of "they," "we," or "you").

3. Participate to the fullest of your ability; community growth depends on the inclusion of everyone's voice.

4. Instead of invalidating someone else's story with your own spin on their experience, share your own story and experience. Although it may be tempting, kindly don't speak for others; your observations can always be framed speaking from your experience, observations, and impressions, which are then open for others to respond to.

5. Try to see and understand the world from another's point of view (i.e., perspective taking).

6. Be conscious of your nonverbal communications, both your body language and other nonverbal responses (e.g., *how* you say something). Awareness of how others experience our communications with them can create learning opportunities for everyone.

III. To facilitate deep sharing and listening, an exercise called "go-arounds" can be used at any time.

1. This is not a dialogue or discussion exercise.

2. It can be used in conjunction with any of the reflection/journaling and classroom exercises in this book.

3. The goal of the exercise is to ensure that everyone has an opportunity to share their truth without interruption or comment from others and to ensure that everyone has the opportunity to listen deeply to others.

4. The process is as follows:
   a. Go around the classroom or small group.
   b. When it's your turn to speak, share your own truth.
   c. When it's not your turn to speak, listen deeply to understand the person who is speaking. Do not comment or respond, either verbally or nonverbally, to anything that is said.
   d. After everyone has had a chance to speak, everyone agrees not to talk to anyone about anything that was said for 24 hours. Just hold the others' truths for that period of time.

Assignment exercises are intended to be written papers that you may write for your own learning, which we encourage. They can also be assigned by your professor for course credit.

All of the exercises in the book, plus all the figures, charts, and tables, are listed by category in the table of contents.

References

Council on Social Work Education. (2015). *Educational policy and accreditation standards.*

Gil, D. (1998). *Confronting injustice and oppression: Concepts and strategies for social workers.* Columbia University Press.

Kivel, P. (2017). *Uprooting racism: How white people can work for racial justice* (4th ed.). New Society.

National Association of Social Workers. (2017). *Code of ethics of the National Association of Social Workers.*

Perlman, H. H. (1976). Believing and doing: Values in social work education. *Social Casework, 57,* 381–396.

Sue, D. W., & Sue, D. (2013). *Counseling the culturally diverse: Theory & practice* (6th ed.). Wiley.

CHAPTER 2

The Foundation
Understanding Social Justice

The dawn of the 21st century brought economic insecurity and structural inequities for a large proportion of the U.S. population, along with unprecedented levels of political polarization, civil uprisings, and racial injustice. The current climate, by shining a spotlight on devastating social and economic injustices, poses both challenges and opportunities for social workers. The primary purpose of this book—to support and prepare professional social workers in efforts to transform oppressive and unjust systems into nonoppressive and just alternatives (Gil, 1998)—is based on a vision of the social work profession as firmly and unequivocally committed to eliminating oppression and promoting social justice in the 21st century.

For most people, to be socially just means to treat everyone equitably (i.e., create a level playing field so there is fairness) and equally (i.e., treat everyone the same regardless of race, gender and gender identity, sexual orientation, ability, age, immigrant status, language, class, religion, etc.). Social justice and diversity are generally understood as going hand in hand. The main premise of this book is that anti-oppression social work practice means (a) engaging with diverse clients based on an understanding of how diversity and labeling people as the "other" is used to create structural inequities and (b) employing interventions that are grounded in a commitment to social and economic justice and to dismantling systems of oppression.

It is important to acknowledge the tremendous challenges we face on the journey from cultural competence to anti-oppression social work practice, particularly during these times. Without arguing about the badness of the

21st century compared with difficult times in the past, the reality is that structural changes in the economy over decades have bestowed fabulous wealth on a tiny sliver at the top while undermining the living standards of the middle class and absolutely crushing the poor and low-wealth people, who are disproportionately people of color (Van Soest, 2012). It can be easy to slip into pessimism, to question whether anything we do will make a difference. But we can find hope by turning to history, to a time in the past when others who faced equal or greater challenges continued, against all odds, to work for and create social change. Historian Howard Zinn (1997), in his essay "Failure to Quit," gave us hope for a vision that social work can be a force for social justice.

> I can understand pessimism, but I don't believe in it. It's not simply a matter of faith, but of historical evidence. Not overwhelming evidence, just enough to give hope, because for hope we don't need certainty, only possibility. Which is all history can offer us. When I hear so often that there is little hope for change. ... I think back to the despair [about the possibilities for change in the United States at the beginning of the 1960s]. Yet, it was on the first of February in that first year of the new decade that four black students from North Carolina A&T College sat down at a "white" lunch counter in Greensboro, refused to move, and were arrested. In two weeks, sit-ins had spread to fifteen cities in five Southern states. By the year's end, 50,000 people had participated in demonstrations in a hundred cities, and 3,600 had been put in jail. That was the start of the civil rights movement, which became an anti-war movement, a women's movement, a cultural upheaval, and in its course hundreds of thousands, no millions, of people became committed for a short time, or for a lifetime. It was unprecedented, unpredicted, and for at least fifteen years, uncontrollable. It would shake the country and startle the world, with consequences we are hardly aware of today ... today there are thousands of local groups around the country—many more than existed in the Sixties—devoted to struggling for tenants' rights

or women's rights or environmental protection ... or to take care of the hungry and the homeless, or those in need of health care. There are now tens of thousands of professionals ... who bring unorthodox ideas and humane values into courtrooms, classrooms, and hospitals. ... History does not start anew with each decade. The roots of one era branch and flower in subsequent eras. Human beings, writings, invisible transmitters of all kinds, carry messages across the generations. I try to be pessimistic, to keep up with some of my friends. But I think back over the decades, and look around. And then, it seems to me that the future is not certain, but it is possible. (Zinn, 1997, pp. 656–661)

Because conceptual signposts can help with the work ahead, we offer in this chapter a brief foundational overview of social justice. We begin with basic definitions and opportunities for you to reflect on your own values, beliefs, intentions, and behavior about fairness and justice, rights and privileges. We present three prescriptive theories to both ground you in conventional social justice thinking and, equally important, raise critical questions about how traditional philosophical perspectives have functioned to rationalize oppression. We then present two normative perspectives—the racial contract that integrates diversity and oppression with social justice and the human rights perspective that builds on and broadens the racial contract to emphasize universal solutions—as the most consistent with anti-oppression social work practice.

Defining Social Justice

The professional mandates that social workers promote social justice and challenge social injustice are clear (Council on Social Work Education, 2015; International Federation of Social Workers, 2021; National Association of Social Workers, 2017). And yet a major critique of social justice content in social work education concludes that a substantive and meaningful focus, both in terms of definition and pedagogical approach, is lacking (Nicotera, 2019). That means the most immediate challenge we face is reaching an understanding about what social justice and social injustice mean.

As an idea, social justice has been highly contested historically and has taken on various meanings over time. As is seen later in this chapter, one's perspective on social justice is often related to one's positionality. In other words, what you consider to be just or unjust is influenced by where you are located in the hierarchy of society based on race, gender, sexuality, class, ability, and other identities. The problem with that, as Reisch (2002) points out, is that people end up marching under one banner of social justice while at the same time promoting radically different ideas about what it is. "Liberals and conservatives, religious fundamentalists, and radical secularists all regard their causes as socially just" (p. 343), and it is not uncommon for some people to claim they are for social justice while others accuse them of not being for social justice at all.

Although there is no one universally accepted definition of social justice in the social work literature, several related definitions can help to discern its meaning. Segal (2016) considers social justice to be fairness that is supported by advocacy and social empathy that integrate social justice and relevant socially just practice (Segal & Wagaman, 2017).

Doman Lum (personal communication, May 9, 2005) combines both social and economic justice in his conceptualization:

> Social justice governs how social institutions deal fairly or justly with the social needs of people as far as access to what is good for individuals and groups. It secures civil and human rights and benefits in terms of social provisions of well being such as nutrition, housing, employment, education, and health care. And, third, social justice addresses historical and current forms of oppression and seeks systemic, legal and societal strategies to correct historical, "normative" abuses and establish an equal playing field for all regardless of ethnicity, gender and gender identity, sexual orientation, social and economic class, age, and other related factors.
>
> Economic justice embodies moral principles regarding the development of equitable economic institutions so that any individual can earn

a living, enter into social and economic contracts (monetary agreements to buy a car, house; obtain assets, e.g., stocks), exchange goods and services to produce an independent material foundation for economic sustenance. It also ensures education and employment to promote flourishing, rather than survival, for all individuals in relation to learning and career development. Also, when people are unable to provide for themselves, economic justice fosters welfare assistance until they can function in a work environment.

In the next section we provide you with the opportunity to reflect on what social justice means to you, after which we present an overview of several widely understood social justice perspectives.

Beginning With Awareness, Reflection, and Critical Thinking

Is life fair? If so, why? If not, why not? If life is fair, why do you consider it to be fair? And so we begin with questioning the origins of our own values, beliefs, feelings, and behaviors about social justice. The purpose of the following two reflection/journaling exercises is to encourage you to reflect conscientiously and think critically about the implications of your current perspective. We encourage you to do freewriting in response to the questions posed. Also, with these reflection exercises, as with others, you may choose to share your thoughts and feelings by using the go-around strategy. Both techniques are described in Chapter 1.

REFLECTION/JOURNALING EXERCISE 2.1

Fairness and Justice

Throughout our lives, often beginning at a young age, we hear expressions such as: "That's not fair!" "You're not playing fair!" and "Life is not fair!"

Such expressions usually coincide with disappointment when something bad happens to us or to someone we care about. The expression is perhaps a manifestation of a belief that life is not fair, at least not to us at that moment, and that it should be. Underlying any expression about fairness lies a social justice perspective, whether or not we know what it is.

When you were growing up, you likely received many messages about fairness and justice. Take a few minutes to do some freewriting about some of them.

- Do you recall a particular situation in which you learned a lesson about what was fair or unfair, just or unjust? What did you learn from the situation?

- What did the adults around you (e.g., parents, other caretakers, teachers) teach you about fairness?

- How do you carry those messages with you today? Which ones do you hold on to? Which ones have you discarded?

- In general, do you believe that the world is a just place? Why or why not?

REFLECTION/JOURNALING EXERCISE 2.2

Rights and Privileges*

Take some time to write your responses to the following questions:

1. What are rights? What do people have a right to (i.e., what do people deserve just because they are human beings)?

2. What are privileges? Do people get them based on doing something? On merit? On doing work? On what they're born into?

3. Is it fair to take (e.g., through taxes) from one group and give to another group? When is it fair and when is it not fair? Does it have to with rights or privileges? When is it a form of justice and when is it an infringement on people's freedom?

4. If there is a situation in which the goods and services produced are inadequate to satisfy everyone's desire for them, on what basis or according to what principles can these goods and services be distributed justly? For example, if you believe that everyone has a right to food but there is an inadequate supply, how do you distribute the food? If you believe that having food is a privilege, then what do people have to do to earn it? And what should be done when people who have not earned it get it or when those who earned it do not get it?

5. If there is a situation in which the goods and services produced are adequate to satisfy everyone's desire for them, on what basis or according to what principles can they be distributed justly?

Reflection and Discussion

Now take a moment to read your responses and reflect on them. What, if any, themes do you see? Do you believe that life is just (fair), and, if so, what does justice mean based on your responses? Do you believe life is unjust (unfair)? Where do your beliefs come from? How comfortable are you with them? In a small group or in pairs, discuss each question and how you think you came to the position that you took.

*This exercise was adapted from Van Soest (2003, pp. 349–350).

Now that you have had an opportunity for personal reflection, we move on to two classroom exercises to further stimulate awareness, this time through dialogue and problem-solving with others about how you use the term "social justice" and what guiding principles you use to make decisions in particular scenarios.

CLASSROOM EXERCISE 2.1

Demands*

Read the scenario and then discuss the questions that follow.

Recently, the workers at a major university went on strike to call attention to their demands. One of the demands was that all staff with salaries up to $60,000 should get an across-the-board salary increase of $400 per month.

1. In your opinion, is the workers' demand a just one? Do you think it is a fair demand? Why?

2. Should the amount of increase be based on the amount of time a person has worked at the university (e.g., a person who just started work a month ago versus a person who has worked there for 10 years)?

3. Is it fair (just) that a worker making $59,000 would get the same amount as a worker who is only making $15,000 a year?

4. Should the cutoff point be $60,000? Why not set it at $30,000? On what basis would you make such a decision?

5. Would it be fair (just) to demand the salary increase only for workers earning salaries in the bottom quartile? Explain why.

6. As you think about your responses to the above questions, what beliefs or principles did you use to arrive at your position?

*This exercise was adapted from Van Soest (2003, pp. 350–351).

CLASSROOM EXERCISE 2.2

Fair Distribution

Provide enough of some kind of food so that every person could have a generous portion (e.g., crackers, nuts, hard candies). Divide the class into small groups. Each group must decide how to distribute the food to the class in a fair way and then present its distribution plan to the class. This is followed by discussion of the following questions:

1. What distribution system did each group select (e.g., everyone should get an equal amount; distribution should be based on need, for example, who hasn't eaten breakfast or lunch yet; distribution should be based on merit)?

2. Which system would you consider to be most fair? Most just?

3. Might there be a situation in which one system would be more fair and just than it would be in another situation? On what basis do you make such a distinction?

If the class can agree on which distribution system is most fair (just), distribute the food based on that system. Whether or not the class can agree on a system, move on to discuss the following questions:

1. Do you think that there is one distribution system to which social work as a profession should adhere?

2. If so, what should that system be? Would it apply to all situations? When might a different system be more fair (just)?

3. Might having more than one system be congruent and consistent with social work values?

4. What are the implications of the strategies discussed in class for real-life situations involving decisions about distribution of resources?

Social Justice Theory

The previous exercises were intended to illustrate the importance of thinking critically about what social justice means for you as an important step in taking social work's social justice mandate seriously. Now we dig deeper into the question of justice. What is it? Is justice equality? Is justice having freedom? Does justice mean meeting needs? If so, how do we distinguish between needs and privileges? Between needs and desires? These and many other questions point to the complexities involved in determining what is just and fair. Whether we are aware of it or not, each of us believes in certain principles and theories about what justice is. And, as noted earlier and illustrated in Figure 2.1, one's perspective on what is just and fair is often related to one's own social position in society.

Figure 2.1   Social Justice Perspectives

Occupying different positions in a hierarchical social order explains, in part, why discussions can become intense when people who consider a situation to be unfair engage with people who consider the same situation to be fair.

Having a knowledge base of frameworks can be helpful. To that end, what follows is an overview of some principles and contemporary social justice theories that are prevalent in the literature. Our goal is to provide a base for you to (a) examine and challenge your personal perspectives; (b) understand which social justice perspectives and principles are coherent and compatible with anti-oppression social work practice; and (c) translate that understanding into effective strategies for promoting justice and fairness on individual, community, organizational, and societal levels.

Types of Social Justice

We start with a long-established conceptualization of three types of social justice—distributive, legal, and commutative—that is grounded in the social contract tradition of political philosophers such as Hobbes, Locke, Kant, Rousseau, John Rawls, and Robert Nozick. Social work is concerned with all three types (see Figure 2.2).

Figure 2.2   Types of Justice

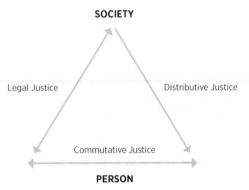

Commutative Justice

When we consider what individuals owe to each other, we are talking about commutative justice, that is, fundamental fairness in agreements and exchanges between individuals and private social groups. Whether working with individuals, families, groups, organizations, or communities, social workers often deal with and facilitate conflict resolution processes aimed at achieving fairness in relationships.

Legal Justice

When we consider what the individual owes society, we are talking about legal justice. Philosophically, this type of justice has focused on the responsibility that citizens have to society to respect and obey its laws (as shown by the arrow pointing from person to society in Figure 2.2). When examined through the lens of cultural diversity and oppression, however, it becomes clear that society is failing to fulfill a corresponding responsibility to its citizens to institute laws that are just, fair, and applied equally to all people (a responsibility shown by the arrow pointing from society to person in Figure 2.2). There are numerous examples of our society's laws throughout history and currently that discriminate between the rights given to different groups: for example, legalization of slavery, laws denying women and Black people the right to vote, denying equal treatment based on sexual orientation.

The disparate outcomes of injustices in the legal system today are well documented. For example, even though studies show that people of all colors use and sell illegal drugs at remarkably similar rates and that white youths are more likely to engage in drug crimes, "our nation's prisons and jails are overflowing with Black and brown people convicted of drug crimes … and the U.S. imprisons a larger percentage of its Black population than South Africa did at the height of apartheid" (Alexander, 2020, p. 8). Racial disparities in laws, legal rules, and procedures at every step of the criminal justice system result in African American youths being six times as likely as whites to be sentenced to prison for identical crimes (Poe-Yamagata & Jones, 2000). Classroom Exercise 2.3 offers an opportunity for you to engage in critical thinking about ways to rectify such disparities in the criminal justice system.

CLASSROOM EXERCISE 2.3

Toward a More Just Legal System*

The United States has the world's highest incarceration rate; 2.3 million Americans are in prison today. Fueled by the "war on drugs" and "tough on crime" mandatory sentencing policies, mass incarceration has had a clear racial impact: 70% of American prisoners are nonwhite. The average American has a 1 in 20 chance of being imprisoned at some point in their life, but that rate is much higher for Latinx men (1 in 6) and African American men (more than 1 in 3) than for white men (1 in 23). Strikingly, one in nine Black men under age 25 live under some form of restrained liberty: in prison, in jail, on probation, or on parole.

In small groups, read the pros and cons of the sentencing proposal aimed at preventing racial discrimination in relation to drug crimes and then discuss the questions below.

Proposed Sentencing Policy: Federal law should not make first-time drug offenders face mandatory sentences. Judges should be allowed more discretion in sentencing these drug offenders.

- **Pro:** Mandatory minimum sentences cause first-time offenders, mostly minorities, to go into an already overcrowded prison system.

- **Con:** Mandatory minimum sentences are needed to show that we are serious in our war on drugs.

In small groups, read the above policy and evaluate it by discussing the following questions:

1. Do you think the sentencing policy would prevent or eliminate structural inequities in the criminal justice system? If yes, why do you think so? If no, why do you not think so?

2. Which of the two pro and con positions do you think would be more fair? To whom?

3. Who, outside of you and your group members, might support the policy? Who might oppose it? Why?

4. What other policies can you think of that could prevent racial discrimination in the criminal justice system? Do you think they would work? Why or why not?

5. Why is it important that the criminal justice system not be perceived as racially biased?

6. Do you think a color-blind legal justice system is possible? Why or why not?

*Source: Equal Justice Initiative (2014).
Adapted from "Class Activity: Toward a Colorblind Justice System," Constitutional Rights Foundation (n.d.)

An alternative approach to legal justice that has been gaining widespread attention has particular relevance for anti-oppression practice. It is called restorative justice. Conventional criminal justice systems focus largely on applying the law, assessing guilt, and administering punishment. By contrast, restorative justice focuses on repairing the damage caused by a criminal action. It is an approach that involves both victims and perpetrators in a process aimed at healing and restoring, as much as possible, the respect, equality, and dignity of those affected by the wrongdoing. The restorative approach, which is increasingly used in many settings such as prisons and schools, has the potential to prevent the intrinsic injustices of the conventional criminal justice system (Umbreit & Armour, 2010).

Fania Davis (2019) called for a convergence of restorative justice practitioners and racial justice activists to disrupt the school-to-prison pipeline, mass incarceration, and state-sanctioned police violence against people of color. In *The Little Book of Race and Restorative Justice,* she wrote:

> In keeping with the worldview and principles of African and other indigenous justice systems, restorative justice invites a paradigm shift in the way we think about and do justice—from a justice that harms to a justice that heals. Our prevailing adversarial system is based upon a Roman notion of justice as just deserts. Causing someone to suffer creates an imbalance in the scales of justice, and the way to rebalance the scales and do justice is to cause the responsible person to suffer; we respond to the original harm with a second harm. Ours is a system that harms people who harm people, presumably to show that harming people is wrong. This sets into motion endless cycles of harm. Restorative justice seeks to interrupt these cycles by repairing the damage done to relationships in the wake of crime or other wrongdoing, and do so in a way that is consonant with indigenous wisdom—Africa's and that of other traditions. Justice is a healing ground, not a battleground. (pp. 24–25)

Distributive Justice

When we consider what society owes the individual, we are talking about distributive justice, that is, the just or fair allocation of resources. This perspective is considered to be the one most closely linked to our professional mission of promoting social and economic justice. Wakefield (1988) argued, in fact, that the organizing value of social work is distributive justice. Beverly and McSweeney's (1987) definition of justice for social work emphasizes its distributive quality as well:

> Justice ... means fairness in the relationships between people as those related to the possession and/or acquisition of resources based on some kind of valid claim to a share of those resources ... the justice or injustice of a particular policy or situation is determined by looking at the fairness of the distribution of resources in relation to the claims or demands made for those resources. (p. 5)

For social workers, the distribution of goods other than political or economic resources, such as counseling, therapy, health services, education, and leisure, also falls within the realm of social justice.

Of these three traditionally recognized types of social justice—distributive, legal, and commutative—we agree that distributive justice has been an important organizing value of social work. However, the distributive paradigm does not sufficiently encapsulate the complexities of injustice (Young, 1990). This is particularly true when we combine the notion that people have a right to have their needs met with multiculturalism issues (i.e., cultural competence and oppression), which is the emphasis of this book. However, as a way to begin thinking about this perspective, Reflection/Journaling Exercise 2.3 focuses on its basic distributive sense.

REFLECTION/JOURNALING EXERCISE 2.3

Fair Distribution

Read the following scenario and then reflect on the questions that follow.

If you imagine that there are 25 people in the world and there are 25 apples cut into quarters or 100 slices, this is how those slices would be distributed into portions proportionate to the way food is distributed to people worldwide:

- Six people would receive nothing or crumbs.
- Seven people would receive one slice each.
- Six people would receive three slices each.

- Five people would receive 10 slices each.

- One person would receive 25 slices.

Write your reactions to the following questions before engaging in classroom discussion.

1. Is this worldwide distribution of food just or unjust?

2. Can you think of any situation or condition in which this kind of disparity might be just?

3. What principles or kinds of situations might be used to conclude that such disparities are just?

Although most people might quickly conclude from the above exercise that the disparities in the way the world eats are clearly unjust, others might consider the possibility that their justness or unjustness might depend on certain qualifying conditions, and still others might even say that the disparities are actually just. How do we account for such different conclusions among social workers as well as among others? What follows is an overview of several theories of distributive justice that illustrate how each might judge the justness of distribution disparities.

Three Traditional Social Justice Perspectives

The following three mainstream philosophical social justice perspectives—utilitarian (see Hare, 1992; Sidgwick, 1966), libertarian (Nozick, 1974), and egalitarian (Rawls, 1971)—are prescriptive, not descriptive. Each perspective presents a case for what social justice should be, and each offers distinct ways of defining social justice. These three traditional conceptualizations provide a beginning theoretical framework from which to examine and critically analyze other perspectives that are more consistent with anti-oppression social work practice.

Utilitarian Perspective

What distribution of goods, what principles of justice, and what ascriptions of rights are such that their acceptance serves the general interest? That is the key question posed by the utilitarian perspective, whose major proponent was John Stuart Mill (Sterba, 1985). According to this theory, we arrive at justice by weighing relative benefits and harms, and by determining what maximizes the greatest good for the greatest number of people. Thus, from a utilitarian perspective, it may be determined that social justice exists even if some people have no rights met and others have all their rights met, as long as it is determined that the imbalance is for the common good. As illustrated in Figure 2.3, the outcome of utilitarian justice tends to be a distribution of goods and services similar to a bell curve, with most people getting their needs met, a small percentage getting none of their needs met, and another small percentage getting more than what they need.

Figure 2.3   Utilitarian Perspective of Social Justice

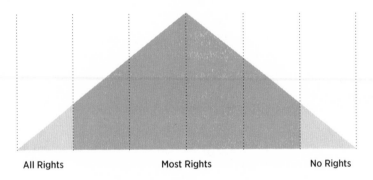

All Rights   Most Rights   No Rights

The common good, however, is open to varied viewpoints, and one's definition determines whether a situation is just or not. For example, some people believe that it is not for the common good to provide for people when they can provide for themselves. By contrast, others may argue that when some groups are not provided for, the common good is not served because there may be unrest or because it harms us all morally, as individuals and as a society. Consider three policymakers, all of whom support utilitarianism and yet take very different positions about whether society's resources should go into education or the military. One, seeing the common good as primarily to protect the country's citizens from external attack by another nation, supports policies that channel resources into weapons of war at the expense of education. The second, seeing the common good as primarily an educated citizenry, supports policies that channel resources into education first, perhaps at the expense of the military. And the third, defining the common good as both an educated *and* a protected citizenry, supports policies that divide resources between education and the military.

Libertarian Perspective

In contrast to utilitarianism, the libertarian position advanced by Robert Nozick (1974) is based on the principle that resources are distributed by a natural and social lottery. The laws of nature that regulate distribution in an uneven and amoral way should not be interfered with. For example, some people are born with higher intellectual capacities than others, some people get lucky in relation to money and others don't, some people are born into rich cultures and some into poor cultures, and so on. Libertarians view this natural distribution as inherently fair because it is not based on morality but rather on chance or the natural order of things. It is a perspective that is incompatible with social work values and ethics in that it ignores any examination of the hardships of people's "actual lives in the assessment of justice" (Sen, 2009, p. xi).

Another problem with the libertarian perspective for social work is its contention that people hold certain rights by entitlement. What they have, they are entitled to by virtue of the fact that they have it. Thus, justice consists in the widest possible latitude of freedom from coercion in what people accumulate and what, how, and when they dispose of it. For example, people opposed to taxation should not be coerced into compliance. Charity is valued and seen as a virtue; however, in a just society each person should have the freedom to determine how much, to whom, and when to give. No institution or person should interfere with that basic freedom or with the natural order of things. On the other hand, tax dollars for the military, when used to protect people's fundamental freedom of ownership, may be seen as acceptable coercion.

While life may seem unfair in the present, according to the libertarian perspective, there is a rebalancing of justice that occurs naturally over time. When we notice that people are oppressed or denied resources, we are only seeing a "snapshot" in time rather than viewing it within a long-term historical context. In other words, when we look backward or forward in time, we might see that an oppressed group was the oppressor in the past and/or may become the oppressor in the future.

Egalitarian Perspective

John Rawls (1971) proposed that to design a society that was really just, we would need to do so under a veil of ignorance. That means that those who attempt to create a fair society would not know in advance what their position in that society would be, and they would thus, at the outset, have a stake in avoiding extreme inequalities. For example, since you might be born with severe developmental disabilities, you would want to ensure that society would provide the resources needed for your care and growth. Similarly, since you might be born into a very poor family, you would want to ensure that there was a distribution system to help you.

In a just society designed under a veil of ignorance, inequalities would not be permitted to achieve a greater common good (utilitarianism) or to maintain individual freedom (libertarianism). The first principle of egalitarianism, in fact, is that basic liberties must be equal, because citizens of a just society have the same basic rights to freedom, to fair equality of opportunity, to access to goods and services, and to self-respect. Thus, if you were born as a poor person into this just society, you would have liberties that were equal to those of the richest person in society. The second egalitarian principle is that, although the actual distribution of income and wealth need not be equal, any inequalities in power, wealth, and other resources must not exist unless they work to the absolute benefit of the worst-off members of society. For example, if you were born with serious medical conditions or developmental disabilities, under this principle you might receive more resources in your early years than are provided to others because you would need them more to have equal opportunity in life. So, even though there would be an inequality in the distribution of, say, educational services, it would work to the absolute benefit of you as one of the worst-off members of society.

From an egalitarian perspective, in contrast to the libertarian view, redistribution of resources is a moral obligation. The unmet needs that should be redressed first should be for those who are most in need. This means that, to provide genuine equality of opportunity, society must give more atten-tion to those with fewer native assets and to those born into less favorable social positions. If justice as fairness is to be attained, no one should be advantaged or disadvantaged through the genetic accidents of one's birth, such as inborn abilities and aptitudes or the contingency of one's social cir-cumstances such as class, family fortune, and social status. A shortcoming of egalitarianism for anti-oppression social work practice is that race, gen-der, and sexuality were not included in Rawls's deliberations. Critical race theorist Charles Mills (2017a) pointed out that this theory of justice does not discuss racial injustice or even mention colonialism and imperialism, and then asks us to imagine the veil of ignorance being lifted and finding yourself to be a person of color in a white supremacist state.

Although Rawls did not restrict inequality to income and material goods, Iris Young (1990) noted that the kind of disrespect and marginalization suffered by some groups cannot be articulated in terms of Rawlsian theory because the elements that would make a difference were ignored. In other words, equality of people in this theory of justice amounts to sameness, to a homogenization of otherness rather than its recognition.

Of the three traditional social justice perspectives, egalitarianism has often been seen as the one closest to traditional social work values and ethics. Wakefield (1988), for example, argues that "social work strives to ensure that no person is deprived of a fair minimum level of those basic social goods to which everyone is entitled" and supports Rawls's inclusion of self-respect in the list of social goods (p. 187). But there is evidence that, while perhaps holding to egalitarian principles as the ideal, social workers may operate more often from a utilitarian perspective in practice (Conrad, 1988; Reisch & Taylor, 1983). For instance, terms such as cost-benefit anal-ysis and triage strategies related to managed health care systems point to a utilitarian approach.

The Racial Contract

In *The Racial Contract*, Mills (1997) challenges the social contract tradition itself with a social justice perspective that is distinctly different from the three conventional theories we've just discussed. Utilitarians, libertarians, and egalitarians use the social contract as a normative tool, that is, as an ideal social contract that explains how a just society, ruled by a moral government, should be formed and regulated by a defensible moral code. Mills, on the other hand, does not use the social contract normatively but, rather, descriptively to explain the actual genesis of a society, a people's moral psychology, and how a government actually functions. In other words, the racial contract focuses on the reality of the injustices that are so prevalent in our society and world.

Mills contends that not only is society currently unjust but that it is also unjust because people who are considered to be nonwhite have always been excluded from the social contract that determines distribution of resources. And that, he concludes, renders the idea that the social contract is the basis of Western democratic societies a myth in and of itself; that the actual (i.e., in practice) basis of Western societies is instead a racial contract.

The basic difference between the racial contract and the three conventional theories, then, is Mills's contention that the social contract is not a contract among everybody, as in "we the people," but is instead a contract only between people who count and have social position, as in "we the white male upper class people." The social contract has always consisted of formal and informal agreements between the members of one subset of individuals who are designated as white (dominant) and who are, by implication, seen as legitimate in comparison to other groups. The remaining subset of individuals, who are designated as nonwhite and thus of a different and inferior moral status of subpersons, is not a participatory, consenting party to the contract—that is, subjects acting on the agreement—but rather the objects being acted on. The main point is that the purpose of the social contract, in reality, has always been the differential and biased privileging of whites in relation to nonwhites.

From the beginning, "race" was not an afterthought or a deviation from ostensibly neutral and unbiased Western ideals of the social contract, but rather a core part of those ideals. This contention is supported by historical facts about specific derivative contracts that were designed to exploit global resources and peoples for the benefit of Europe. For example, the slavery contract, colonial contract, and expropriation contract granted Europeans absolute dominion over all territories of the world, not by virtue of conquering them, but as a right acquired simply by "discovery."

Mills was originally inspired by Carole Pateman's (1988) *Sexual Contract* theory of male gender domination as a contract among men to subordinate women. He, in turn, theorized white racial domination in terms of a contract among whites to subordinate people of color. So in all three cases (class, gender, race), the contract is limited to the privileged group, entrenching their group privilege, rather than being universal (Mills, 2017b). Pateman & Mills (2007) then integrated their conceptions of sexual and racial contracts. Rather than disjoining patriarchy from white supremacy, Mills began to think in terms of racial patriarchy, where race is gendered and gender is raced. In other words, although one's race (Black) may be subordinate, at the same time one's gender (male) may be dominant. The issue of intersectionality of multiple identities is explored in more depth in the next chapter. The racial contract and, by implication, the sexual and other domination contracts, provide the best conceptual tool for social workers to move from cultural competence to anti-oppression social work practice.

REFLECTION/JOURNALING EXERCISE 2.4

Social Injustice and the Social "Dominator" Contract

Think about a time when you personally experienced a social injustice, a friend or family member experienced a social injustice, or you witnessed a social injustice. Write at least one paragraph that describes the social injustice and on which "dominator" contract (i.e., race, gender, class, etc.) it was based. If you cannot think of an example, you can either make up a scenario to write about or write about an example from history. Consider sharing using the go-around strategy described in Chapter 1.

Universal Human Rights

A human rights approach to social justice represents a shift from a "defensive stance against oppression and injustice to an affirmation of the right to satisfaction of material and non-material human needs and equitable participation in the production and distribution of resources" (United Nations, 1994, p. 6). From this perspective, social justice "encompasses satisfaction of basic human needs and the equitable sharing of material resources" (United Nations, 1994, p. 16). Although we support the concept of human rights based on the intention to support freedoms for choice, growth, and development, we do so with the understanding that the concept has been appropriated at times to support individual rights over social justice rights. Our profession is still challenged to articulate the voices of individuals within the context of domination and to identify and implement specific advocacy actions. It is important to understand human rights as basic rights that are inherent in our nature; without them, we could not live as human beings, as they are integral to a life with dignity and respect. Human rights are a universal and basic entitlement for all, regardless of race, gender, class, or other diverse identities.

Basic rights include the assurance of freedom, certainty of social justice, and institution of the social and international order needed to realize these rights and freedoms. They include the right to develop and exercise our human capabilities, such as intelligence, talents, and conscience. They promote dignity in people's lives. Human rights include much of what is discussed in the capabilities approach to social justice (Nussbaum, 2000, 2001, 2013). These rights include the freedoms that people value, such as the ability to live to an old age, freedom of choice, imagination, thought, emotions (e.g., forming attachments and not having emotional development limited by fear and anxiety), affiliations, play, and control over one's physical and social environment. From this perspective, human rights promote quality of life. Figure 2.4 provides a short summary of the basic instruments concerning human rights, with the dates when they were adopted by the United Nations General Assembly. The list illustrates the comprehensive nature of the human rights perspective.

Figure 2.4　Human Rights Instruments Adopted by the United Nations

INSTRUMENTS PROVIDING GENERAL PROTECTION

The Universal Declaration of Human Rights (1948)

The Covenants on Human Rights (1966)

The International Covenant on Civil and Political Rights

- Right to life, liberty, and security
- Right not to be subjected to torture and cruel, inhuman, or degrading treatment or punishment
- Prohibition of slavery
- Right not to be detained arbitrarily
- Rights to freedom of expression, religion, assembly, association, including trade union membership
- Right to freedom of movement and residence
- Right to vote through universal suffrage
- Right to a fair trial
- Rights of minorities to protection

The International Covenant on Economic, Social, and Cultural Rights (1976)

- Right to work
- Right to social security
- Right to protection of family
- Right to an adequate standard of living
- Right to education
- Right to health
- Right to join trade unions

INSTRUMENTS PROVIDING PARTICULAR PROTECTION

International Convention on the Elimination of All Forms of Racial Discrimination (1965)

Convention on the Elimination of All Forms of Discrimination Against Women (1979)

Convention Against Torture & other Cruel, Inhuman & Degrading Treatment or Punishment (1987)

Convention on the Rights of the Child (1989)

International Convention on the Protection of the Rights of All Migrant Workers and Members of Their Families (1990)

RULES REGARDING DETENTION AND TREATMENT OF OFFENDERS

Standard Minimum Rules for the Treatment of Prisoners (1955)

Principles of Medical Ethics (1982)

Standard Minimum Rules for the Administration of Juvenile Justice (1985)

OTHER HUMAN RIGHTS INSTRUMENTS

The highest aspiration: A call to human rights (2020)

Declaration on the Right to Development (1986)

Declaration on the Elimination of All Forms of Religious Intolerance (1981)

Declaration on the Protection of Women and Children in Armed Conflicts (1974)

Declaration on the Rights of Mentally Retarded Persons (1971

These instruments are described in more detail in United Nations (1994).

Critical Analysis of Diverse Social Justice Perspectives

When we talk about social workers viewing social problems and individual troubles through a social justice lens, which social justice lens and which underlying value assumptions about what makes something just or unjust are we talking about? Classroom Exercise 2.4 examines a situation from the five different social justice perspectives we've just discussed.

CLASSROOM EXERCISE 2.4

Determining What Is Just During a Health Crisis

While beliefs about social justice are usually deep-seated and not readily available to our consciousness, they are particularly influential during times of crisis. Consider the 2020 global COVID-19 pandemic that killed hundreds of thousands of people in the United States. Despite consensus in the scientific community—Center for Disease Control, World Health Organization, and public health experts—that masks helped prevent the spread of the virus, confusion and political divisions arose about when and where to wear masks. As a result, the United States had the highest number of cases and deaths than any other country in the world. People of color and people without resources disproportionately contracted and died from the virus at much higher rates than whites and those with resources. Most of those who did not contract the virus were those with the most resources (money, ability to work from home, etc.). It could be argued, from a utilitarian perspective (see diagram) that such an outcome might be considered to be just if most people who were infected recovered and if the common good was seen as keeping the economy going.

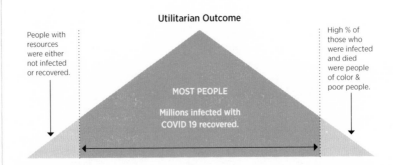

Utilitarian Outcome

People with resources were either not infected or recovered.

High % of those who were infected and died were people of color & poor people.

MOST PEOPLE

Millions infected with COVID 19 recovered.

Review the five views about social justice that were presented in this chapter— utilitarian, libertarian, egalitarian, racial contract, and human rights. In small groups, consider the use of masks as a strategy to distribute health and life to a population by reducing the number of people who would get sick and die from the virus, and discuss the following questions:

1. Some people decided to never wear a mask. If you asked these people why they wouldn't wear masks, what do you think they would say? Which social justice perspective(s) might be used to justify their decision and why? Which perspective would be least likely to justify not wearing a mask and why?

2. Some people decided to wear a mask outside at all times. If you asked those people why they made that decision, what do you think they would say? Which social justice perspective(s) might justify their decision and why? Which perspective would be least likely to justify always wearing a mask and why?

3. Some people decided to wear a mask outside, but only when social distancing was not possible. If you asked those people why they made that decision, what do you think they would say? Which social justice perspective(s) might be used to justify their decision and why? Which perspective would be least likely to justify their decision and why?

Next Steps: Identifying, Analyzing, and Responding to Social Injustices

In this chapter, we presented several perspectives to help you reflect and think critically about your own beliefs about social justice. The next step will be to analyze how the values and concepts of the social contract underlying those divergent views function either rationalize and support or question and challenge oppressive conditions for diverse populations. We begin that process with a review of the various social justice perspectives, which for our purposes, we have grouped into two categories.

The first category is the world of mainstream philosophy, which conveys an abstract view of justice and rights. The three normative perspectives (egalitarian, utilitarian, libertarian) in this category are useful ways to think about what social justice should be, but they do not acknowledge or explain why certain groups of people are consistently denied justice. With that limitation in mind, social work values and ethics do seem more closely aligned with the philosophical principles of the egalitarian perspective, but the realities of practice may often require a utilitarian compromise.

The other category is the world of the -isms (domination, conquest, imperialism, colonialism, racism, slavery, apartheid, reparations, etc.), which focuses on the very real impact of oppression on people's lives both historically and in the present. The racial contract provides a bridge between the normative world (i.e., what should be) and the realities of the world as it is. It equips social workers with tools that enable us to see how the dynamics of oppression operate in practice to produce disparate outcomes for diverse populations. The human rights perspective can be seen as building on the racial contract's description of what is by proposing a universal meeting of the human needs of all, without discrimination, as a solution—that is, a vision of social justice to strive for.

It is right and good for social work as a profession to endorse and implement an ideal social contract, such as that laid out in the egalitarian principles of justice. But to advocate and work toward an ideal vision of social justice, the nonideal contract as it exists needs to be demystified and discarded. That is what the racial contract does, and why, of all the perspectives, it is the one most consistent with our premise that diversity and social justice are inextricably entwined, that culturally competent practice is anti-oppression practice. The racial contract invites us to recognize how notions about social justice are race- and gender- and "other"-based. It helps us to understand how people seen as expendable or undeserving are excluded from the realm of social justice. How those who have not been included in or benefited from the social contract have been negatively labeled because of the group with which they are identified. How their exclusion is premised on stereotypes and prejudicial attitudes related to ethnocentrism.

At all levels of social work practice—micro, meso, and macro—concerns about human rights, structural inequities, oppression, and other forms of injustice need to be identified. Critical thinking about the beliefs and value assumptions underlying the decisions made at all three levels is required to understand the systematic and ubiquitous ways that oppression operates. What follows are two exercises aimed at stimulating that kind of critical thinking, one involving an individual client and the other an agency situation.

CLASSROOM EXERCISE 2.5

Resource Limitations

Mary is a social worker in a public welfare agency with limited and increasingly shrinking resources. Her caseload consists of 50 individuals and families, most of whom are Native American people living on a nearby reservation. One of Mary's clients is a single mother of three small children. Her refrigerator has been malfunctioning, so milk and other dairy products spoil within a few days. Mary's supervisor denies her request for a new refrigerator for her client, saying there are several families on the reservation who don't have a refrigerator at all, and the agency's severely limited resources should be used to obtain refrigerators for them first.

In small groups, read the case situation and the discuss the following questions:

1. Was the supervisor's decision just (fair) or unjust (unfair)?

2. On what principle did Mary's supervisor base her decision? Which social justice perspective?

3. What other decisions might be made in this situation? Based on which social justice perspectives?

4. What would decisions based on the racial contract and human rights perspectives look like?

ASSIGNMENT 2.1

Social Justice Analysis of an Agency Policy

Choose an agency policy from your field placement or agency of employment with which you have some concerns and analyze the policy from a social justice perspective. You may provide your analysis in a paper or as a presentation to the class. The analysis should include the ways in which the policy perpetuates oppression of clients or staff. You should defend your position and discuss the pros and cons of alternative positions about the policy. Include strategy steps for advocating change in your analysis. The following statements and questions are suggested as guides:

1. Describe the policy in detail.

2. Discuss how the policy negatively affects clients or staff; be specific about who is being harmed and how.

3. Discuss who is benefiting from the policy; be specific.

4. On what basis would you determine that the policy is unjust? Make your case specifically and clearly.

5. Which of the five social justice perspectives presented in this chapter are you using to make your case that the policy is unjust?

6. What are alternative and differing views about the policy? Be sure to discuss fully a view about the policy that is different from yours.

7. Which of the five social justice perspectives presented in this chapter does the opposing view use?

8. What strategy steps do you propose for advocating for change? Be specific and realistic.

References

Alexander, M. (2020). *The New Jim Crow*. The New Press.

Beverly, D. P., & McSweeney, E. A. (1987). *Social welfare and social justice*. Prentice Hall.

Conrad, A. P. (1988). The role of field instructors in the transmission of social justice values. *Journal of Teaching in Social Work, 2*(2), 63–82.

Constitutional Rights Foundation. (n.d.). *The color of justice*. https://www.crf -usa.org/brown-v-board-50th-anniversary/the-color-of-justice.html

Council on Social Work Education. (2015). *Educational policy and accreditation standards*.

Davis, F. E. (2019). *The little book of race and restorative justice: Black lives, healing and U.S. transformation*. Good Books.

Equal Justice Initiative. (2014, October 1). *Race and the criminal justice system*. https://eji.org/news/history-racial-injustice-race-and-criminal-justice/

Gil, D. (1998). *Confronting injustice and oppression: Concepts and strategies for social workers*. Columbia University Press.

Hare, R. M. (1992). Justice and equality. In Sterba, S. P. (Ed.), Justice: Alternative political perspectives (pp. 185–199). Wadsworth.

International Federation of Social Workers. (2021). https://www.ifsw.org

Mills, C. W. (1997). *The racial contract*. Cornell University Press.

Mills, C. (2017a) *Black rights/white wrongs: The critique of racial liberalism*. Oxford University Press.

Mills, C. (2017b, January). Philosophy and the racial contract. In N. Zack (Ed.), *The Oxford Handbook of Philosophy and Race. Oxford Handbooks Online*.

https://www.oxfordhandbooks.com/view/10.1093/oxfordhb/9780190236953
.001.0001/oxfordhb-9780190236953-e-4

National Association of Social Workers. (2017). *Code of Ethics of the National Association of Social Workers.*

Nicotera, A. (2019). Social justice and social work, a fierce urgency: Recommendations for social work social justice pedagogy, *Journal of Social Work Education, 55*(3), 460–475, https://doi.org/10.1080/10437797.2019.1600443

Nozick, R. (1974). *Anarchy, state, and utopia.* Basic Books.

Nussbaum, M. (2000). *Women and human development: The capabilities approach.* Cambridge University Press.

Nussbaum, M. (2001). *Upheavals of thought: The intelligence of emotions.* Cambridge University Press.

Nussbaum, M. (2013). *Creating capabilities: The human development approach.* The Belknap Press of Harvard University Press.

Pateman, C. (1988). *The sexual contract.* Stanford University Press.

Pateman, C., & Mills, C. W. (2007). *Contract and domination.* Polity Press.

Poe-Yamagata, E. & Jones, M. A. (2000). *And justice for some: Differential treatment of youth of color in the justice system.* Building Blocks for Youth.

Rawls, J. (1971). *A theory of justice.* Harvard University Press.

Reisch, M. (2002). Defining social justice in a socially unjust world. *Families in Society, 83*(4), 343–354.

Reisch, M., & Taylor, C. T. (1983). Ethical guidelines for cutback management: A preliminary approach. *Administration in Social Work, 7*(3/4), 59–72.

Segal, E. A. (2016). *Social welfare policies and social programs: A values perspective* (4th ed.). Brooks/Cole Cengage Learning.

Segal, E. A. & Wagaman, M.A. (2017). Social empathy as a framework for teaching social justice. *Journal of Social Work Education, 53*(2), 201–211. http://dx.doi.org/10.1080/10437797.2016.1266980

Sidgwick, H. (1966). *The methods of ethics.* Dover.

Sterba, J. P. (1985). From liberty to welfare. *Social Theory and Practice, 11*(3), 285–305.

Sen, A. (2009). *The idea of justice.* The Belknap Press of Harvard University Press.

Umbreit, M., & Armour, M. P. (2010), *Restorative Justice Dialogue: An Essential Guide for Research and Practice.* Springer.

United Nations. (1994). *Teaching and learning about human rights: A manual for schools of social work and the social work profession.* Centre for Human Rights, International Association of Schools of Social Work United Nations.

Van Soest, D. (2003). Advancing social and economic justice. In D. Lum (Ed.), *Culturally competent practice: A framework for understanding diverse groups and justice issues* (pp. 350–351). Brooks/Cole.

Van Soest, D. (2012). Confronting our fears and finding hope in difficult times: Social work as a force for social justice, *Journal of Progressive Human Services, 23*(2), 95–109.

Wakefield, J. C. (1988, June). Psychotherapy, distributive justice, and social work. Part I: Distributive justice as a conceptual framework for social work. *Social Service Review, 62,* 187–210.

Young, I. M. (1990). *Justice and the politics of difference.* Princeton University Press.

Zinn, H. (1997). *The Zinn reader: Writings on disobedience and democracy.* Seven Stories Press.

CHAPTER 3

A Conceptual Framework for Anti-Oppression Social Work Practice
Uniting Cultural Diversity and Social Justice

There are many definitions of cultural competence, including self-awareness, knowledge of culturally diverse groups, awareness of within-group differences, and specific clinical skills that include helping responses such as engaging in therapeutic alliances and conducting interventions at different levels of practice (Sue & Sue, 2013). The main premise of this book moves beyond cultural competence to focus on anti-oppression practice. In other words, culturally competent social work practice means engaging in effective interventions that are grounded in a commitment to promote social and economic justice with diverse clients. To begin to understand the implications of this assertion, we start by breaking it down into parts and identifying our premises. We explore the details in this and following chapters.

First, culturally competent practice and anti-oppression practice cannot be practiced in isolation from each other. Together, they embody a core social work value that, in practice, has the ultimate goal of transforming "unjust and oppressive social, economic, and political institutions into just and non-oppressive alternatives" (Gil, 1998, p. 1).

Second, to be culturally competent requires understanding the connection between the individual difficulties that people face and the social problems or conditions that create those difficulties.

Third, to be culturally competent means making informed choices about two necessary and interrelated interventions:

1. Provide direct assistance, safety nets, and service systems that meet the needs of individuals, families and communities that are experiencing problems.

2. Engage in actions aimed at dismantling and transforming the oppressive and inequitable systems that create those problems (i.e., the root causes).

Fourth, to be culturally competent requires asking critical questions about why people who experience problems disproportionately also share particular characteristics—is there a dynamic at work that is targeting certain groups? For example, why are a disproportionate number of the 140+ million poor and low-income people in the United States disproportionately Black, Indigenous, Latinx, women, and people with physical or mental disabilities? What are the forces that create such structural inequities, and how do they work?

Fifth, moving from cultural competence to anti-oppression practice means focusing on how systems of oppression operate to confer power and advantage on people who are regarded as the norm (i.e., white, male, heterosexual, cisgendered, able-bodied, English-speaking, U.S. born, and otherwise privileged) and deny power and advantage to those regarded as "other" or different (i.e., Black, Indigenous, Latinx, other people of color, female, people with disabilities, noncisgendered, nonheterosexual, non-English-speaking or U.S. born, and otherwise nonprivileged).

Sixth, cultural competence is grounded in an understanding of intersectionality, encompassing our own positions of advantage and disadvantage in oppressive systems based on the groups with which we identify.

Seventh, when we are advantaged (i.e., privileged) based on our membership in one or more groups considered to be the norm, culturally competent practice entails distributing our own power and resources. We do this as allies and accomplices with those who are targeted for marginalization and disadvantage; in other words, working in solidarity and partnership with them to challenge, disrupt, and dismantle barriers to structural inequities.

Eighth, culturally competent means (a) understanding how the dynamics of oppression operate to reproduce structural inequities and (b) employing anti-oppression strategies and interventions at all three levels of practice (micro-individual, meso-institutional, macro-structural) as illustrated in Figure 3.1, which focuses on homelessness.

Figure 3.1 Homelessness and Culturally Competent Anti-Oppression Social Work Practice

If you have come here to help me you are wasting your time.
But if you have come because your liberation is bound up with mine,
then let us work together.
—Lilla Watson, Aboriginal elder, activist and educator, Queensland, Australia

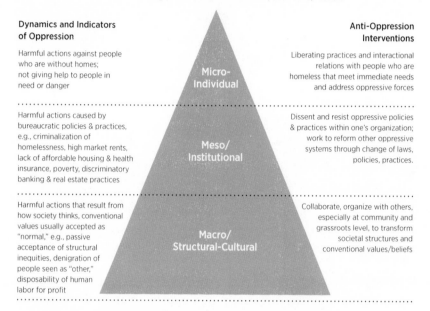

Dynamics and Indicators of Oppression		Anti-Oppression Interventions
Harmful actions against people who are without homes; not giving help to people in need or danger	**Micro-Individual**	Liberating practices and interactional relations with people who are homeless that meet immediate needs and address oppressive forces
Harmful actions caused by bureaucratic policies & practices, e.g., criminalization of homelessness, high market rents, lack of affordable housing & health insurance, poverty, discriminatory banking & real estate practices	**Meso/Institutional**	Dissent and resist oppressive policies & practices within one's organization; work to reform other oppressive systems through change of laws, policies, practices.
Harmful actions that result from how society thinks, conventional values usually accepted as "normal," e.g., passive acceptance of structural inequities, denigration of people seen as "other," disposability of human labor for profit	**Macro/Structural-Cultural**	Collaborate, organize with others, especially at community and grassroots level, to transform societal structures and conventional values/beliefs

As you can see, the call to be a culturally competent social worker is a tall order. You need to know what oppression is and how it works, as well as its patterns, dynamics, and consequences. You need to know how oppressive systems discriminate against and harm selected groups of people based on race, ethnicity,[1] gender, sexual orientation, gender identity, disability, age, religion, and other characteristics. You also need to know what oppression looks like at the four levels of intervention (see Figure 3.2) and that the levels are interconnected: (1) the individual—attitudes that people have been socialized to believe are true about themselves and others; (2) the interpersonal—interacting with others based on what people have been taught

---

1 We use the terms "ethnicity," "people of color," and "race" interchangeably to refer to what have been called ethnic minorities. All of these refer to the values, beliefs, heritage, and life experiences that influence the formation of social identity. In that all groups have national origin heritage, these terms are applied to all groups in relation to their social and racial identity. The term "race" is used with the understanding that is a social construct with no biological evidence. This will be discussed further in this text.

Figure 3.2   The Four Levels of Oppression

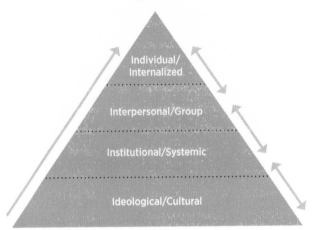

If you are going to hold someone down,
you're going to have to hold on to the other end of the
chain. You are confined by your own system of oppression.
—Toni Morrison

through institutions and supported by family, peers, and community; (3) the institutional—systematic ways that policies and practices control access to resources and power; and (4) the ideological—assumptions, beliefs, messages, and symbols that reinforce what is considered "normal," "superior," and "right" and condemn deviations from those norms; these are beliefs that justify discrimination at the other three levels.

Each level supports, undergirds, and interacts with the other levels to maintain intractable systems of oppression. What follows is an illustration of how a culturally competent social worker applies a lens of oppression through which she makes culturally competent decisions at each level.

- Individual: A school social worker recognizes and acknowledges her own unconscious belief that students of color tend to be undisciplined and cause problems in the classroom; she examines her own pattern of using discipline versus treatment based on race.
- Interpersonal: She monitors her previously unexamined beliefs and makes sure they don't get played out in how the problem is defined and how issues are talked about during her interactions with students of color.

- Institutional: She works to help her colleagues see how biased beliefs and interactions at the individual and interpersonal levels of oppression are being reinforced by the school's norms, policies, and practices, and she develops strategies to reduce those that result in a disproportionate number of African American boys being sent to the school social worker for help with "classroom behavior problems."

- Ideological/cultural: The social worker recognizes that this level of oppression is more difficult to grasp because it manifests itself in passive acceptance of inequalities and deprivations as "just the way things are" and beliefs that are reinforced by avoidable social indicators, such as high dropout and low graduation rates of Black males. She invites her colleagues to join her in learning more about this and interrupting the ways in which their beliefs, values, and symbols of a dominant worldview—such as that white is "normal," "better," "smarter," "well-behaved"—undergird and give rise to oppression at the institutional, interpersonal, and individual levels.

As you can see, learning about oppression and how it operates is a daunting task. It is a lifelong journey with obstacles along the way. We discuss two of them in the next sections: feelings that arise when you consider the ways you benefit from and/or are harmed by oppressive systems and the challenges posed by current social and political realities.

REFLECTION/JOURNALING EXERCISE 3.1

Cultural Diversity for Social Justice

1. *Cultural diversity.* What does that mean to you? Write down all the thoughts and feelings these words evoke in you.

2. In the same way, consider the words "social justice."

3. Finally, combine the two—cultural diversity for social justice—and reflect on any thoughts and feelings that phrase evokes. Just brainstorm without censoring yourself, knowing that no one else will see what you wrote.

Why Is Learning About Cultural Diversity and Social Justice So Difficult?

> I am a white woman. I am standing beside a black woman. We are facing a group of white people seated in front of us. We are in their workplace and have been hired by their employer to lead them in a dialogue about race. The room is filled with tension and charged with hostility. I have just presented a definition of racism that includes the acknowledgement that whites hold social and institutional power over people of color. A white man is pounding his fist on the table … yells, "A white person can't get a job anymore!" I look around the room and see forty employees, thirty-eight of whom are white. Why is this white man so angry? … Why are all the other white people either sitting in silent agreement with him or tuning out? I have, after all, only articulated a definition of racism. (DiAngelo, 2018, pp. 1)

Why is it so hard to talk openly and honestly about diversity and social justice issues? Because it's personal, that's why. Because it's hard to listen and talk about how our access or lack of access to social and economic power is based on the groups to which we belong. It makes us feel anxious, fearful, and angry. So we don't talk about it. Or we talk about it disingenuously, reluctantly, or defensively. And when we do that, we don't learn what we need to learn. To help overcome this obstacle, we offer an opportunity in the following section to face fear and anger head-on.

Confronting Our Fear and Anger Means Facing the Issue of Privilege

> Fear is a powerful emotion, one that immobilizes, traps words in our throats, and stills our tongues. Like a deer on the highway, frozen in the panic induced by the lights of an oncoming car, when we are afraid it seems that we cannot think, we cannot speak, we cannot move. (Tatum, 2017, pp. 331)

Much of the fear and anger that gets triggered in discussions related to diversity and oppression is rooted in a deep need to be seen as "good" persons. That need comes from having been socialized into and having, unavoidably and unconsciously, internalized either-or beliefs about what is good versus bad, right versus wrong. Whether we're aware of them or not, each of us has also been assigned multiple social identities within which there is a hierarchy, a social status of dominant and nondominant groups. So, if a conversation implicates us as beneficiaries in a dominant system that harms others, then it can feel like our identity as good, moral people is being challenged. And that, inevitably, produces feelings of discomfort, anxiety, and shame. Phrases like "I am not a racist, but" or "I don't mean to sound sexist, but" or "I didn't mean to imply that you weren't able to ..." reveal such discomfort. They also reveal a view of racism, sexism, ableism, and other -isms not as systems of oppression but instead as discrete acts committed by individuals. And, since only bad people commit acts that are racist, sexist, or ableist, and I don't, then "I am not a racist."

The very concept of "unearned" privilege by itself can trigger intense emotions. Strong forces in U.S. culture have socialized many of us to believe that the world is a just place, that a person's merit and fate are closely aligned, and that people get what they deserve (Lerner, 1980). The very idea that dominant groups can bestow benefits to people whom they deem normal and limit opportunities to people who fall into other categories "violates everything we've been told about fairness and everything we've been told about the American Dream of hard work paying off and good things happening to good people" (Oluo, 2018, p. 63). To consider the idea that privileges are granted simply due to the circumstances of birth, such as race and gender, is to make the world feel less safe, less predictable, not kind, not fair. While a desire to believe that the world is just is understand-able, holding onto that belief contributes to a world that is the opposite of that. Studies show that some social and political consequences of the belief in a just world include acceptance of existing discriminatory institu-tions, a tendency to denigrate and blame victims of social injustice, and not engaging in activities to alleviate the plight of social victims or to change society (Rubin & Peplau, 1975).

Discussions about privilege become even more difficult and emotion-laden when we talk about specific privileges enjoyed by dominant group members and specific limitations, disadvantages, and disapproval experienced by nondominant group members. In all systems of advantage, the core privilege denied to those in the nondominant group and offered only to those in the dominant group is to be deemed inherently normal, regular, legal, right—in other words, superior to and better than those who are not given that privilege. While members of the nondominant group are constantly aware of how they are perceived and what opportunities and resources they are denied, members of the dominant group enjoy the privilege of not having to know, see, hear, or talk about the fact that they even have privileges.

Talking about privilege is further complicated in that everyone has multiple social identities and experiences disadvantages and abuse based on a combination of race, physical and mental ability, gender, sexuality, class, education, and other factors (see Figure 3.3). All forms of oppression cause deep suffering, and trying to decide whether one is worse than others is problematic because it diminishes people's lived experiences, disregards the impact of multiple identities in shaping lives, and divides us when we need to be working together to achieve social and economic justice. The reality is that the health and well-being of large numbers of people are often determined by a combination of advantages and disadvantages conferred upon them. That means the same person can be more privileged among some groups of people and less privileged among other groups (Collins & Bilge, 2020). When a person belongs to multiple oppressed social groups, the intersectionality of those oppressions overlaps and causes that person even more hardship (Crenshaw, 1989). The point is, when we address one form of oppression, we need to take other forms into account. That means asking big, difficult questions, such as: How do women of color experience gender privilege differently than white women? And how do men of color experience gender privilege differently than white men?

Figure 3.3 Types of Privilege

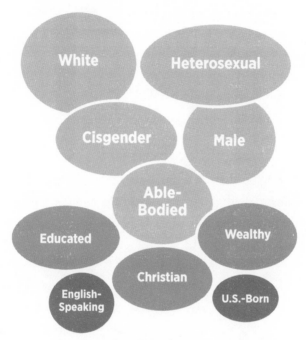

PRIVILEGE DEFINED

The advantages, benefits, or degrees of prestige and respect conferred on individuals by virtue of their membership in certain social identity groups.

The process of developing cultural competence requires us to ask those hard questions and more. In the next sections, we invite you to start with questions about yourself, such as: In what ways do you enjoy power, privilege, and advantage? In what ways are you denied power, privilege, and advantage?

We intentionally begin with centering racism as the core system of oppression for several reasons. The United States was founded as a white nation based on a system of racial oppression. A deep-seated belief in white supremacy justified the genocide, ethnic cleansing, and enslavement of Indigenous people of color and the importation and enslavement of people of African descent. Systemic racism is woven into the very fabric of American culture, society, and laws. It has proven itself to be intractable over and over again, both historically and in the present. It is a system of oppression that defines us as a nation and affects all of us as individuals. It is, metaphorically speaking, embedded in the DNA of all white Americans. That is why we believe that, if we are ever to overcome and eliminate racism, a soul-searching critique of white privilege, and of whiteness itself, is needed. And finally, we focus on racism as an important and essential step in helping to understand and eliminate the other systems of oppression such as sexism, heterosexism, cisgenderism, ableism, classism, ageism, and anti-Semitism.

Facing White Privilege

White people are particularly afraid to talk openly and honestly about their own privilege, a fragility that, according to DiAngelo (2018) serves to maintain their dominance within the racial hierarchy and holds the system of racism in place. Even when one's privileges are understood as part of a complex, interconnected system,

> that isn't to say that understanding privilege won't make you feel bad. It might make you feel very bad, and I'm convinced that is why so many of us are quick to dismiss discussions on privilege before they even get started. We may not fully "get" privilege, but we have a feeling that understanding our privilege will change what we feel about ourselves and our world, and not in a good way. (Oluo, 2018, p. 59)

So why is it so hard to talk about race, especially for white people? Some people are afraid they will inadvertently say something that will sound offensive, even racist. And that is often exactly what does happen. And, yes, it is painful. And embarrassing. It triggers feelings of shame. That's why it's so important to understand how this happens. One explanation is that the system of white privilege is grounded in what is called *implicit bias*: the process of associating stereotypes or attitudes with categories of people without conscious awareness. It's that lack of awareness that trips us up, because it makes it possible not to admit that we even have implicit biases. But, everyone does have them, both positive and negative ones. Why wouldn't we, when biases have been poured into us since birth like air and water into our bodies? We have them even when they contradict our stated values. We have them even when we think we don't. We discover new biases even when we admit we have them and think we've identified all of them.

Consider this true story. A white social worker with decades of experience as a diversity trainer is walking her dog when she sees a woman who appears to be Latinx walking out of her home and what immediately pops into her head is "housekeeper." Despite her commitment to fairness and justice, close relationships with Latinx friends, and her knowledge of implicit bias, her brain made a potentially harmful snap judgment about who someone was. So what does she do in the face of this discovery? She starts by reflecting on when and how her implicit bias might influence her thoughts and decision making. She takes the time to examine the structural inequities that result from implicit biases such as hers, the cycle whereby these biases produce inequitable outcomes for Latinx in the job market, and how harmful stereotypes are used to justify inequitable hiring practices. By becoming aware of and acknowledging her implicit bias, she has taken an important step in countering discrimination (Hahn & Gawronski, 2019).

The following exercise is intended to stimulate classroom discussion about how people experience discussing implicit biases about race. Again, we remind you that in exercises throughout this book, the terms "race" and "people of color" are used interchangeably.

CLASSROOM EXERCISE 3.1

Talking About Race and Implicit Bias

Like the diversity trainer in the story, working on our implicit biases starts with ourselves and being willing to look at when and how our own thoughts and decision making can be influenced by them. It all starts with personal reflection. So, before engaging in this discussion exercise, think about the questions below. You might want to write down your answers.

- What do you remember from childhood about how you made sense of human differences? What confused you? What made it hard for you to understand?

- What childhood experiences did you have with friends or adults who were different from you in some way?

- When were you first aware of your race?

- What was your earliest experience dealing with race and/or racism?

- How, if ever, did any adult help you to think about racial differences?

- What is an example of implicit bias that you have experienced, witnessed, or heard about?

- How might that type of bias be used to justify inequitable practices or behaviors?

- How might you adjust your practice as a social worker based on your answers above?

After reflecting, review the ground rules you've agreed on for classroom exercises (see Chapter 1), and then share with one other person or with a small group what you learned about your own implicit bias from this exercise.

The phrase "check your privilege" is often used in conversations about race. It can be difficult to hear. The words can sting. To some white people, it may feel like a dirty secret has been exposed, the secret that some of what they have is unmerited (Jensen, 1998), which can trigger fears about not being special, of not being worthy, that success is more a function of being born white than a result of brains and hard work, and that they are being told to give up their advantages. And anyone who truly believes in meritocracy does not want to compete in a system in which certain groups of people are excluded or disadvantaged. To quote Wilkerson (2020), "A win is not legitimate if whole sections of humanity are not in the game" (p. 385).

"Check your privilege" also shines a spotlight on advantages that whites receive on a daily basis and take for granted, such as not having to think about their race or racism every day; not being racially profiled while driving, shopping, or jogging; and not worrying about being murdered by the police. When made aware of one's own privileges, there's a strong societal urge to perpetuate racial biases, both to justify them and to reduce one's cognitive dissonance. For instance, if people believe that Black people are more prone to criminal behavior, they can then justify police racial profiling, and that, in turn, justifies their white privilege not to be racially profiled (Davis, 2016).

Talking about race may trigger particularly primitive feelings for well-meaning people who abhor racism but are not consciously aware of being part of the problem. Sometimes the extent to which they benefit becomes clear when they are made aware for the first time or in a new way that they enjoy the most basic of privileges, such as getting to live 3.5 years more than people of color (Kendi, 2019). They often feel genuine shock when they realize that they don't know what it really means to have to deal with unresponsive institutions whose cooperation is required to meet one's basic needs such as employment, a living wage, housing, career, equitable salary, and medical services. It takes deep humility for white people to listen to what it means to have to navigate through hostile, unwelcoming terrain when the terrain through which they have navigated has functioned in their best interests.

The opposite is the reality for most people of color. In an article titled "Whites in Multicultural Education: Rethinking Our Role," Gary Howard wrote:

> Throughout most of our history, there has been no reason why white Americans, for their own survival or success, have needed to be sensitive to the cultural perspectives of other groups. This is not a luxury available to people of color, [whose] daily survival depends on knowledge of white America. ... To be successful in mainstream institutions, people of color in the U.S. need to be bicultural—able to play by the rules of their own cultural community and able to play the game according to the rules established by the dominant culture. For most white Americans, on the other hand, there is only one game, and they have traditionally been on the winning team. (1993, p. 38)

People of color are targets of microaggressions on a regular basis, slights and insults that, when chalked up over a lifetime, amount to oppression on a huge scale. Microaggressions will be discussed in more detail in the next chapter.

The tremendous gulf between individuals who are positioned differently in terms of access to sociopolitical power and privilege makes it difficult to talk with each other about it. So people tend to not talk about it. And when they do, they talk in general, safe terms. Reflection/ Journaling Exercise 3.2 focuses on how the system of advantage based on the color of your skin affects you. You will probably become aware, when doing the exercise, that the reason behind how you are treated is not necessarily clear and/or known to you. For example, someone may insult you, not because of your skin color, but because of your accent or your gender or your last name or your sexual orientation or your disability or some combination of factors. Put everything on your list even if you aren't sure you benefited or were targeted due to your skin color. Sorting that out in relation to all the "unpacking your privileges" exercises is part of the learning process.

REFLECTION/JOURNALING EXERCISE 3.2

Unpacking/Packing White Privilege: Part 1

If you are white, imagine you are unpacking, from your invisible, weightless knapsack, all the privileges that make your life easier and that you can count on at every stage of your life. These are not things that you earned but rather were made to feel were yours by birth and by virtue of being a conscientious, law-abiding, "normal" person of goodwill. Make a list of as many as you can think of, at least six things.

If you are a person of color or of mixed race, imagine you are unpacking from your invisible and heavy knapsack all the stones, pebbles, and even bricks that are memories of racist, oppressive, dehumanizing things you are aware of, have seen or experienced, the microaggressions (slights, insults, and put-downs) that have targeted you because of your skin color. Make a list of as many as you can think of (including things you're not sure were based on your skin color or on something else), at least six things.

Look at your list. How does it feel to reflect on what's on it? Consider having a straightforward discussion in class about your list. What excites you about having that discussion? What fears might you have?

*Reflection Exercises 3.2, 3.3, and 3.4 are based on the work of Peggy McIntosh (1995) and Antoinette Kavanaugh (2020).

Facing Male Privilege

The difficulties inherent in talking about a system of advantage for whites isn't the only obstacle we face in our attempts to address issues of diversity for social justice. Gender in the United States also consists of unearned advantage and dominance for males. Again, the secret related to gender is that some of what males have is unmerited. Fear and anger rooted in this secret make it difficult for males to take what females say seriously, particularly in relation to male privilege, in the same way that white privilege makes it difficult for white people to listen to people of color. In her essay, "White Privilege and Male Privilege," Peggy McIntosh (1995) describes how the system of gender privilege, like racial privilege, becomes invisible to the males who benefit from it. And yet it affects the everyday life of both males and females, although in different ways depending on one's race, sexual orientation, ability, and other social identities.

Acknowledging that men have advantages doesn't deny that bad things happen to them, just as acknowledging that white people have advantages doesn't deny that bad things happen to them. Remember, we are talking about an institutionalized system of advantage, not a judgment about the goodness or badness of people with privileges based on that system. The outcomes, however, are that men make the most money; that men dominate government and corporate boards; that men, not women, occupy virtually all of the most powerful positions in our society; that men continue to control and dominate women in areas of physical and sexual abuse. To be male and oblivious to the ways that men are advantaged is the first big privilege. This is the way it is with all systems of advantage; the first substantive privilege of being white, male, heterosexual, cisgendered, able-bodied, and so forth, is the privilege of being oblivious to your privileges.

REFLECTION/JOURNALING EXERCISE 3.3

Unpacking/Packing Male Privileges: Part 2

If you are a male, imagine you are unpacking, from your invisible and lightweight knapsack, all the privileges that make your life easier, not things that you earned but rather were made to feel were yours by birth. Make a list of as many as you can think of, at least six things. Compare your list of male privileges with your previous list of advantages or disadvantages based on race.

If you are a female, imagine you are unpacking, from your invisible and heavy knapsack, all the stones, pebbles, and even bricks that are memories of sexist, oppressive, dehumanizing things you are aware of, have seen, or experienced, all the microaggressions (insults and put-downs) that have targeted you because of your gender. Make a list of as many as you can think of (including things you're not sure were based on your gender or on something else), at least six things. Compare this list with your previous list of advantages or disadvantages based on race.

Look at your lists. What did you learn? How does it feel to reflect on what's on your lists? Consider having a straightforward discussion in class about what you've learned. What excites you about such a discussion? What concerns and fears might you have?

Facing Sexual Privilege

I was born Black, and a woman. I am trying to become the strongest person I can become to live the life I have been given and to help effect change toward a livable future for this earth and for my children. As a Black, lesbian, feminist, socialist, poet, mother of two including one boy and a member of an interracial couple, I usually find myself part of some group in which the majority defines me as deviant, difficult, inferior or just plain "wrong." … From my membership in all of these groups I have learned that oppression and the intolerance of difference come in all shapes and sexes and colors and sexualities; and that among those of us who share the goals of liberation and a workable future for our children, there can be no hierarchies of oppression. I have learned that sexism and heterosexism both arise from the same source as racism. …Within the lesbian community I am Black, and within the Black community I am a lesbian. Any attack against Black people is a lesbian and gay issue, because I and thousands of other Black women are part of the lesbian community. Any attack against lesbians and gays is a Black issue, because thousands of lesbians and gay men are Black. There is no hierarchy of oppression. (Lorde, 1983)

Lorde's words about multiple identities make clear that using racism as a template for understanding all other oppressions, as we do in this text, does not negate the reality that all forms of privilege and disadvantage come with real consequences on real people's lives in complicated ways. And so we now turn to McIntosh (1995), who moves beyond race and gender to discuss other systems of privilege. She asserts that there is an even bigger taboo to talking about heterosexual privilege than about race privilege due to "the daily ways in which heterosexual privilege endows some persons with comfort or power; and provides supports, assets, approvals, and rewards those who live or expect to live in heterosexual pairs. Unpacking and owning those privileges, she says, is more difficult owing to the deep embeddedness of heterosexual advantage and dominance with religious and other taboos surrounding these" (p. 85).

The same is true of cisgender privilege; if you identify with the gender you were assigned at birth, you are considered normal and can reasonably assume that you can walk through life without worrying about getting or keeping a job because of your sexual or gender identity. The risks of not being cisgender are even greater if you have multiple identities; for example, if you are a Black, transgender woman, you face a higher chance of being murdered (Dinno, 2017). As with the other systems of advantage, the more cognizant you are of your own privileges, the more you start to realize how much work it is for those who don't have access to those privileges.

REFLECTION/JOURNALING EXERCISE 3.4

Unpacking/Packing Our Heterosexual and Cisgender Privileges: Part 3

Imagine unpacking, from your invisible and lightweight knapsack, all the privileges that have been given to you because you are cisgender and your sexual orientation is heterosexual. Make a list of all the special circumstances and conditions that you experience that you did not earn but that you have been made to feel are yours by birth, by citizenship, and by virtue of being a conscientious, law-abiding, "normal" person of goodwill. Compare this list with your lists of privileges from the previous two reflection exercises.

If you are a gay, lesbian, bisexual, or transgender person, imagine unpacking from your invisible and heavy knapsack all the stones, pebbles, and even bricks that are memories of heterosexist, oppressive, dehumanizing things you are aware of, have seen, or experienced—the microaggressions (insults and put-downs) that have been targeted at you because of your sexuality. Make a list of as many as you can think of (including things you're not sure were based on your gender or sexual identity or on something else), at least six things. Compare this list with your lists of privileges from the previous two reflection exercises.

Look at all three of your lists. What did you learn? How does it feel to reflect on what's on them? Consider having a straightforward discussion in class about what you learned. What excites you about such a discussion? What concerns and fears might you have?

Facing Multiple Privileges

Now let us look at the full and complex picture. Reflection Exercise 3.5, a self-assessment tool developed by the California Partnership to End Domestic Violence, is an opportunity for you to look at the intersection of your multiple identities and the corresponding privileges conferred and not conferred.

REFLECTION/JOURNALING EXERCISE 3.5

Oppression and Privilege Self-Assessment Tool*

In a quiet and safe space, take some time to read through the disadvantages and advantages identified below, circling those that apply to you. As you go through the statements, identifying the areas in which you have privilege or find yourself at an intersection of oppression and privilege, be kind to yourself. The more we deepen our understanding of ways in which we can advocate for spaces free of violence, the more we learn about ourselves even though this can result in some personal discomfort. We invite you to lean into this discomfort and allow these feelings to provide a space for genuine understanding and empathy for yourself.

Disadvantages OPPRESSION	Advantages PRIVILEGE
• I worry about not having enough money to pay for housing, food, clothing, or education.	• I, or my family, can afford to live in a comfortable home and have enough money to meet our needs.
• I cannot talk openly about who I am dating or in love with.	• I can talk openly about my partner or loved one.
• I face physical barriers accessing public buildings and using the transportation systems.	• I can easily use public buildings and transportation systems.
• I don't own a car.	• I own a car.
• I cannot afford to travel nationally or internationally, whether it be for pleasure or educational purposes.	• I can afford to travel, nationally or internationally, whether it be for pleasure or educational purposes.
• I worry that people may not hire me because of the color of my skin, my name, the way I look, or my gender.	• I don't worry about being hired because of the color of my skin, my name, the way I look, or my gender.
• I have a disability.	• I don't have a disability.
• At home, while growing up, my family spoke a language other than English.	• At home, while growing up, my family spoke English.
• I worry about being harassed or attacked because of my gender or sexual orientation.	• I don't worry about being harassed or attacked because of my gender or sexual orientation.
• My gender does not match the gender I was assigned at birth.	• My gender matches the gender I was assigned at birth
• I tend to see people of my racial or ethnic group portrayed negatively in newspapers, television, movies, and advertisements.	• There are many positive images of people from my racial or ethnic group portrayed in newspapers, television, movies, and ads.
• Because of financial hardship, I tend to put up with a number of problematic situations.	• When problematic situations arise, I tend to have the financial means to solve them.'
• I need to hide, change, or minimize parts of my identity to reduce the chances of mistreatment.	• I don't need to hide, change, or minimize parts of my identity to reduce the chances of mistreatment.
• The holidays I tend to celebrate are not observed as national holidays.	• The holidays I celebrate are recognized as national holidays.
• I am not white.	• I am white.
• I am not a man.	• I am a man.

*California Partnership to End Domestic Violence https://www.cpedv.org/sites/main/files/oppression_and_privilege_self_assessment.pdf

What should be clear at this point is that the issue of unmerited privileges is complicated. We are all affected by systems of advantage—sometimes we benefit and sometimes we pay. No wonder delving into conversations about privilege is like roaming into an area rife with emotional land mines. Yet the understanding and insight gained are not only worth the effort, but they are also essential to anti-oppression social work practice. When you are able to identify and talk about your unearned privileges, you are in a position to think critically and reject dominant ideological beliefs that maintain the system(s) of oppression that advantage you. You have then taken steps toward becoming an ally to those disadvantaged by whatever system advantages you.

So what does it mean to be an ally? According to the Guide to Allyship website (https://guidetoallyship.com/), an ally is someone who takes on the struggle as their own; uses their privilege in the service of those who lack it; amplifies the voices of the oppressed before their own; acknowledges that even though they feel pain, the conversation is not about them; stands up even when they feel scared; owns their own mistakes; and understands that their education (i.e., awareness building) is up to them and no one else. An ally decenters themself and supports moving the voices of those affected by oppression from the margins to the center. Moreover, being an ally means that you are willing to be a resource for others (University of Michigan, Intergroup Dialogue, n.d.), to appreciate the collective struggle (i.e., to act with others), and to value having power with as opposed to power over (Bishop, 2002).

REFLECTION/JOURNALING EXERCISE 3.6

Negotiating Your Privileges Through Social Justice Efforts

Now that you've identified some of the privileges you have due to your membership in different groups (in Reflection Exercises 3.2, 3.3, and 3.4), reflect on the following questions:

1. When I look at my list of privileges, what are my thoughts about what to do with them?

2. What does "check your privilege" mean to me now?

3. What are some of the ways that I can use my position of privilege in the service of social justice?

4. Are there any privileges I would be willing to give up to create a more just and fair society? Which ones would be hard to give up?

5. Which of my privileges can I use to be an ally to those who don't have the same privileges?

6. In what areas of my life (e.g., school, job/career, home) could I use my privileges to promote social and economic justice? How?

7. How might I give or share power with those who are systematically excluded from decision making?

Whereas an ally mostly engages in activism by standing with an individual or group in a marginalized community, an accomplice focuses more on dismantling the structures that oppress that individual or group and engages in such work as directed by the stakeholders in the marginalized group. Being an accomplice is committing to action and using your privileges to interfere with and dismantle oppressive systems. Anti-oppression social workers are both allies and accomplices. At the micro level of practice, the social work ally focuses on individuals, while at the meso and macro levels, the social work accomplice focuses on the structures of decision-making activity.

Being both ally and accomplice begins with acknowledging that you have unearned privileges and a willingness to be confronted and to consider change. It means having the deep humility of never being truly culturally competent and recognizing that the pursuit of critical examination is a lifelong process.

Current Social and Political Realities: An Obstacle and Opportunity

The deeply troubled, inequitable, and increasingly polarized nation and world in which we live poses another substantial obstacle to moving beyond cultural competence to anti-oppression practice for social justice. It also poses an increased opportunity and need for the social work profession, as a product of society, to integrate its historical response to individual social injustices with an equal commitment to change the discriminatory and oppressive systems that produce those injustices. The challenges are daunting and the stakes high. We face a power structure that is constructed and controlled by a privileged class based on race, ethnicity, and socioeconomic status. At the same time, the possibility to bring about social change may be greater than ever due to the convergence of four interconnected societal realities of our time: intensified/institutionalized social divisions, economic collapse, a global pandemic, and exposed racism.

For more than a quarter of a century, our country has been experiencing an increasingly volatile polarization. Tatum (2017) attributed the divisiveness to trauma-inducing anxiety about threats to the status quo given that white people will soon be a numerical minority, combined with other anxieties about a ruptured sense of security after the 9/11 terrorist attacks in 2001 and fear that the United States could lose its prominent position in the world, a growing sense of financial insecurity during the last months of George W. Bush's presidency, and the 2008 election of President Barack Obama that disrupted the usual narrative of white victory. Obama's election proved to be a catalyst for intense and successful voter suppression efforts, a sharp rise in white supremacist hate groups, increased American nationalism, and anti-immigrant sentiment.

The election of a Black man as president also gave rise to the myth that we were now a postracial, color-blind society when, in reality, we had simply learned to avoid noticing and talking about race (Tatum, 2017). This was especially true with regard to racial wealth disparities. The economic collapse in 2008, known as the Great Recession, had a systematically more disastrous effect on Black, Indigenous, and Latinx families who lost their homes and their jobs. And, despite the national recovery that followed, disparate unemployment rates continued to raise the racial wealth and income gap between whites and people of color to its highest in 25 years. Although racial wealth disparities today are the same as there were in 1950, Americans have largely not noticed or have ignored the depth of financial struggle. A 2019 study found that, although most Americans believe that

Black households hold $90 in wealth for every $100 held by white households, the actual amount is $10 (Kraus et al., 2019).

Since the 1990s there has been a rise in voices purporting that white identity is under attack by "multicultural forces" that used "social justice" to undermine white people and "their" civilization. Those voices have been countered by a growing activism of those advocating for social justice. The decade of 2010 saw a greater surge in grassroots social justice organizing than at any time since the Great Depression, including new movements such as Occupy Wall Street, Black Lives Matter, #MeToo, and a 2018 revival of Rev. Martin Luther King Jr.'s 1968 Poor People's Campaign. The outcome of the 2016 presidential campaign stirred unprecedented numbers of people to protest, volunteer, and donate to social justice causes, many for the first time. In 2016 the majority of white voters chose Donald J. Trump for president, and the majority of voters of color did not, making it clear that our nation was not only sharply divided, but it was also sharply divided along racial lines. Tatum (2017) provided an age-related perspective of the years 2008 to 2016:

If you were born in 1997, you were eleven when the economy collapsed, perhaps bringing new economic anxiety into your family life. You were still eleven when Barack Obama was elected. You heard that we were now in a post-racial society and President Obama's election was the proof. Yet your neighborhoods and schools were likely still quite segregated. And in 2012, when you were fifteen, a young Black teenager named Trayvon Martin, walking home in his father's mostly White neighborhood with his bag of iced tea and Skittles, was murdered and his killer went free. When you were seventeen, Michael Brown was shot in Ferguson, Missouri, and his body was left uncovered in the streets for hours, like a piece of roadkill, and in the same year, unarmed Eric Garner was strangled to death by the police, repeatedly gasping "I can't breathe" on a viral cell phone video, to name just two examples of why it seemed Black lives did not matter, even in the age of Obama. When you were nineteen, Donald J. Trump was elected president and white supremacists were celebrating in the streets. (pp. 71–72)

Continuing from the above, think about 4 years later, when you were 24. A virus called COVID-19 swept across the globe in 2020, wreaking death and destruction in our country more than any other, infecting millions and killing several hundred thousands of people, and bringing the U.S. economy to its knees. The pandemic shone a light on the life and death consequences of previously existing systemic racism as Black, Indigenous, and Latinx people died in staggering numbers compared to their proportion of the population. Hardest hit were low-paid service workers who prepared and served food and cared for children and the elderly—who were most susceptible to the virus—and people like farmworkers and meatpackers, disproportionately people of color, many undocumented immigrants, who supply our food (Barron-Lopez, 2020). Even as the pandemic showed the country that those workers were the critical engine of our economy, our country did not take care of them by providing health insurance, protective equipment, sick leave, adequate pay, and other necessary supports. After waiting the longest for new opportunities after the 2008 Great Recession, people of color who were non-essential workers and least likely to be able to work from home were among the first to lose their jobs. They were increasingly targeted for attacks—Asian Americans physically assaulted, the virus called "kung flu," Black men racially profiled as criminals when wearing protective masks against the virus, and other acts of violence (Poor People's Campaign, 2020).

In 2020, unemployment rose to the highest levels since the Great Depression. Our country reeled from a convergence of four interrelated pandemics. Social divisions, already exacerbated by institutions at the highest levels of government and fueled by economic anxiety, intensified during a global pandemic that collapsed the economy and exposed the already existing crisis of systemic racism. It all came to a head in June 2020, when a Black man named George Floyd cried out "I can't breathe" while being murdered by Minneapolis police officers. Decades of educating, organizing, and protesting against anti-affirmative action backlash, mass incarceration, and deep economic inequalities, combined with increased social media exposure of untold numbers of unarmed Black people being murdered by police, culminated in a large, long, and multicultural movement. Tens of thousands took to the streets for weeks, protesting police brutality and calling for widespread, deep, systemic change. The groundswell of protesters included mothers and grandmothers protecting their offspring from militarized forces sent in to silence their voices.

There were calls for hiring more social workers as a way to address the problem of police murdering Black people, which elicited considerable soul searching within our profession. Although there seemed to be agreement within the profession that more social workers were needed to address individual and social problems, controversy swirled about the idea of social workers being hired by, and thus being part of, police departments and the feasibility of social workers being able to stop police from murdering people of color. Difficult questions were raised—about the injustices that social work has perpetuated and benefited from—about how seductive and powerful it is to comfortably move with the current and go along with the way things are. The following comments about the idea of embedding social workers in police departments stirred some critical self-examination within the profession.

- Embedding us social workers in police departments would endorse a system that needs to be radically reimagined.
- We should not be party to any police "reform" that listens more to the voices of the oppressors than those of the oppressed.
- We do need more mental health social workers so the police don't have to intervene.
- Our profession has been tempted from the beginning to give a thin veneer of respectability to institutions that keep them from transforming.
- Social workers should be swimming against the current of injustice, not joining it.
- We have to stop police brutality, but social workers aren't the answer.
- We need to acknowledge how, both as individuals and as a profession, we contribute to and uphold racist systems, and we must commit to deconstructing and dismantling them.

Current social and political realities and issues of privilege are two substantial obstacles in our work to develop cultural competence practice and, at the same time, they offer considerable opportunities. In the next section we address a third obstacle, the lack of a coherent conceptual framework for uniting diversity and social justice that can be applied to a wide range of professional knowledge and practice areas.

A Conceptual Framework for Competent Social Work Practice That Unites Cultural Diversity and Social Justice

The ultimate goal of uniting anti-oppression social work practice is the transformation of "unjust and oppressive social, economic, and political institutions into just and non-oppressive alternatives" (Gil, 1998, p. 1). The following questions are essential to the task:

- Why are some groups systematically excluded from and denied the privileges and advantages of the dominant group?
- Who benefits from their exclusion?
- What benefits are accrued for what groups via this relegation to the margins of society?
- How do systems of oppression shape the life experiences of both those who are disadvantaged and those who are advantaged by them?
- How do social workers respond to the symptoms and consequences of oppressive systems and to the source of oppression?

Let us return to the beginning of this chapter and premise that anti-oppression social work practice recognizes and develops strategies to eliminate the structural roots of people's problems. That includes a rigorous effort by practitioners and the organizations in which they work to reevaluate their own role, on personal and professional levels, in creating or maintaining oppression. In the second part of this chapter, we present a conceptual practice framework for uniting cultural diversity and social justice that:

- Is applicable to a wide range of professional knowledge areas such as assessment and engagement with individuals and families; theories of human behavior; policy formulation, implementation, and analysis; working with communities; and conducting research.

- Examines the values, beliefs, and practices related to issues of power, privilege, and oppression regarding aspects of the life experiences of clients, workers, organizations, and communities.
- Is premised on a willingness to look at the white side of the racist equation and to not dismiss the historical context and social power position of people of color.
- Approaches the development of a sensitivity toward people targeted for exclusion by multiple oppressive systems by exploring the factors associated with their exclusion.
- Avoids language such as "the Black problem" and "the immigrant problem" that places the burden of responsibility and blame on those who are systematically disadvantaged and ignores factors related to social power.
- Refutes the myth that cultural diversity is about the "other" and as such is an entitlement program that provides undeserved benefits for people of color, women, LGBTQ people, poor people, people with disabilities, and so forth.

What follows is discussion of four components of a fundamental framework for examining cultural competency from a social justice perspective: (1) the centrality of race and racism, (2) the role of socioeconomic class, (3) the complex interaction of multiple identities and their associated privilege statuses, and (4) transformative learning processes.

The Centrality of Race and Racism

> *If you're white, you're all right.*
> *If you're brown, stick around.*
> *If you're black, get back.*
> —African American folk saying

As noted earlier, we have centered racism as the core system of oppression for several reasons. Our country was founded on the ideology of white supremacy. Racism is and always has been the principal force in building, sustaining, and shifting the social and political structures and organizational arrangements that control the distribution of opportunity and resources. While the dynamics of all forms of oppression are not fully informed only by race, understanding how racism is maintained is central to comprehending how oppression operates with other groups based on gender, sexual orientation, gender identity, ability, and so on.

REFLECTION/JOURNALING EXERCISE 3.7

Race-Based Experiences Growing Up

When were you first aware of yourself as a member of a particular racial group?

When were you first aware of people from other races? What races? What were the messages you grew up with about "others"?

When did you first witness or experience someone being treated differently because of his or her racial group?

At what point did you feel proud of your racial identity?

Was there a time when you realized that you would be treated differently because of your race?

What are some of the times when you had or have friends from different racial groups?

Are any other significant event(s) in your life related to race or racism?

*From Wijeyesinghe et al. (1997, p. 90).

The Concept of Race: A Social Construct

The dominant view in United States, since its founding, is that race is an inherent, innate quality, and that the races are biologically different. It is these differences that create a hierarchy of value. "Yet, race has no biological or genetic basis; the nation deliberately constructive this pseudoscientific notion to justify slavery's unspeakable terrors. 'white' people and 'black' people are historiosocial inventions. Neither the people nor designations existed before slavery" (Davis, 2016, p. 31). However—as evidenced by our country's racist legacy of conquests and genocide of its Indigenous Native peoples, colonialism, slavery, and segregation—racism is all too real.

Because it is a social construct, the meaning of race changes over time, by legal statute. It is subject to personal definition. Historical examples abound regarding the changing categorization of racial groups in our country. For example, Japanese Americans, who were once considered nonwhite and Oriental, are now identified in the broad category of Asian and Pacific Islander (Omi & Winant, 1986). At the time of their arrival, Jewish people were kept at the margin of dominant white society, because they were not Christians, and Catholics were not regarded as white. Census data and immigration policies have gone through changes, with Italian Americans, Irish Americans, and Latinos viewed at different times as both white and nonwhite (Hacker, 1992).

It is clear that the question is not "who is white?" but instead "who *may* be considered white?" Race categorization is based on arbitrary factors related to power and validation. In a sense, those who have already received the "white" designation are members of a club, from whose sanctum it is decided whether new members are needed or wanted as well as the proper pace of new admissions. The "white club," as much as anything else, is one of privilege, and its members have always had the power to expand its domain. While it has admitted people of all ethnicities over time, it has been persistently unwilling to absorb people of African descent (Hacker, 1992, p. 9). As Wilkerson (2020)wrote, pointing to our entire American social structure as an unrecognized caste system:

> By extending the dream of dominion over the land and all others in it to anyone who could meet the definition of white, the American caste system became an all-or-nothing gambit for the top rung. Those permitted under the white tent could reap the rewards of full citizenship, rise to positions of high status (or as far as their talents could take them), get access to the best the country had to offer or, at the very least, be accorded respect in everyday interactions from subordinate groups who risked assault for any misstep. A two-tiered caste system raised the stakes for whiteness, leading to court dockets filled with people on the borderline seeking admission to the upper caste. (p. 126)

Racism, a system of oppression based on race, is different from prejudice. Prejudice is a personal, behavioral, psychological phenomenon characterized by prejudgments and biased beliefs about individuals. Racism is also different from discrimination, which refers to actions taken against others based on biased beliefs. Racism is set apart from prejudice and discrimination because it is an institutionalized system of advantage grounded in social, political, and economic power that deprives and diminishes people of color while offering preference, support, and opportunity to those perceived as white (Knowles & Prewitt, 1969). Prejudice is not necessary for individuals to carry out racist institutional practices, because the specific practices are part of systematic, program-based policies.

The institutional nature of racism can be difficult to grasp. For people who are considered to be white, racism is often seen as something external to them, rather than as a system that shapes the daily experiences of all of us and distorts everyone's sense of self, regardless of ethnic or racial background. It is more comfortable to see racism as a problem that people of color face and with which they have to struggle; after all, they are the ones being disadvantaged in disproportionate numbers.

But viewing the people who are the targets of racism as "the problem" has far-reaching consequences for social workers. It can lead to a view of antiracism work as an act of compassion for others, maybe as an optional extra project, perhaps even an important commitment, but not one intimately and organically linked to one's own life. This view makes it possible to avoid concerns about our own racism and thus to be able to say, "I am not a racist." Making such a statement, according to Kendi (2019), signifies neutrality, a claim that you are not a racist even when you are not aggressively against racism.

But there is no neutrality in the racism struggle. The opposite of "racist" isn't "not racist." It is "antiracist." What's the difference? One endorses either the idea of a racial hierarchy as a racist, or racial equality as an antiracist. One either believes problems are rooted in groups of people, as a racist, or locates the roots of problems in power and policies, as an antiracist. One either allows racial inequities to persevere, as a racist, or confronts racial inequities, as an antiracist. There is no in-between safe space of "not racist." ... The good news is that racist and nonracist are not fixed identities. We can be a racist one minute and an antiracist the next. What we say about race, what we do about race, in each moment, determines what—not who—we are. (Kendi, 2019, pp. 9–10)

Just as Kendi sees the movement from racist to antiracist as always ongoing, so too is our learning about racism and our own privileged or nonprivileged place in its system. Engaging in actions to dismantle it and, beyond that, standing ready to fight at racism's intersection with other systems of oppression is a lifelong journey.

Whiteness

Just as understanding white privilege is essential to eradicating racism, understanding its corresponding investment in whiteness is equally important. As Lipsitz (1998) eloquently notes: "Although reproduced in new form in every era, the possessive investment in whiteness has always been influenced by its origins in the racialized history of the United States" (p. 3). Political science professor Andrew Hacker (1992), in his book, *Two Nations: Black and White, Separate, Hostile, Unequal*, provided overwhelming evidence of exactly how, more than any other oppression, skin color is used to assign status and power. Of all the forms of exclusion, discrimination, and power assignment in this country—and there are many—"none is so deeply rooted, persistent, and intractable as that based on color" (Hopps, 1982, p. 3).

> White people: I don't want you to understand me better. I want you to understand yourselves. Your survival has never depended on your knowledge of white culture. In fact, it's required your ignorance. (Ijeoma Oluo, 2018)

People of color experience the grave consequences of racism everyday but they are not the problem. The root of the racism problem is whiteness.

Regardless of how much they may detest racism, white people are the sole reason it has flourished for centuries. So, we need to ask: What does it mean to be white in America? How does whiteness shape people's lives? Who benefits from the social construction of "whiteness as the norm"? If the white race is a private club that grants privileges to certain people who look white, how does the loyalty of its members sustain a system of oppression based on race? How do white people benefit from problematizing "blackness" and "the other" instead focusing on the construction of whiteness as the source of systemic racism?

> In the same way that both men's and women's lives are shaped by their gender and that both heterosexual and lesbian women's experiences in the world are marked by their sexuality, both white people and people of color live racially structured lives. In other words, any system of differentiation shapes those on whom it bestows privilege as well as those it oppresses.... [thus] in a social context where white people have too often viewed themselves as nonracial or racially neutral, it is crucial to look at the "racialness" of white experience. (Frankenberg, 1993, p. 1)

Using the term "whiteness" shifts it from the unnamed status that is a consequence of dominance and is taken as normal. It reveals that, hidden behind the daily practices of hard-working, well-meaning people, whiteness is at the core of the institutionalized racism that shapes all our lives and identities in ways that are inseparable from other facets of daily life. Institutionalized racism isn't the ugly kind, it's the subtle and slippery kind that silently and invisibly tears at the fiber of our schools and our society. It's not the kind of racism that is expressed through hostile, racial slurs, but the kind wrapped in righteous proclamations of tradition, fairness, and high standards.

To look at whiteness is to look head-on at the site of dominance in our country. And that is not easy to do. It is much more difficult to say, "Whiteness has nothing to do with me—I'm not white" than it is to say, "Race has nothing to do with me—I'm not racist" (Frankenberg, 1993, p. 6).

To speak of whiteness is to assign everyone a place in the system of racism. It refutes the idea that white people have the option of whether or not to deal with racism.

When looking at whiteness, there are a couple of key points that need to be emphasized. First, there is a gulf of difference between how white people and people of color experience racism. Second, at this time in U.S. history, whiteness as an ethnic identity is often presented in terms of "white pride" by the politically conservative far right. When North Americans of European descent celebrate being white, that is far different from ethnic white people affirming their cultural, national heritage. The former—celebrating whiteness—symbolizes, like Confederate statues in the present political moment, a white supremacist act, an act of backlash.

Some culturally or racially specific ways in which whiteness shapes people's lives were described by DiAngelo (2018). She wrote that, while no person of color in our country can make the same claims, all white people in the United States:

- Are born into a culture in which they belong, racially.
- Are free to move in virtually any normal, neutral, or valuable space.
- Are "just people" whose race is held up as the norm for humanity and is, in fact, rarely if ever named.
- Experience white solidarity or racial bonding, the unspoken agreement to protect white advantage and not cause another white person discomfort by confronting them about something racially problematic.
- Can reminisce about the good old days and wish for a return to former ways while remaining oblivious to our national racial history.
- Can position themselves as innocent of race identification.
- Are the group most likely to choose racial segregation (schools, workplaces, neighborhoods, etc.) and most likely to have the resources to do so.

The next two exercises address the issues related to the first component of our conceptual framework: the centering of race and racism as a gateway to understanding other oppressions. Reflection Exercise 3.7 asks you to consider your personal experiences from an early age in relation to issues of race, and Assignment 3.1 addresses the institutional nature of racism.

ASSIGNMENT 3.1

Analyzing the White Culture of an Organization*

Once an agency's culture has been assessed, the organization is able to identify goals and develop a plan for bringing about institutional change. Choose a dominant (i.e., mainstream white) organization that you are or have been part of (your field agency, place of employment, organization in which you volunteer, or an institutional entity that you are a member of, such as a church). In relation to your particular organizations, answer the bulleted questions under each of the five characteristics of a white agency culture.

I. **White culture defines what is considered normal, creates the standard for judging values.** For example, think about who and how these terms are defined: good parenting, stable family, well-raised child, individual self-sufficiency, effective leadership.

    • In your organization, what are the characteristics of a good employee? How were you informed about what they were? If unwritten rules, how did you learn about them?

II. **White culture privileges a focus on individuals (not groups).** Independence and autonomy are valued and rewarded. An individual is in control of their environment—"you get what you deserve."

    • In your organization, what is rewarded? Are people encouraged to compete? Collaborative decision making? Decisions based on the common good?

III. **White culture assigns a higher value to some ways of behaving than others.** It often defines the "other" behaviors as dangerous and/or deviant. For example, right to comfort, avoid conflict or emotion, be polite. Comfort level is defined by whites, and those who cause discomfort or are involved in conflict can be marginalized. Individual acts of unfairness, which daily target people of color, become equal to the pain and discomfort of systemic racism.

    • In your organization, what behaviors are considered uncomfortable (e.g., conflict, loud voice, crying)? How does the organizational culture respond when these behaviors happen?

IV. **Decision making often reflects white cultural assumptions about the primacy of individuals, standards of behavior, and use of power over others.** For example, deciding and enforcing, either/or thinking, and those less affected define the problem and solution.

- Reflect on different groups you belong to—who is included in the decision-making process? What is the rationale? Is the process different on paper versus in reality?

- Consider your agency's practice guidelines: Do they include advocating for systems change?

V. **White culture values certain ways of knowing and not others.** For example, if you can't measure it, then it is not of value. Focus on cause-and-effect relationships and rational linear thinking.

- In your organization, who or what informs you that a program or service is working? How is success defined? Who decides what is sufficient time?

*White culture characteristics, descriptions, and questions developed by Potapchuk (2012).

The Powerful Role of Socioeconomic Class

The second component of a conceptual framework for anti-oppression social justice practice addresses the role of socioeconomic class in conferring privilege. In conversations about race, legitimate questions are often raised, such as: What about class? Isn't class just as important as race? In absolute numbers, aren't there more white people who are poor and of low wealth in the United States than people of color in those circumstances? Our conceptual framework explores such questions, based on the following concepts and assertions:

- The prevalence of poverty and class privilege in the United States is deeply correlated with racism.
- Oppression has always functioned in our country to create a class system based on race (Howard, 1993).
- Just as science has been used to prove the biological inferiority of people of color, science was also used in the 19th century to "prove" the biological inferiority of poor people and to make a causal

connection between poor people's lack of wealth and their lack of accomplishment and merit.

- Similar to how oppression has been used to exploit and create a class system based on race, it has also been used to exploit various other ethnic groups for different purposes and at different points in history.
- When people from different ethnic and racial groups recognize their shared experience as targets of oppression and economic exploitation, they are able to develop bonds of solidarity that are necessary to the success of social justice advocacy efforts.
- There is considerable class inequality among white people as well as between white people and people of color and other identities. For example, of the more than 140 million people of all races and ethnicities in the United States who were poor or of low wealth in 2020, almost half of them were white (Poor People's Campaign, 2020).
- When poor and low-wealth people of all races and ethnicities recognize that the same elements of oppression are used to exploit all of them economically, they are able to come together in solidarity to take actions to eliminate systemic poverty (Poor People's Campaign, 2020).
- Social power differences based on socioeconomic position can mediate the effects of racism and other systems of oppression. While it is unproductive to engage in comparative ranking about who is most oppressed, it is useful to recognize how class affects people's lives differently. For example, the consequences of oppression are not the same for an upper-class, married African American female as they are for a white, single, undereducated mother of three minor children.
- People's behavior and life circumstances need to be considered in their historical context. The harsh realities of history lay bare the many secrets of white privilege, the creation of an economically privileged class, and the effects of class privilege.
- When historical perspectives and cultural experiences of other races are inconsistent with the image of a democratic nation based on fairness, the result is cognitive dissonance. Approaching the

past and present with a new sense of honesty often activates new, uncomfortable feelings of guilt. It is important to resist disillusioned confessions about the sins of one's ancestors or a tendency to minimize the differences in life experiences based on race and class in an attempt to make them all equal, as well as other strategies aimed at lessening discomfort.

Intersectionality: The Complex Interaction of Multiple Social Identities

The third component of our conceptual framework highlights the many ways in which racism interacts with the dynamics of socioeconomic class, gender, and other systems of oppression. Everyone has a constellation of identities that intersect in ways that affect how they are viewed, understood, and treated.

The intersection of five privileged positions—white, male, heterosexual, cisgender, and able-bodied (see Figure 3.3.)—is the subject of considerable, sometimes heated, disagreement in many corners of personal and public life. Questions arise and arguments abound related to which institutional advantage brings the most power and which form of oppression came first or is the worst in a game of competitive oppressions. Advocacy and organizing efforts against social injustice are often threatened and undermined by divide-and-conquer tactics based on false divisions. Such efforts have been particularly effective in relation to race. Because the effects of racism are so deep and powerful, potential bonds for joining in advocacy against social injustice and exploitation have often been effectively undermined due to prejudice and discrimination based on race. That pattern was disrupted in 2020, however, when the convergence of four pandemics—intensified social divisions, economic collapse, a global virus, and exposed racism—brought Black, Indigenous, Latinx, Asian, and white people of all ages, classes, abilities, and religions together in a broad-based coalition movement for social justice.

Ideological Underpinnings of all Systems of Oppression

Justifications for oppression based on gender, sexual orientation, gender identity, class, and ability are often similar to those that justify racism.

Although the denigration of an entire people on the basis of race is justified by an ideology of white supremacy and racial inferiority, likewise the depreciation of all females on the basis of gender is justified by an ideology of male superiority that insists that females are less intelligent and logical and more emotional and irrational. Similarly, the disparagement of an entire people on the basis of sexual orientation or gender identity is justified by insistence on mental and moral deficiencies, and discrimination against anyone with a physical or mental disability or who is poor is based on a belief that their lives are less worthy and, in essence, disposable.

Kendi (2019) recognizes the racist grounding of the other forms of oppression in several ways. He defines sexism as gender racism with a historical example: "White-male interest in lynching Black-male rapists of white women was as much about controlling the sexuality of white women as it was about controlling the sexuality of Black men" (pp. 190). In regard to oppression based on class, "when we say Black poor people are lazier than poor whites, ... we are speaking at the intersection of elitist and racist ideas—an ideological intersection that forms class racism" (p. 152). In relation to oppression based on gender, which Kendi calls queer racism:

I am a cisgendered Black heterosexual male—"cisgender" meaning my gender identity corresponds to my birth sex, in contrast to transgender people, whose gender identity does not correspond to their birth sex. To be queer antiracist is to understand the privileges of my cisgender, of my masculinity, of my heterosexuality, of their intersections. To be queer antiracist is to serve as an ally to transgender people, to intersex people, to women, to the non-gender-conforming, to homosexuals ... to be queer antiracist is to see homophobia, racism, and queer racism—not the queer person, not the queer space—as the problem, as abnormal, as unnatural. (p. 197)

Moving from cultural competence to anti-oppression practice means examining the effects of the interlocking oppressions on individual and group experiences related to power and privilege. It is important to understand that the dynamics of oppression operate in a complicated yet systematic way. For example, the overrepresentation of certain populations among those who are poor and of low economic status is not a chance occurrence, and people who are deemed to be inferior or defective in more than one way (e.g., being Black, female, lesbian, and with a disability) are even more likely to be negatively affected. The defamation of everyone on the basis of low economic status is then subsequently justified on the basis of class superiority.

Multiple Social Identities

It is often assumed that because one is targeted by oppression based on one identity—such as being gay, lesbian, or transgender; being Jewish; being a woman; being a Muslim—that person will automatically have empathy toward other oppressed communities. There is a widespread belief that participation in one kind of liberation movement, such as feminism or gay rights, leads automatically to antiracism. However, this is not the case, and we need to understand why it isn't. To maintain power and advantage, oppressive systems operate in ways that create divisions between oppressed populations. Internalized oppression, whereby persons may celebrate a part of their acceptable social identity while denigrating their own devalued, unacceptable part(s), also plays a role in inhibiting coalition building.

Everyone has multiple social identities based on race, ethnicity, gender, sexual orientation, gender identity, ability, age, class, and/or other factors. Thus, most people are both targets of oppression and agents of oppression (Bell, 1997). Although people may be targets of discrimination based on one aspect of their social identity, the same people may be advantaged based on another social identity. The issue of privilege gets complicated, given that one aspect of an individual's identity may confer unmerited privilege, while, at the same time, another aspect of that same person's identity may create disadvantages.

Examine multiple identities within a framework of power and privilege can be uncomfortable. Noticing one's privileges might mean having to give them up. When power and privilege are threatened in a broader sense, attempts are always made to hold on to them. As the population of people of color in the United States grows, white Americans are nervous about losing their dominant position, as evidenced by an alarming increase in the number of white supremacy groups and acts of overt and violent racism. Men who are uncomfortable with the transition from their dominant gender status to participating with more equity in relationships with women find covert and overt ways to hang on to their gender privilege, while not appearing to do so. Heterosexual and cisgender people who are committed to their position of dominance defend and legitimize their privileges—and even justify hate crimes in the name of God. Anti-transgender bias and hate are growing in the United States, as evidenced by the large numbers of transgender and gender nonconforming people being murdered, the majority of whom are Black transgender women. Most people who enjoy economic advantage do not even consider the possibility of giving up their position of dominance and privilege or supporting policies that would make accumulation of wealth possible for everyone.

Even while the world is rapidly changing, there remains a deep-seated commitment to dominance, power, and privilege by those who have them. A peaceful transition to a new kind of America, in which no group is in a dominant position, will not be easy. The creation of a just and equitable society will require considerable change in education and personal values. It will require deep psychological shifts: from overestimation of self for those in dominant positions and from underestimation of self for those in subordinate positions. What must take place in the lives of white people, of males, of heterosexuals, of cisgender people, of economically advantaged people, of able people, for them to see that now is the time to begin their journey from dominance to shared power? From marginalization and dismissiveness to acceptance and inclusion? What are the issues that must be addressed in the current practice climate that need to be addressed if social work is to play an effective role in such change?

As always, the questions and answers begin with oneself. The following exercise is aimed at helping you to explore issues related to your own multiple identities, power, and privilege.

CLASSROOM EXERCISE 3.2

Identity Circles

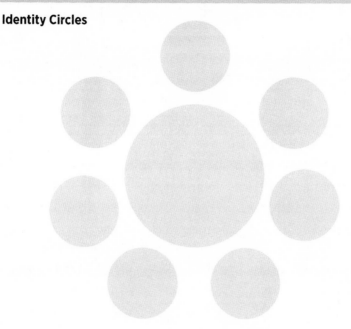

Write your name in the center circle and respond to the question "who am I?" by filling in the other circles with other identities that you consider to be important to your sense of self. Be specific, for example, write woman or female and not gender.

Write your answers to the following questions:

- Which identity feels the most primary to you? Which is least important? Why? What issues come up for you about integrating your diverse identities into one identity?

- What dominant group identities surfaced in your discussion that you did not include?

When everyone has finished writing, we'll break into pairs to share our thoughts about what we wrote.

Transformative Learning Processes

On the journey from cultural competence to anti-oppression social work practice, we will undergo a major transformation, a paradigmatic shift in how we think about difference toward a way of thinking that includes but also goes beyond appreciating difference to extinguishing oppressive systems of domination, power, and advantage based on difference. Because facilitating such a major shift is a challenging learning process, we need to grasp and understand the following elements, even when engaged in it.

- First and foremost, constructing an antiracist, antisexist, antiheterosexist, antiableist identity, consciousness, and behavior is an intensely personal process.

- It is a process that will challenge one's sense of self and basis of self-esteem. The struggle for a positive social identity varies depending on one's unique experiences and background related to social status and power. Ultimately, the struggle for social workers requires that they develop a positive social identity for themselves to better value their clients' identities and related struggles (Pinderhughes,1989).

- Transformative learning is not linear, nor does it always proceed in sequential stages. It takes unpredictable twists and turns when previously unexamined feelings are aroused and new learning opportunities present themselves.

- When engaged in learning about diversity and social justice, people often uncover contradictions between the principles they verbalize and their behaviors, between inherited ideas they have been socialized into and new information, and between their self-image and the feedback they receive from others.

- People who engage in this work can expect to find themselves moving beyond familiar points, out of their comfort zones. The changes they experience will inevitably be coupled with substantial distress.

- Learning about diversity and oppression involves questioning one's assumptions and exploring alternative ideas in a spirit of critical inquiry. This is not only difficult, but it can also be psychologically explosive (Brookfield, 1990).

- People doing this work must counter their own experience of discomfort with a willingness to confront and work through unresolved conflicts in relation to their own role, status, and participation in an oppressive society.

- Each new learning challenge that is faced ignites a search for new ways to think and act. This search motivates continued learning.

Educational frameworks that unite cultural diversity and anti-oppression practice for social justice challenge one's worldview, which is why personal turmoil and reevaluation are inevitable parts of the process. The challenges can feel overwhelming at times. No one can do this work in isolation—it is too complex. This work requires multiple voices in dialogue and struggle. It requires connecting and networking with others who also value this learning process. It requires knowledge building about skills, concepts, theories, and history. It requires emotional support from people who understand its demands and can help us keep the focus on growing in the midst of a lot of heat. It requires patience and gentleness—both with oneself and with each other. It requires cutting each other a break while not letting each other off the hook. Finding, developing, and using peer and collegial support are essential. As one navigates the learning process, it helps to know that everyone is affected by injustice and everyone needs to be in the struggle to find solutions.

Conclusion

This chapter highlighted some of the issues and obstacles everyone faces on the journey to develop a cultural competence characterized by an integration of diversity and social justice. A conceptual framework was presented with four essential components aimed ultimately at the elimination of oppressive systems. What is proposed is nothing less than a transformation on the most fundamental level of knowledge creation. What does this mean? It means exposing the ways in which implicit cultural assumptions, frames of reference, and biases within our profession influence what social workers think about what they know about people and their environments and the helping strategies they adopt. It means examining how knowledge is created and influenced by factors such as race, ethnicity, gender, class, ability, gender identity, and sexual orientation. It means identifying and examining the human interests and value assumptions of those who create knowledge. And, finally, it means creating a learning environment that critically challenges the facts, concepts, paradigms, themes, and explanations routinely accepted in mainstream academia (Banks, 1993).

In the next chapter, key concepts and definitions provide theoretical grounding for your further understanding of the complex elements that compose cultural competence.

References

Banks, J. A. (1993, September). Multicultural education: Development, dimensions, and challenges. *Phi Delta Kappa, 75*(1), 22–28.

Barron-Lopez, L. (2020, April 29). *Hispanic caucus calls on Trump administration to investigate working conditions for meatpackers.* https://www.politico.com/news/2020/04/29/hispanic-caucus-trump -meatpackers-221686

Bell, L. A. (1997). Theoretical foundations for social justice education. In M. Adams, L. A. Bell, & P. Griffin (Eds.), *Teaching for diversity and social justice: A sourcebook* (pp. 3–15). Routledge.

Bishop, A. (2002). *Becoming an ally: Breaking the cycle of oppression* (2nd ed.). Allen and Unwin.

Brookfield, S. (1990). Using critical incidents to explore learners' assumptions. In J. Mezirow & Associates (Eds.), *Fostering critical reflection in adulthood: A guide to transformative and emancipatory learning* (pp.177–198). Jossey-Bass.

Collins, P. H., & Bilge, S. (2020). *Intersectionality* (2nd Ed.). Polity Books.

Crenshaw, K. (1989). Demarginalizing the intersection of race and sex: A black feminist critique of antidiscrimination doctrine, feminist theory, and antiracist politics. *University of Chicago Legal Forum,* 139.

Davis, L. (2016). *Why are they angry with us? Essays on race.* Lyceum Books.

DiAngelo, R. (2018). *White fragility: Why it's so hard for white people to talk about racism.* Beacon Press.

Dinno, A. (2017). Homicide rates of transgender individuals in the united states: 2010-2015. *American Journal of Public Health, 107*(9), 1441–1447.

Frankenberg, R. (1993). *The social construction of whiteness: White women, race matters.* University of Minnesota Press.

Gil, D. (1998). *Confronting injustice and oppression: Concepts and strategies for social workers*. Columbia University Press.

Hacker, A. (1992). *Two nations: Black and white, separate, hostile, unequal.* Scribner.

Hahn, A., & Gawronski, B. (2019). Facing one's implicit biases: From awareness to acknowledgement. *Journal of Personality and Social Psychology: Interpersonal Relations and Group Processes, 116*(5), 769–794.

Hopps, J. (1982). Oppression based on color [Editorial]. *Social Work, 27*(1), 3–5.

Howard, G. (1993). Whites in multicultural education: Rethinking our role. *Phi Delta Kappa, 75,* 36–41.

Jensen, B. (1998, July 9). Wake up to white privilege [Editorial]. *Baltimore Sun.*

Kavanaugh, A. (2020, July 27). *Black, indigenous, and people of color are unpacking their invisible knapsack.* https://medium.com/an-injustice /black-indigenous-and-people-of-color-are-unpacking-their-invisible -knapsack-b5df602d4230

Kendi, I. X. (2019). *How to be an antiracist.* One World.

Knowles, L., & Prewitt, K. (1969). *Institutional racism in America.* Prentice-Hall.

Kraus, M., Ivuoma N. O., & Daumeyer, N. M. (2019). The misperception of racial economic inequality. *Perspectives on Psychological Science.* https://doi .org/10.1177%2F1745691619863049

Lerner, M. (1980). *The belief in a just world: A fundamental delusion.* Plenum Press.

Lipsitz. G. (1998). *The possessive investment in whiteness: How white people profit from identity politics.* Temple University Press.

Lorde, A. (1983). There is no hierarchy of oppressions. In *Homophobia and education.* Council on Interracial Books for Children. https://sites.williams .edu/engl113-f18/marr/there-is-no-hierarchy-of-oppression/

McIntosh, P. (1995). White privilege and male privilege: A personal account of coming to see correspondences through work in women's studies. In M. L. Andersen & P. H. Collins (Eds.), *Race, class, and gender: An anthology* (pp. 76–87). Wadsworth.

Oluo, I. (2018). *So you want to talk about race.* Seal Press.

Omi, M., & Winant, H. (1986). *Racial formation in the United States from the 1960's to the 1980's.* Routledge.

Pinderhughes, E. (1989). *Understanding race, ethnicity, and power: The key to efficacy in clinical practice.* Macmillan.

Poor People's Campaign (2020). https://www.poorpeoplescampaign.org/

Potapchuk, M. (2012). *Transforming white privilege: A 21st century leadership capacity.* CAPD, MP Associates, World Trust Educational Services.

Rubin. Z., & Peplau, L. A. (1975). Who believes in a just world? *Journal of Social Issues, 31*(3), 65–89.

Sue, D. W., & Sue, D. (2013). *Counseling the culturally diverse: Theory & practice* (6th ed.). Wiley.

Tatum, B. D. (2017). *Why are all the Black kids sitting together in the cafeteria and other conversations about race.* Basic Books.

Wijeyesinghe, C. L., Griffin, P., & Love, B. (1997). Racism curriculum design. In M. Adams, L. A. Bell, & P. Griffin (Eds.), *Teaching for diversity and social justice: A sourcebook* (p. 90). Routledge.

Wilkerson, Isabel (2020). *Caste: The origins of our discontents.* Random House.

PART II

Concepts, Definitions, and Processes

CHAPTER 4

Understanding the Dynamics of Oppression

In the previous chapters we discussed a foundation for understanding social justice and a framework for addressing the socioeconomic and personal barriers to moving from cultural competence to anti-oppression social work practice. Now we examine in more depth how oppressive systems operate and the inequities they produce. We begin with the concepts of cultural diversity and multiculturalism, first as generally understood and valued, and then through an anti-oppression and social justice lens. We include all social identities—regardless of positionality—and how they are granted either privilege status/advantage or target status/disadvantage. We then move on to scrutinize the dynamics of power, how oppression is based on social identity, and how systems of oppression are maintained. As with all the chapters in this book, we emphasize the significance of self-awareness and the role of historical context, lived experience, and social power.

From Cultural Competence to Anti-Oppression Practice: Essential Concepts and Definitions

Cultural Diversity and Multiculturalism

Cultural diversity is generally seen as a focus of one's identity that can be used to differentiate groups and individuals from one another. Although the terms *cultural diversity* and *multiculturalism* are often used interchangeably, there are widely acknowledged differences between the two. Diversity is usually understood as real or perceived differences between people, such as race, gender and gender identity, sexual orientation, religion, background, and so on. Multiculturalism, while similar and connected to diversity, is generally focused on inclusiveness, understanding, and respect. Those who promote multiculturalism view the demographic changes in our country as an enrichment of communities through the introduction of new immigrant groups, greater integration of diverse cultural contributions (e.g., food, music, art) into the mainstream culture, and increased inclusion of diverse groups into the community and professional settings. Multiculturalism increases interaction with those different from ourselves, challenges old perceptions and attitudes, and, in the best of circumstances, stimulates new perspectives and behaviors.

Understanding and accepting others, in all their cultural and social dimensions, involves understanding and accepting ourselves. The goal of Classroom Exercise 4.1 is to explore your own background. Depending on your relationship to the dominant culture, you may experience discomfort such as the following when doing the exercise:

- If your social identity benefits by validation and recognition from the dominant culture, you may have a sense of not having a specific culture with which to identify. However, close scrutiny of day-to-day practices, holidays that are honored, and celebrations in which your family participates will illuminate cultural beliefs and values that organize your life experiences.

- If you identify more strongly with a traditional or ethnic culture, you may often encounter experiences in which your culture is disparaged by the dominant culture. For example, when you were a child, a teacher may have insisted that your parents stop speaking with you in their native language instead of exploring ways of maintaining your native language and simultaneously mastering English. This exercise provides an opportunity for you to validate your identity over others' judgments.

- If you have multiple ethnic backgrounds, you may find that you are not comfortable categorizing your social identity as associated with one culture and may instead identify with several. This exercise provides an opportunity for you to affirm a perspective about who you are that honors all facets of your identity, even though others may insist on identifying you with only one facet.

CLASSROOM EXERCISE 4.1

Creating Your Cultural Chest

Prepare a chest filled with symbolic cultural treasures such as religious or ethnic artifacts that represent who you are. Decorate the outside of the chest to represent what you let others see in regard to who you are. Bring your chest to class and present it to others as a way to show them who you are.

As an alternative to actually preparing a chest, imagine what you would put into such a chest and how you would decorate the outside. You may then share with others in class by describing your virtual chest.

Debriefing Questions:

1. What feelings did this exercise trigger in you?

2. What was your experience in putting together your chest?

3. What connections did you make, if any, with your life experiences?

4. What did you learn from this activity?

Assignment Exercise 4.1 is an opportunity for you to explore your ethnic/racial roots in more depth and examine the unique experiences of significant individuals who have shaped your path in life. The emphasis is on how learning about and dealing with diversity from an anti-oppression perspective means taking responsibility for (a) exploring how you have benefited from or have been targeted by the institutionalization of racism and other forms of oppression, (b) examining how these have affected your identity, (c) managing privilege in a responsible way, and (d) considering change strategies you can take to dismantle oppressive structures.

Ethnic Roots Paper

The purpose of this assignment is to explore your ethnic/racial roots and examine the unique experiences of your parents, grandparents, great-grandparents, and beyond or other significant individuals who have shaped your path in life. Your paper should be 6–7 pages long and address the following set of questions:

I. Background: Very briefly describe yourself in relation to age, birthplace, socioeconomic class, and status when you were growing up, current cultural identification(s), and other significant factors.

II. Background of parents, grandparents, and great-grandparents, and important information:

   a. Describe what you know about your mother, father, maternal grandparents, paternal grandparents, maternal and paternal great-grandparents, and other persons of significance for you. If you are adopted, consider your birth parents and/or adoptive parents in your response—whichever best fits your sense of identity.

   b. If your ancestors immigrated to the United States, how did they arrive and enter (e.g., voluntary immigrants, involuntary through conquest or brought here as enslaved people, time period of entry)? If they were not immigrants, what was their experience with the imposition of the U.S. political system on their lives?

   c. What were their experiences with white supremacy and conformity, as well as other factors affecting inclusion?

III. By the standards of the dominant white culture, do you perceive individuals related to you as included in or excluded from American society?

   a. How did they avoid, attempt, or achieve assimilation, acculturation, and integration? How did they attempt to be or resist being accepted by the dominant culture? For example, were names changed to fit into mainstream American society? Were ethnic roots emphasized or downplayed?

   b. Were traditions, language, and/or customs suppressed or passed down through the generations?

c. What role did social class and social power play in your family's experiences?

IV. Conclusion

a. What conclusions can you draw about your own current identity based on your ethnic roots, socialization, and personal experiences?

b. How have you benefited from or been a target of racism and oppression based on your ethnic roots?

c. What responsibility do you feel today to engage in anti-oppression change strategies based on your identity and ethnic roots?

As our country becomes more and more diverse, we are likely to encounter a shift in roles, interactions, and ambiguous situations that require more interpersonal negotiation than what we customarily face. While this may be demanding and stressful, it also increases the potential for developing new interpersonal skills essential for engaging in diverse interactions. By legitimizing difference as something to be appreciated and understood, processes cam be activated that lead to increased awareness of our own belief systems and interpersonal behavior. When there is curiosity and risk taking, interactions with unfamiliar individuals in new settings can result in new connections. These interactions and connections can stimulate new ways of thinking about our own identity and what we value. Multiculturalism and cultural diversity lead to changes in customs for interactions and the possibility of gaining understanding of different perspectives is enhanced.

Bridging differences leads us into new experiential terrain that requires a sense of humility, both emotionally and intellectually. It involves active engagement and negotiation with others whose communication and interaction styles are different from our own. It may be tempting, perhaps as a way to lessen our discomfort, to look for a set of easy rules, like the "five things that we need to know to work with a particular population." However, this inevitably involves using subjective impressions and knowledge about diverse groups in a boilerplate fashion, as if unfamiliar cultures are static or all individuals within that group are the same. A way to avoid that is to treat new information about diverse groups as hypotheses and then continually match them with each interaction we have. Developing a more complex and accurate knowledge about other individuals and cultural groups requires change and adaptation fueled by a robust curiosity. In the following assignment, you will have an opportunity to do just that by walking in the shoes of a person from a different cultural group.

ASSIGNMENT EXERCISE 4.2

Immersion "Shadow" Experience Paper

The purpose of this exercise is for you to observe and experience the life of a person from a cultural group different from your own. You will be asked to reflect on the similarities and differences between your own cultural group and another cultural group.

Select a person from a culture different from your own who is willing to allow you to shadow, that is, be present, at five different events in their life. The person must also be willing to have candid discussions with you about their life experiences and the impact of their culture on those experiences. The person selected must not be a friend or acquaintance whom you have known for more than a month.

The three to five events in the person's life that you will shadow are as follows:

1. You will participate in a family meal in the person's home.

2. You will participate in a family special event, such as a birthday or anniversary party, wedding, graduation, coming of age, and the like.

3. You will attend a spiritual or religious event or engage in a discussion about the person's spiritual or religious life (e.g., baptism, bar mitzvah, Ramadan, Purim).

4. You will observe the person in his or her workplace.

5. You will attend a recreational or leisure activity with the person.

Reflection Paper

At the end of each event, write a 2-page reflection paper on the experience. By the end of your three to five events spent with your person, you should have 6–10 pages as the core of your reflection paper. Your reflection on each event should be no more than 2 pages long and should include the following:

1. Observations about the interactions among the people participating in the event.

2. Your comfort level at the event and the group's comfort level with your presence.

3. Similarities to and differences from your own life experiences.

4. Myths, stereotypes, biases, and prejudices that you had about the person's cultural group that were challenged as a result of your experience at the events.

5. Impact of the experience on your personal and professional life.

Debriefing Questions

1. What feelings were triggered in you as you did this exercise?

2. What was your experience in doing this?

3. What connections did you make, if any, with your life experiences?

4. What learning do you take from this activity?

Although multiculturalism and appreciating diversity are essential for effective social work practice, they are not enough. Anti-oppression practice with people across diverse cultures and identities requires a comprehension of how diversity is used to create oppressive systems and structural inequities. Think, for example, about who you, as a social worker, are serving when you consider your organizational context and your client's needs. Are you, as an agent of an organization, primarily meeting organizational needs or are your client's needs primary? As shown in the following chart, a progressive way of addressing diversity moves from helping people assimilate into the dominant culture to cultural competence to anti-oppression practice.

Table 4.1   From Cultural Competence to a Critical Anti-Oppression Approach Social Work Practice[1]

There must exist a paradigm, a practical model for social change that includes an understanding of ways to transform consciousness that are linked to efforts to transform structures. —bell hooks

APPROACH	CONTEXTUALIZING FRAMEWORK	OBJECTIVES
I. Social work with the "other"	Group-specific practice, cross-cultural communication, learning about other cultures	Learn to work effectively with a diverse client population by avoiding decontextualizing their experience; by studying the cultures, values, lifestyles, and worldviews of individual identity groups; and by helping them assimilate into the dominant culture.
II. Cultural sensitivity and tolerance	Human relations, intergroup relations, tolerance, celebrating diversity, pluralism	Develop awareness of and sensitivity toward diversity, particularly through an examination of your personal biases.
III. Cultural competence	Multicultural competence, culturally relevant/responsive practice, understanding multiple perspectives, culturally appropriate intervention	Gain the knowledge and practical skills necessary to implement multicultural intervention strategies that will enable you to engage with diverse clients.
IV. Practice within sociopolitical context	Critical theories and analyses of systems, social justice theories	Engage in a critical examination of the systemic influences of power, oppression, dominance, inequity, and injustice in all aspects of the profession, from your own practice to institutional policies and practices. Learn how to be an ally.
V. Anti-oppression practice	Theories of oppression; power, advantage, and privilege; critical race theory (Abrams & Moio, 2009); structural change; social movements	Prepare to be a change agent through a critical examination of individual, institutional, and structural levels of practice, and develop anti-oppression intervention skills. Learn how to be an accomplice.

[1] Table adapted from Gorski (2009).

Cultural Diversity and Multiculturalism:
An Anti-Oppression Perspective

We now move our discussion about cultural diversity and multiculturalism beyond inclusion, understanding, and acceptance to addressing difference within a sociopolitical power context of racist exclusions that have been and are "calculated, brutally rational, and profitable" (Goldberg, 1993, p. 105). Anti-oppression multicultural practice means "interrogating, challenging, and transforming those cultural practices that sustain racism" and "linking the struggle for inclusion with relations of power in the broader society" (Giroux, 2000, p. 499). In other words, multiculturalism requires an undoing of oppressive systems, which means a fundamental change of institutional structures and dominant cultural beliefs and norms.

To understand cultural diversity and multiculturalism within an antioppression framework is to acknowledge the following:

- Members of some groups enjoy privileges and dominant status, based on white supremacy, socioeconomic status, and other advantages, while members of other groups are relegated to low status in society and do not have access to privilege.
- Social identity groups that are considered to be diverse experience historical and ongoing oppression in our society.
- Race is the central mechanism of oppression in the United States, and understanding institutional racism as a structural phenomenon is foundational to understanding all other forms of oppression.
- Socioeconomic class is a primary element of both diversity and oppression.
- The very creation and maintenance of a class system based on difference is a function of oppression.

At the core of oppressive systems is the assumption of diversity, not just as being different, but as being deviant from the norm; in other words, in violation of dominant cultural values, beliefs, practices, and phenotype (how one looks). To view diversity as "the other" is a way to marginalize some individuals and groups and to uphold the dominance and social power of one segment of society. A view of diversity as other obscures the most basic privilege of the dominant group, which is defining and naming the norm. As Kendi (2019) pointed out, "whoever creates the cultural standard usually puts themself at the top of the hierarchy" (p. 91).

Thus, viewing and addressing diversity through an anti-oppression practice lens means doing the following:

- Recognizing that race is the scaffolding that undergirds all oppressive systems; that race, racialization, and racism are the centralizing forces of oppression (Abrams & Moio, 2009).
- Not labeling any person or group as "other" and not defining or explaining any person or group based on one single aspect of or stereotype about their social identity.
- Developing and using critical thinking skills to identify assumptions, examine evidence, and expose the myopic, shortsighted thinking that often underlies value judgments based on difference.
- Understanding the significance and impact of diversity in the everyday lives of all persons, not just those identified as "the other."
- Knowing that diversity issues matter immensely to everyone and, therefore, expecting that discussions about difference and diversity will often evoke intense feelings and become conversational lightning rods.
- Engaging, especially during moments of tension, in open dialogue and exploring your own biases and beliefs instead of making judgments about those who are perceived as different.
- Exploring your own unique diverse national origins and other social identities and how they influence your views about yourself and others.

Anti-oppression social work practice requires us to value the lived cultural experiences of diverse individuals and to change our personal attitudes and behaviors toward those who are perceived as different from us. It requires us to examine our own power position in relationships. It requires us to see the parallels, intersections, and distinctions between all forms of oppression and the ways they are manifested in our own lives as well as within the organizations and the multicultural society in which we work and live.

In the 21st century the United States will become more racially and ethnically diverse, and immigration will continue to be a major and contentious force in shaping demographics. Yet, even though diversity is most salient in relation to ethnicity, most people identify with not just one but several cultural groups based on values and interests. Those different identities play out in their lives in various ways depending on the status of each identity within oppressive systems. When we include all aspects of a person's uniqueness —such as socioeconomic class, gender, sexual orientation, disability, religion, age—we find that one person can be vulnerable to harm in some situations and at the same time be privileged in other situations.

In Reflection/Journaling Exercise 4.1 you will have an opportunity to map out your own social identity profile, including the various social groups to which you belong. We encourage you to reflect on how your life experiences are shaped by the intersection of your different statuses (power, privilege, marginalization) based on different parts of your identity. The goal is to increase your awareness of intersectionality on a personal level as a precursor to understanding the dynamics of and your role in oppressive systems.

REFLECTION/JOURNALING EXERCISE 4.1

Social Group Membership Inventory*

Social identities are socially constructed categories often based on the physical, social, and cultural characteristics of individuals within a group. Identification in a social group can be self-claimed or ascribed by others. For instance, racial groupings may be ascribed as well as self-claimed. The government, schools, and employers may ask an individual to claim a racial identity group or may ascribe a racial category to an individual based on visual perception. Social groups hold different positions in society. A *target group* is a social identity group that is disenfranchised, exploited, or marginalized. An *agent group* is a social identity group that holds unearned privilege and power in society.

For the purpose of this self-examination, put an X in the column that most closely matches the social group memberships you claim or those ascribed to you. Please note that unlike the agent (privilege) group list, the list of examples for the target (marginalized) group is not exhaustive, but rather illustrative. Feel free to add your own language for your identities.

SOCIAL IDENTITY CATEGORY	X	AGENT (PRIVILEGED) GROUP	X	TARGET (MARGINALIZED) GROUP
Race		white people		People of color, multiracial, etc.
Ethnicity		Western-European		Chinese, Iranian, Colombian, Navajo, etc.
U.S. nationality		U.S. born		Immigrant, foreign born
Sex		Assigned male at birth		Assigned female, intersex
Gender		Cisgender, gender conforming		Transgender, genderqueer, etc.
Class		Rich, wealthy, upper-middle		Working class, poor, low-wealth people
Sexual orientation		Heterosexual		Lesbian, gay, bisexual, asexual, queer
Age		Young adults, adults		Children/youths, older adults, elders >55
Ability		Able-bodied people		People with disabilities
Religion		Christian, Protestant, Catholic		Pagan, Muslim, Jewish, Buddhist, Wiccan, atheist, etc.
Body size		Thin, fit, slim		Fat, bigger body
Other				
Total				

Count the number of target identities you have and total them at the bottom of the columns.

1. Review the social identity categories and circle the identities that are most salient (significant) to you. Write about why some are most salient and others are not.

2. Is there a pattern between agent and target status and salience? Write about why you think this might or might not be the case.

*Dr. Adriana Aldana (2018) CSUDH MSW 524: Critical Race Studies in Social Work Practice. Adapted from Gisella Zuniga, 2001 and the SJTI 2001 Manual. Mark Brimhall-Vargas, OHRP, University of Maryland

Structural and Interpersonal Dynamics of Oppression

Levels of Anti-Oppression Practice Interventions

When we come to understand how oppressive systems operate, it becomes apparent that factors related to individual characteristics are often overrated, while contextual and structural factors, such as socioeconomic class, privilege, entitlement, negative stereotyping, and marginalization, go unnoticed. On the one hand, when we don't have a balanced view of situations that includes contextual as well as individual factors and focus only on people's choices as a way to explain their difficulties (e.g., substance abuse, domestic violence, homelessness), we can easily end up "blaming the victim." On the other hand, if we gloss over individual factors and focus only on environmental, historical, and situational obstacles as a way to explain behavior, we can end up disempowering people by assuming that individual effort is ineffective in dealing with those obstacles. The key to anti-oppression practice, as illustrated by Figure 4.1, is to inquire about the connections between interventions at all levels: from meeting human needs to securing human rights, from social service to social control to social justice, and from individual to piecemeal to structural change (Brenden & Van Soest, 1987).

Figure 4.1   Intervention Levels

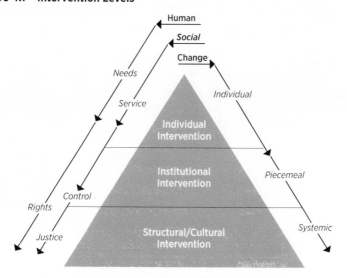

The boundaries between the intervention levels—individual, institutional, structural—in the above model are permeable and interrelated. To both meet human needs and attain human rights and social justice, all three levels are required. Interventions beginning in the sphere of individual services are often based on the values of compassion, benevolence, and a charitable ideology. However, when interventions focus solely on meeting the needs of individuals and families, they tend to do so with considerable inequity and inefficiency and do not eliminate the need itself. For example, at this level, welfare may be given as a form of charity through means-tested, temporary assistance that is not designed to prevent or end poverty. When interventions are restricted to the individual level, as Gil (1990) suggested, they perpetuate the problems they are meant to address and may even become a powerful underlying cause of the problem.

As the diagonally descending arrows in Figure 4.1 indicate, individual interventions need to be complemented by interventions at the next two levels. Anti-oppression interventions at the institutional level are based on values of equity, equality, and fairness (in other words, creating laws and policies that are more responsive to people's needs) and seek to eliminate punitive, exclusionary practices aimed at controlling behavior and restricting opportunities. Limiting interventions to the first two levels, however strong they may be, can perpetuate injustice if changes at the structural level are not addressed. For example, without challenging the faulty assumption that the economy and the system of capitalism are basically sound and dynamic enough to meet the needs of all citizens, highly successful job-training programs can result in people continuing to live in poverty even while fully employed.

An integration of individual, institutional, and structural interventions is at the core of anti-oppression practice. Moving from a focus solely on individual interventions to a focus on institutional and structural interventions represents a movement from adhering to conventional beliefs and systems to alternative visions and structures:

- From traditional values and ideologies characterized by a sense of compassion and benevolence for "the other" (those who deviate from some norm as determined by the dominant culture) to questioning of the dominant values and beliefs that support oppressive societal structures (e.g., patriarchal and racist ideologies that benefit white males in our society).

- From an expression of social responsibility based on prevailing norms and perceptions of reality—which entails changing the individual to fit the norm—to a critical consciousness of the need for fundamental, systemic change in societal norms and structures.

- From adherence to the status quo of social roles and economic class to an increased emphasis on social and economic development aimed at the liberation and fulfillment of all individuals. For example, operating food shelves in the community maintains the status quo by treating poverty as a marginal concern at the individual level; creating community microbusinesses impacts economic development at the institutional level and changes ideology at the structural level.

Common Elements of Oppression

"Oppression" is defined as a situation in which one segment of the population acts to prevent another segment from accessing resources or acts to inhibit or devalue them to dominate them (Bulhan, 1985). Oppression is a multidimensional phenomenon that can be unintentional because it is incorporated into the functioning of social and political institutions as well as individual consciousness. It is driven by social power, not individual power, and is realized via interpersonal interactions that reflect contextual power dynamics. This means that the experience of having advantage or disadvantage can be influenced situationally, depending on the context. Oppression is a social injustice that is perpetrated through social institutions, practices, and norms on individuals who suffer the injustices of oppression due to their membership in targeted social groups. Oppression inflicts harm that is both psychological, such as reducing one's self-image through microaggressive behaviors that denigrate and humiliate, and material, such as reducing access to resources such as wealth, income, health care, and jobs (Cudd, 2006).

Those targeted and harmed by oppressive systems are not just people from any one social group. People of color, women, LGBTQ people, persons with physical or mental disabilities, non-English speakers, the elderly, and children are members of oppressed groups. Correlative groups—such as whites, men, straight and cisgendered persons, able-bodied, English speakers, and nonelderly adults—are privileged persons who are not members of those oppressed groups. Most people are members of several social groups, so depending on the circumstances, all individuals are involved in the role of both oppressor and oppressed at one time or another, whether or not they are consciously aware of their privilege or nonprivileged status (Cudd, 2006; Gil, 1998; Mullaly, 2002).

According to Young (2000), the presence of any one of "five faces" or experiences—exploitation, marginalization, powerlessness, cultural imperialism, and violence—constitutes oppression, and most people experience some combination of these. While the origins of different kinds of historical oppression may differ and the effects of oppression on various groups may diverge, there are four elements that are common to all oppressions regardless of the target population: power and advantage, institutionalization, invisibility, ideology, and violence (Pharr, 1988).

All Oppressions Grant Power and Advantage

All forms of oppression bestow power and advantage on certain groups and/or people who are regarded as the norm and deny power and advantage to others who are labeled as the other. The defined norm is the standard to which the other is compared and thus is perceived to be inferior to and deviant from the norm. For example, a white, heterosexual man is the standard of rightness that is valued and against which all others are judged. The other is nonwhite, not male, or not heterosexual. Such judgment justifies dehumanization of the other and confers advantage and privilege on those who fit the norm, to the disadvantage of the other (Garcia & Van Soest, 2019).

Oppression is about social power, not individual or personal power. Racism, sexism, heterosexism, and other -isms are sociopolitical, systemic, and structural phenomena. They are neither personal prejudices based on individual power and stereotypes nor exclusively behavioral. There is a difference between prejudice and discrimination (personal power) and the system of advantage that confers economic, social, judicial, and political power on people who fit the norm. To understand oppression, we can look at indicators and patterns in institutional practices and policies. For example, in the political arena, very few U.S. senators are Black, Indigenous, Latinx, female, or openly homosexual. During the 2020 COVID-19 health crisis, of the hundreds of thousands of people who died there were disproportionately more people of color, of low income, elderly, and people with compromised health.

All Oppressions Are Institutionalized

A second element common to all systems of oppression is that they are *institutionalized,* woven into the norms, traditions, laws, and policies of society. Thus, even those who don't hold oppressive beliefs are compelled to act in accordance with institutional interests—to adhere to "business as usual." Institutionalized racism illustrates how the process works with all other forms of oppression by ensuring entitlement and benefits for the dominant white group regardless of the intentions of individuals in those institutions. According to Pinderhughes (1989), not only does institutional racism ensure that whites benefit, but it also exonerates them from responsibility, and it sanctions the blaming of people of color for the restrictions and limitations imposed by oppression.

Chart 4.1 is a timeline of sample events throughout history that illustrate how systems of oppression are woven into the very foundation of American culture, society, and laws. It shows how racism is an institutionalized sociopolitical phenomenon based on a social system of power and advantage that is distinct from personal prejudice based on individual power and stereotypes. We recognize that the list does not capture all events that bear attention and hope that it will stimulate further exploration.

**Chart 4.1   Sample of Racist Institutional Practices and Policies in the
United States, 1600–2020***

1600+	International Native American slave trade began in 13 colonies.
1619	Jamestown colonists started a school to convert Indigenous children to Christianity.
1641	Colonial laws supported killing, scalping Indians, raping and enslaving any Native woman or child.
1700+	Indian slave trade was the colonies' primary economy, with 30,000 to 50,000 Indians enslaved.
1790	Naturalization Act of 1790, in which citizenship was restricted to free whites.
1819	Civilization Act to assimilate Native Americans and convert them to Christianity.
1830	Indian Removal Act; Trail of tears began the next year, estimated 8,000 deaths.
1848	Treaty of Guadalupe Hidalgo ceded Mexican territory in Southwest to the United States.
1850	Fugitive Slave Law allowed federal marshals to capture runaway slaves with no legal recourse; California Indian Act of 1850 authorized slavery of Native children.
1857	*Dred Scott v. Sanford* denied possibility of citizenship to African Americans.
1864	Congress made it illegal for Native Americans to be taught in their native languages, sent children to boarding schools. U.S. Army massacred 300 Cheyenne Indians.
1870	Naturalization Act of 1870 revised Naturalization Act of 1790 and 14th Amendment to exclude Chinese and other Asian immigrants.
1879	Boarding School policy removed Native children from their communities to kill the Indian, save the man.
1882	Chinese Exclusion Act
1883	Supreme Court struck down 1875 Civil Rights Act.
1887	Dawes Act dissolved tribal lands and granted land allotments to individual families.
1890	Wounded Knee massacre; final suppression of Plains tribes by U.S. Army.
1896	*Plessy v. Ferguson* upheld doctrine of "separate but equal" for Blacks and whites.
1902	U.S. courts appointed white American guardians over Indigenous minors' interests in allotment process.
1922	Cable Act: Any female U.S. citizen who marries an alien ineligible for citizenship loses her citizenship.

(continued)

Chart 4.1 (continued)

1923	Supreme Court: South Asians may be "Caucasian" but not white, ineligible for citizenship.
1931	Nine African American men arrested in Scottsboro affair.
1942	120,000 Japanese Americans sent to relocation camps.
1953	Congress began a 13-year period of terminating Native tribes and selling their lands.
1954	Castle Bravo, largest U.S. hydrogen bomb test, was detonated over Bikini Atoll; U.S. government studied effects on residents of Marshall Islands without their informed consent.
1954	Operation Wetback expelled more than 2 million Mexicans.
1955	14-year-old Emmett Till was brutally beaten and killed for allegedly whistling at a White woman. Two White men acquitted by an all-white jury.
1965	"Bloody Sunday": police teargassed and whipped civil rights workers marching for voting rights at the Edmund Pettus Bridge in Selma, Alabama.
1974	*Milden v. Bradley* allowed for legal segregation of students of color in inner-city districts from white students in white suburban districts.
1979	Largest U.S. nuclear accident on Navajo (Dine) reservation in New Mexico; people not notified immediately of deadly radioactive uranium waste in water supply; cleanup continues in 2020.
1985	Supreme Court ruled that Oregon Klamath tribe does not have exclusive rights to hunt, fish, and gather on reserved lands, according to 1864 treaty.
1986	Immigration Reform and Control Act criminalized the employment of undocumented workers and mandated intensification of the Border Patrol.
1990	Supreme Court ruled that states can outlaw religious practices of the Native American Church.
1991	African American Rodney King was severely beaten by four Los Angeles police officers, who were acquitted.
1996	Welfare reform set public assistance time limits, disproportionately negative effect on women of color.
2001	Patriot Act gave power to detain suspected "terrorists," more than 1,000 Arab, Muslim, and South Asian men detained.
2004	Proposition 200 stated that Arizonans must present proof of U.S. citizenship for basic public services and to vote.
2013	Supreme Court struck down key provisions of the 1965 Voting Rights Act.
2017	President Trump signed executive orders banning entry of people from Muslim-majority nations.

(continued)

Chart 4.1 (continued)

2018	Thousands of children separated from their asylum-seeking parents at Mexican border and held in cages at detention centers; record-keeping failed to keep track of family members' locations.
2019	Black Americans killed by police at three times rate of white Americans from 2013 to 2019 with only 1% resulting in convictions (Bult, 2020).
2020	President Trump issued executive order banning federal government, its contractors, subcontractors, and grantees from offering diversity training on racial and gender biases, calling it a "malign ideology."

Sources: Timeline adapted in part from Adams and Adams (2007) and Walters (2020).

Despite the historical and present evidence of racist policies and practices listed in Chart 4.1, there is still considerable resistance to comprehending the institutional aspect of racism. The process of understanding its systemic nature can be very painful, especially for white people who see themselves as different from whites whom they view as racists. It is particularly devastating for those who have been involved in civil rights activities to face the implication that they, along with other whites, are the beneficiaries of racism. They may experience a sense of injury when they recognize that they are trapped in the systemic process of racism that benefits them and exploits people of color. This sense of injury is exacerbated further by the realization that, while for many people of color this reality has been obvious, for many whites it has been obscure.

Cudd (2005) suggested, however, that as long as you struggle against the social system, you do not have to be an oppressor, even if you are a member of a privileged group and are powerless to renounce that membership. Cudd maintained that to be an oppressor, you need to (a) be a member of a privileged group, (b) gain from oppression of another social group, (c) intend to so gain, and (d) act to realize that intention by contributing to the oppression of the oppressed group from whose oppression you benefit. Kendi (2019) offers a similar perspective with his definition of a racist (i.e., oppressor) as someone "who is supporting a racist policy through their actions or inaction or expressing a racist idea" and an antiracist (antioppressor) as "one who is supporting an antiracist policy through their actions or expressing an antiracist idea" (p. 13). The point is that institutionalized systems of oppression will continue unabated until those who benefit from them take action to dismantle them.

The Invisibility of All Oppressions

A third common element of oppression is the invisibility endured by groups who are oppressed. By keeping the oppression structurally invisible, individuals and groups are socially defined in a way that inhibits recognition of the group's heterogeneity by the dominant group. Invisibility at a societal level, for example, makes it possible to cast all immigrants as criminals or terrorists, all parents on welfare as irresponsible, or all women who have abortions as uncaring for their offspring. The complexity of individuals and the lived experiences that play a role in human behavior can lead, for example, to a view of African American women in relation to only one feature, as a woman *or* as an African American, and miss the complexity of the combination of the two (Collins & Bilge, 2016; Crenshaw, 1991).

The concept of intersectionality (Collins & Bilge, 2016) illuminates the complex dynamics of oppression and how social and political factors influence social identity in ways that render parts of one's self invisible. *Intersectionality,* a term developed by Crenshaw (1991), refers to the multifaceted discrimination experienced by individuals who belong to multiple groups that are targets of oppression. A Black woman who identifies as a lesbian, for instance, may face prejudice based on her race, gender, and/or sexuality. As Crenshaw explained in a 2017 video:

> Consider an intersection made up of many roads. The roads are the structures of race, gender, gender identity, class, sexuality, disability. And the traffic running through those roads are the practices and policies that discriminate against people. Now if an accident happens, it can be caused by cars traveling in any number of directions, and sometimes, from all of them. So if a Black woman is harmed because she is in an intersection, her injury could result from discrimination from any one or all directions. (National Museum of African American History and Culture, 2017)

Because people have multiple identities, the same person can be both the target of oppression based on membership in some groups and at the same time be granted privileges based on membership in other groups, such as a high-income Black lesbian or a disabled white male. When different degrees of social power, privilege, and constraints coexist in a person's life, some experiences and realities may be denied or minimized, especially when identity is considered to be merely personal. But identity is, in reality, an expression of sociopolitical influences that result in some aspects being visible and others being invisible. And when systemic factors are ignored, intragroup heterogeneity is also rendered invisible. That makes it impossible for us to explore the ways in which we are similar to and different from each other (Cho et al., 2013), which is essential to recognizing identity as a "source of strength, community and intellectual development [as well as] the source of empowerment" (Crenshaw, 1991, p. 1241).

When people internalize the sociopolitical judgments that devalue aspects of their identity, they may undervalue and even ignore substantive parts of their own origins and history. Depending on their privilege or target status, they may over- or underestimate their abilities, thus making invisible some aspect of themselves. When a part of their identity that was previously denied or minimized begins to emerge, they may not be aware of the complicated ways that issues of power, privilege, and constraints are operating in other aspects of their lives. For example, a gay white male who is in the process of accepting his sexuality and is not yet out may not realize how he is exercising his white privilege, while at the same time, he is in the process of resolving and managing the disadvantages of his homosexual identity. Or someone whose phenotype is white may choose to ignore other less socially valued parts of their heritage until they have resolved and integrated their social identity. Reflection/Journaling Exercise 4.2 provides an opportunity for you to explore the complexity of your own social identities in relation to power, privilege/disadvantage, and visibility/invisibility.

REFLECTION/JOURNALING EXERCISE 4.2

Multiple Identities: Power and Nonpower

Take all of the identities that you recognized in Reflection Exercise 4.1, map of yourself, and categorize them in the chart below. For your identities that are seen as "superior," "normal," or "the best group to be in" by the norms of dominant society, place that identity in the first column. For your identities that are seen as "inferior," "disadvantaged," "discriminated against," or "needing help" by the norms of dominant society, place that identity in the second column. Reflect on your profile as a person with many identities. Which aspects of who you are confer privilege and power? Which aspects do not? Which aspects are you most comfortable with? Which ones do you "own" or "disown"?

Aspects of My Identity That Confer Privilege and Power and Are Seen as Dominant	Aspects of My Identity That Do Not Confer Privilege or Power and Are Seen as Subordinate

Reflect on your profile as a person with many identities. Which aspects of who you are receive benefits and advantages from dominant society? Which aspects are disadvantaged? Which parts of your identity are you most comfortable with? Most uncomfortable? Which ones are visible to others? Which ones are invisible? Have you at any point in your life kept any identity invisible to yourself?

All Oppressions Are Held in Place by Ideology and Violence

The fourth element that is common to all oppressions is that they are supported by ideology and maintained by violence or the threat of violence. The ideology of all oppressive systems is, at its core, the idea or belief that the privileged group is superior to the disadvantaged group and therefore has the right to control it. This ideology is expressed in many ways purporting that dominant group members are more intelligent, harder working, stronger, more capable, more deserving, more advanced, chosen, normal, superior— ultimately, more human. Conversely, the opposite qualities are ascribed to people who are the targets of oppressive systems purporting that they are stupid, lazy, weak, incompetent, worthless, less deserving, backward, abnormal, immoral, inferior—ultimately, less human. People who are the targets of oppressive systems and who are treated as "less than" all their lives and find those beliefs reflected in and perpetuated by institutions may come to believe it themselves—in other words, to internalize their oppression.

All oppressive systems are grounded in an ideology of white supremacy. Wilkerson (2020) went beyond institutionalized racism when she maintained that, beyond race, class, or other factors, there is a powerful caste system in our country based on an ideology of white supremacy that influences people's lives and behavior, a racial system that the Nazis studied to plan their outcast of the Jews. "Through no fault of any individual born into it," she writes,

> a caste system centers the dominant caste as the sun around which all other castes revolve and defines it as the default-setting standard of normalcy, of intellect, of beauty, against which all others are measured, ranked in descending order by their physiological proximity to the dominant caste. They are surrounded by images of themselves from cereal commercials to sitcoms, as deserving, hardworking and superior in most aspects of American life, and it would be the rare person who would not absorb the constructed centrality of the dominant group. (Wilkerson, 2020, p. 268)

Violence, justified by an ideology of superiority, is used to enforce and maintain all oppressions. Violence is defined as any act or situation in which a person injures someone, including both direct attacks on one's physical or psychological integrity and destructive actions that do not involve a direct relationship between the victims and perpetrators (Bulhan, 1985; Van Soest, 1997). This definition of violence broadens traditional perspectives in four ways: (1) it emphasizes the consequences of violence from the victim's perspective. (2) it treats all types of violence equally, whether the perpetrators are individuals, groups, institutions, or society. (3) it includes socially sanctioned violence, unintended violence, and subtle or covert violence that causes nonphysical harm, and violence causing long-term consequences. and (4) it includes any avoidable action that violates a human right in the broadest sense or that prevents the fulfillment of a basic human need (Salmi, 1993).

As this definition illustrates, violence comes in many forms, and its victims and survivors bear indelible scars that are often unrecognized or disregarded (Van Soest & Bryant, 1995). The violence may be physical—for example, lynching, raping, battering, and gay bashing. It may be doing harm to oneself. It may be interpersonal and psychological—for example, name-calling based on negative stereotypes and personal threats. It may be indirect, like microaggressions that are subtle put-downs, often unconsciously delivered in the form of backhanded compliments or snubs or dismissive gestures directed toward racial groups, women, people with disabilities, and other groups that society ranks as having lesser value. It may be institutionalized—for example, the predominance and treatment of men of color in the criminal justice system and on death row and condoned police brutality. Whatever form it takes, violence against its targets is justified and undergirded by an ideology of superiority.

Poverty, Violence, and Oppression: Illustrating the Common Elements of Oppression

> *The opposite of poverty is not Wealth . . .*
> *the opposite of poverty is justice.*
> —Bryan Stevenson

Systems of oppression based on race, gender, ability, and other aspects of social identity create and hold in place disparities in wealth, which ensure that economic class functions as a system of oppression. Based on our broadened definition of violence and an understanding of its consequences for its victims, poverty itself is a form of violence. It injures those who suffer under its conditions, even though direct links to obvious perpetrators usually cannot be made. It destroys life, not with a single blow as with physical violence, but by blocking the full development of the life potential of millions of people. Poor and low-income people suffer from undernourishment and malnourishment, they are more vulnerable to disease and high stress, their health is undermined, and they have higher infant mortality rates and reduced life expectancy. And, as discussed in the Chapter 3, people who are poor and have limited resources are disproportionately Black, Indigenous, Latinx, women, children, and people with disabilities.

As illustrated by Figure 4.2, poverty is a form of violence that creates and maintains oppression at three levels—individual, institutional, and structural/cultural. These three interconnected and inseparable levels weave a tight web of poverty and low economic status into the fabric of several other oppressive systems.

Figure 4.2   Violence of Poverty at Three Levels

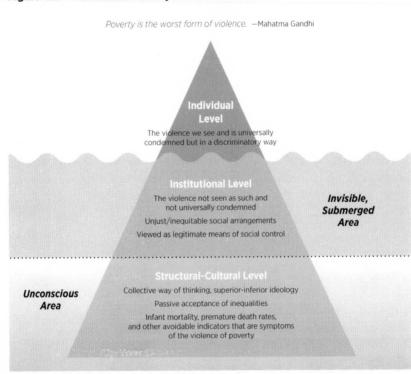

Poverty is the worst form of violence. —Mahatma Gandhi

Individual Level
The violence we see and is universally condemned but in a discriminatory way

Institutional Level
The violence not seen as such and not universally condemned
Unjust/inequitable social arrangements
Viewed as legitimate means of social control

Invisible, Submerged Area

Structural-Cultural Level
Collective way of thinking, superior-inferior ideology
Passive acceptance of inequalities
Infant mortality, premature death rates, and other avoidable indicators that are symptoms of the violence of poverty

Unconscious Area

Like the submerged root of an iceberg, the base of the triangle in Figure 4.2 represents the firmly embedded ideological foundation that undergirds the institutional and individual levels of oppression and violence. It contains the conventional values and everyday social realities and relations that form a collective way of thinking, which in the United States is white supremacy, patriarchy, and other superior-inferior categorizations. This structural level of violence is difficult to grasp because it is rendered invisible by a passive acceptance of inequalities and deprivations such as "the poor will always be with us." It is also difficult to grasp because social and economic indicators of inequities—such as differential infant mortality, premature death rate, and other avoidable differences—serve to reinforce beliefs in white, male, and other superiorities instead of being accurately perceived as symptoms of violence.

The institutional level of violence is submerged from view so that its forms are almost completely invisible. Violence at this level includes harmful actions by social and economic institutions (e.g., low wages, decline in social welfare services, and rise in corporate welfare) that obstruct the development of human potential through the use of discriminatory economic policies and practices. Violence at this level is not universally condemned because it is often subtle, indirect, and covert, and it involves long-term rather than immediate consequences. It is a form of "violence not seen as such" (Keefe & Roberts, 1991).

The top of the triangle represents harmful actions taken by individuals or groups against people or property. Like the tip of an iceberg, this is the violence that can be seen. Yet it is not seen in a critical way in relation to systemic or structural factors. Instead, it is perceived in a discriminatory fashion based on a superiority ideology and dominant beliefs at the structural-cultural level. For example, wealthy people who benefit from our inequitable economic system are admired for being ambitious and successful; poor and low-wealth people who are unable to provide nutritious meals or housing for their children are condemned for being lazy or poor money managers rather than as targets who are disadvantaged by an oppressive system. Individuals without wealth and resources who are accused of committing acts of violence, such as homicide and rape, are punished more severely than are those with resources.

The interrelated individual, institutional, and structural-cultural levels of the violence of poverty cannot be understood apart from one another. The violence of institutions and individuals gives expression to the dominant ideology of superiority at the structural foundation. Dominant beliefs and norms at the foundation rationalize institutional violence and depersonalize and decontextualize individual violence.

The violence of poverty at each of the three levels can be viewed as being of three different types: omission, repression, and alienation (Salmi, 1993). Violence by omission involves not helping those in need or danger, whether the person in need is oneself or others. Violence by repression includes infractions of the civil, political, economic, and social rights of individuals or groups. Violence by alienation deprives people of higher rights, such as emotional, cultural, and intellectual growth. Chart 4.2 gives examples of each type of violence at the individual, institutional, and structural-cultural levels.

Chart 4.2   Examples of Poverty as Violence by Type and Level

VIOLENCE TYPE	INDIVIDUAL LEVEL	INSTITUTIONAL LEVEL	STRUCTURAL-CULTURAL LEVEL
Omission: not helping people in need/danger	A homeless person asks a passerby for a sandwich and is ignored; person in need refuses to seek help.	Restrictive work requirements deny food stamps and welfare assistance to people in need.	Needs of people who are poor or of low wealth are not seen.
Repression: infractions of civil, political, economic, and social rights	Homicide, rape, assault, abuse; white supremacy group murders a Black man.	Welfare worker treats clients differently based on race, sexual orientation, immigrant status; harsher penalties for crack cocaine than other drug offenses.	Easy acceptance of the use of violence as a form of social control and the solution to problems.

(continued)

Chart 4.2 (continued)

VIOLENCE TYPE	INDIVIDUAL LEVEL	INSTITUTIONAL LEVEL	STRUCTURAL-CULTURAL LEVEL
Alienation: depriving people of emotional, cultural, or intellectual growth	High school boys paint swastikas on the school; mob burns a cross on a Black family's lawn.	Voter suppression and other violations of voting rights. Job training program is demeaning to women, culturally insensitive, and results in dead-end jobs that leave poor people worse off.	A persistent belief in one "American" culture, acceptance of mainstream culture's stereotypical negative assessment, and denigration of "the other."

Conditions of poverty form an intractable cycle of violence. Figure 4.3 illustrates how the seemingly senseless and irrational forms of violence reveal their inner logic as a form of counterviolence to societal practices and conditions when viewed in the context of poverty, discrimination, and inequity (Gil, 1990). It is within the context of structural and institutional impoverishment that individual acts of violence by those who are targets of oppressive systems may be best understood. Maintain perspective on the differences between equality and equity as you engage in the following exercises.

CLASSROOM EXERCISE 4.2

Case Vignette

Sarah and John are a Black couple who have been married for 9 years and have two children, Anna, age 7, and Brian, age 4. They both grew up in multicultural, urban neighborhoods and in working-class families where none of their parents went to college. Sarah, the oldest in her family, finished college and has been a fifth-grade teacher for 10 years. John, the youngest of three brothers, worked as a cashier at a computer and electronics store while working on a 2-year community college degree, and over the years he has moved into a middle-management position. While looking for their first home, the couple encountered several obstacles with realtors, such as the realtor not showing homes that had been advertised or saying that a home was just taken off the market or went into escrow. They finally found a home that they loved in a neighborhood not far from their families and with easy access to their workplaces.

When they approached their bank about a mortgage, Sarah and John had to wait for another customer, who was known to the bank staffer, to be served before them, even though he had arrived after they did. The bank staffer explained that he had noticed the other customer was in a hurry and, thinking that Sarah and John were probably unfamiliar with bank protocols and would take more time, had decided to serve the late-arriving customer first. Then, as he looked over their loan application, the bank staffer pointed out that the Federal Housing Administration and Veterans Administration had warned banks not to insure mortgages in that neighborhood. As an aside, he made a friendly comment about the white, middle-class community in which he lived and that there was an African American family that attended his church.

Questions for Discussion:

1. Imagine that you are both Sarah and John. What factors would you consider to understand what you were experiencing?

2. Consider the bank staffer. Would you describe his behavior as prejudiced? Discriminatory? Racist? Discuss the rationale for your response.

3. What aspects of institutionalized racism/oppression are at play in this situation?

4. The bank home mortgage policy and practice were guided by concern for (supposedly) maintaining property values. Identify the pros and cons of banks refusing to insure mortgages in neighborhoods that had been redlined.

5. Given that home ownership is perhaps the most important factor in accumulating wealth that has significant implications for future generations, what are the short- and long-term consequences of these obstacles to home ownership? Consider economic, psychosocial, and community factors. What viable alternatives, if any, offer the stable base for accumulating wealth that home ownership provides?

6. Using Chart 4.2 as a guide, list the different types of violence at individual, institutional, and structural levels can you identify in this situation.

Figure 4.3   Cycle of Violence and Poverty

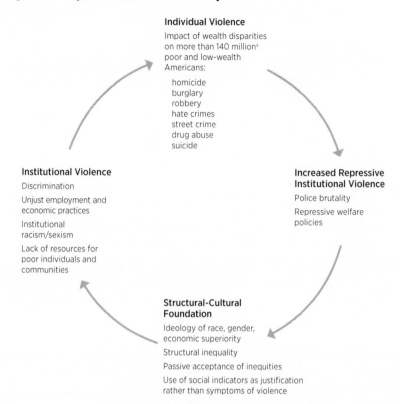

Individual Violence

Impact of wealth disparities on more than 140 million[a] poor and low-wealth Americans:

homicide
burglary
robbery
hate crimes
street crime
drug abuse
suicide

Institutional Violence

Discrimination

Unjust employment and economic practices

Institutional racism/sexism

Lack of resources for poor individuals and communities

Increased Repressive Institutional Violence

Police brutality

Repressive welfare policies

Structural-Cultural Foundation

Ideology of race, gender, economic superiority

Structural inequality

Passive acceptance of inequities

Use of social indicators as justification rather than symptoms of violence

[a] Based on the Supplemental Poverty Measure, which takes into account income as well as the costs of food, clothing, housing/utilities, and government programs that have assisted low-income families and individuals who are not otherwise designated as poor, 43.3% of the U.S. population (or 140 million people) were poor or low-income in 2017 because the wealth and resources of our country have been flowing to a small number of elites and federal programs are not meeting the growing needs of the people (Poor People's Campaign, 2020). Based on a Federal Reserve survey (May 24, 2019) almost 40% of American adults couldn't cover a $400 emergency with cash, savings, or a credit card charge they could quickly pay off.

ASSIGNMENT EXERCISE 4.3

Structural Inequities, Oppression, and Violence

Review the previous section about poverty as a system of oppression and violence that creates and maintains structural wealth inequities. Other structural inequities are similarly created by oppressive systems that are supported by ideology and maintained by violence or the threat of violence. Select one of the five structural inequities and then do research and write a paper based on the instructions that follow.

1. **Structural inequity: Education:** Students in low-income neighborhoods receive an education that is inferior to the education received by students in wealthier areas; poor children must attend public schools while rich children can attend private schools; before the 1950s, school segregation was allowed by federal law.

2. **Structural Inequity: Housing:** Systemic segregation exists through zoning, government redlining of historically underrepresented population areas, and discriminatory mortgage practices.

3. **Structural Inequity: Health Care:** People with good jobs have the best access to health care and a care system dominated by private health insurance; millions are without health insurance despite the Affordable Care Act.

4. **Structural Inequity: Race:** Racial inequity is rooted in U.S. slavery and Jim Crow laws. Racial disparity in neighborhoods; for example, minority families with incomes above $75,000 are more likely to live in poor communities, meaning more violence and schools of lower quality, compared to white families with incomes below $40,000.

5. **Structural Inequity: Gender:** Gender biases are present in the workplace. Men are more likely to be given leadership roles in both male-dominated fields and female-dominated fields. Because only paid work is considered work, the unpaid work women do as caregivers and homemakers has no recognized, visible economic value.

Instructions: Write a 5- or 6-page paper that addresses the following:

1. Indicators of structural inequity. One to two paragraphs that provide documented statistics and examples of inequities in an above area that you selected.

2. Levels of violence. Using Figure 4.2 as a guide and the broad definition of violence in the previous section, consider the ways in which violence is used to maintain the system of oppression and to produce the structural inequities.

   a. On the structural-cultural level, write about two or three beliefs or conventional values that undergird and justify the inequities you've identified.

   b. On the institutional level, write about two or three discriminatory policies and practices by social and economic institutions that create and/or maintain the inequities.

c. On the individual level, discuss two or three harmful behaviors or acts of violence taken by individuals or groups that are related to the inequities. Discuss how perpetrators are dealt with when they are members of the group advantaged by the oppressive system compared with how perpetrators are dealt with when they are members of the group(s) targeted by the oppressive system.

3. Types of violence—omission, repression, alienation. Using Chart 4.2 as a guide, list at least one example of each type of violence at the individual, institutional, and structural-cultural levels that maintain the inequities.

4. Conclusion. Summarize what you learned from conducting this assessment. What are the implications for you based on your membership in either the advantaged or disadvantaged group? For social work practice? What questions do you want to pursue further?

How Oppression Is Maintained

Levels and Impact

According to DeRosa (1988), the dynamics of oppression are maintained at four levels—individual, interpersonal, institutional, and ideological—all working together. DeRosa's four levels complement Pharr's (1988) four common elements of all oppressions presented in the previous section.

Individual level: Negative stereotypes are internalized. Throughout our lives we are socialized—within our families, through friends, mentors, media, and other sources—into a dominant culture that values some groups and not others. Regardless of background, we internalize negative stereotypes that influence how we think and feel about others and ourselves. The result is that we adopt one-dimensional images of diverse groups; in other words, we view one facet or characteristic as the whole portrayal of a group rather than recognizing its complexity. Our internalized stereotypes are a major source of discomfort when we try to engage with others different from ourselves.

For those at whom the negative stereotyping is directed, the criticism and judgment of one's own cultural group by others creates internal conflict. Racial identity theory, which is discussed in the next chapter, describes the developmental stages involved in reaching a wholesome sense of identity. The process of change is often triggered when people of color become aware of a discrepancy between the negative stereotypes that they have internalized and what they observe and experience in real life. For example, someone who is gay observes that not all gay men are in unstable, brief relationships as he has been taught to believe; someone with a disability who has been treated as helpless sees others with disabilities leading fully developed, productive lives. In a similar way, the process of change is triggered for white people when they become aware of a discrepancy between their experiences with people of color and the negative stereotypes about them that they had internalized.

Interpersonal level: Group activity and interpersonal interaction. The ways in which we interact and behave with others are influenced by institutions such as schools and churches and are supported by family, peers, and the community. Negative stereotypes based on the dominant standards and conventions of language, terminology, and ideas are maintained through interactions with others. Then, when we interact with people different from ourselves, we experience a conflict between what we were taught and what we encounter. This is poignantly illustrated by college students who, for the first time, become aware of the intensity of family prejudices when they return home for the holidays after being exposed to new experiences with diverse groups.

Institutional level: Systemic policies and organizational practices, "business as usual," personal prejudice not needed to engage in discriminatory practices. At the institutional level, resources and power are controlled in a systematic way that reflects dominant cultural values. Because we may not be aware of how these values affect us, exploring them can stir up conflicted feelings and discomfort. Disparities in quality-of-life measures—such as health, education, income, housing, mental health, and access to services—are indicators of the institutional level of oppression as discussed in the previous section.

Ideological level: Societal beliefs, values, and practices. The normative and ideological roots of oppression at this level undergird and give rise to how institutions function and shape how individuals think. An ideology and collective psychology, mostly unconscious, at this level defines what is "good" and guides everyday activities. For example, symbols that reinforce particular esthetic behavioral qualities and norms about what is beautiful and good dominate all types of media. Underlying ideologies establish the criteria about what is unacceptable, inappropriate, and/or inferior (e.g., same-sex marriage, immigrant status, having a disability).

The four levels of oppression operate in unison to systematically violate people's basic rights, as illustrated by examples in the following six domains (Bulhan, 1985):

- *Space*: limited and constrained options about where and how one lives. Consider the consequences of low socioeconomic power on housing location and type. Instances of large families living together may arise more out of economic necessity than choice. What are the implications of these restrictions for those who own their home versus rent? How does home ownership affect day-to-day quality of life? How does ownership affect the possibility of accruing wealth?
- *Time*: constraints imposed by responsibilities and limited resources. Consider the degree to which people have control over their time versus having to work for and/or serve others.
- *Energy*: constraints on activities in which people can be engaged. When people have limited resources and have to function at a survival level to meet basic needs for food, shelter, and clothing, then control over their emotional, physical, and psychological energy is seriously limited. A woman may exhaust her energy working as a caregiver for others' children at the cost of energy needed for her own children.
- *Bonding*: the increased challenge of developing the human bonds essential for "good enough parenting," family and peer relationships, and intimate connections. How do people navigate the ups and downs associated with closeness when they don't have stable and supportive contexts for these tasks? How do the effects of marginalization,

poverty, and low social power create obstacles that can interfere with the bonding needed for a wholesome, balanced, and active life?

- *Mobility*: limits on where people feel welcome, safe, and at home. What are the effects of segregated schools or beaches or community covenants that legally restrict who can purchase property in a given area? Can everyone with a substantive economic record such as a stable job and good salary purchase a home where they choose? Consider the places you frequent. If you were alone and in a wheelchair, how would you fare in getting around? Consider how females take extraordinary caution about where they go and, when assaulted, are blamed for using poor judgment. Consider how LGBTQ individuals restrict their activity for fear of making themselves vulnerable.

- *Identity*: constraints on the degree to which people feel that their social identity is validated by society. Consider how populations, as targets of negative stereotypes, are invisible to others (e.g., pronunciation of their names, historical context, values, and interests). How does invisibility affect how they see themselves? How does the devaluation and marginalization of a person's group affect their sense of confidence and identity?

Moral Exclusion

Moral exclusion is the process of placing those who are different from oneself or one's group outside the boundaries of fair treatment by invoking assumptions about who deserves just treatment and who should enjoy society's benefits (Deutsch, 1990). The concept of moral exclusion—meaning disengagement practices that make it possible to justify exclusion (Opotow, 1990)—provides a useful framework for explaining how oppression is maintained by exclusionary behavior at individual and interpersonal levels. It presumes that some populations are subordinate in their level of development on moral, intellectual, or spiritual grounds, and that is what provides the rationalization for exclusion. Persons outside one's moral boundaries are seen as expendable or undeserving, and thus harming them is acceptable, appropriate, benign, or even just. The process of categorizing groups negatively and excluding them from the realm of acceptable norms or values is linked to stereotypes and prejudicial attitudes related to ethnocentrism. Persons excluded from the realm of the norms and values of social justice include people of color, women, LGBTQ persons, people with disabilities, low-income populations, and others.

The concept of moral exclusion can help us understand ourselves in relation to different groups in society. While seldom conscious of them, we all have beliefs about which people should be treated justly, and the broadness or narrowness of our moral boundaries is influenced by prevailing cultural norms. For example, it is no longer considered acceptable in the United States to own people as slaves or to make interracial marriages illegal, but it is still acceptable to exclude immigrants and gay men and lesbians from certain benefits. The identification and exclusion of an out-group from the norms of fairness is a cognitive, affective, and behavioral phenomenon that enables otherwise considerate people to engage in self-serving behavior or inaction in everyday situations to gain benefits, even at injurious costs to others. The following exercise provides an opportunity for you to explore and broaden your own moral boundaries. It is important to keep the perspective that socialization into certain ways of thinking and believing does not make one a bad person. The problem arises when, in line with dominant societal values, we believe that *this* way of being is *the* way to be.

REFLECTION/JOURNALING EXERCISE 4.3

Exploring Your Moral Boundaries

Imagine that the circle below represents your moral boundaries. List the individuals or groups you believe deserve just treatment and should enjoy society's benefits inside the circle. Place the names of the individuals or groups you believe should not enjoy some of society's benefits or just treatment outside the circle. For those listed outside the circle that represents your moral boundaries, note your rationale for their exclusion (e.g., moral, intellectual, spiritual reasons). In addition, note the benefits or rights that you believe they should not be entitled to. In some cases, you may believe that they should not be entitled to some benefits and should be entitled to others; in those instances, be sure to note your beliefs and your rationale for each. For example, some people believe that gay and lesbian individuals should not enjoy the benefit of marriage, which would be outside the circle, but should not be discriminated against in the workplace, which would be inside the circle. Another example might be the belief that people with severe disabilities should not be allowed to marry, vote, or live independently, which would place them outside the circle.

Reflection/Journaling Exercise 4.3 Questions:

1. Look at who is inside your circle. What is your life experience with these individuals and groups? How similar to or different from you are they? What messages did you get about each as you were growing up and from whom or where? What messages do you get today from people around you and from the media? Are there people inside the circle today who would not have been there in the past? What changed?

2. Look at who is outside your circle. What is your life experience with these individuals and groups? How are they similar to or different from you? What messages did you get about each as you were growing up and from whom? What messages do you get today from people around you and from the media? Are there people outside the circle today who would have been inside in the past? What changed?

3. When you look at the individuals or groups outside your moral boundaries, imagine that they are clients and you are their social worker. What are the implications for practice?

4. What was it like to do this exercise? What feelings were triggered? What did you learn?

Bystander Behavior

> *We must always take sides.*
> *Neutrality helps the oppressor, never the victim.*
> *Silence encourages the tormentor,*
> *never the tormented.*
>
> —ELIE WIESEL

In June 2020 a Minneapolis police officer was videotaped as he choked an unarmed Black man named George Floyd to death by pressing his knee on his throat for almost 9 minutes. Several other officers watched and did nothing. Onlookers were heard saying things like "get off his neck," "he's a human," and "he's dying." But why didn't any of the officers or onlookers stop Mr. Floyd from being murdered? What attempts did the bystanders make to intercede as he struggled to breathe, and how were they responded to?

For decades psychologists have researched and tried to understand the circumstances in which bystanders fail to intervene versus circumstances under which they stand up (Fischer et al., 2011). Bystanders are defined as people who see, hear, or otherwise become aware of a behavior that inflicts physical, emotional, or psychological harm on someone else. Bystander effect occurs when the greater the number of bystanders, the less likely it is for any one of them to provide help to a person in distress. Latané and Darley (1970) attributed the bystander effect to two factors: diffusion of responsibility and social influence. Perceived *diffusion of responsibility* means that the more onlookers there are, the less personal responsibility individuals will feel to take action. *Social influence* means that individuals monitor the behavior of those around them to determine how to act.

As cries for justice echoed across the country after the murder of George Floyd and several other Black people by police, Murrell (2020) called for closer examination of several questions about bystander behavior. What factors determine or affect the likelihood that help will or will not be provided to a victim in critical situations of racial violence, aggression, or discrimination? How can we influence the behavioral responses of bystanders and equip them to provide proactive intervention in situations of racial bias, discrimination, and aggression? What does the growing research on moral trauma tell us about the traumatic consequences for individuals who witness and feel a party to behavior that harms another individual and goes against their sense of morality?

Without minimizing that racism and other -isms are created by and embedded in institutional and structural constructs, we focus here on bystander behavior at individual and interpersonal levels and how it either supports/maintains or interrupts/disrupts the operation of oppressive systems. The following five-step psychological process proposed by Latané and Darley (1970) is aimed at helping us avoid the bystander effect and find ways to intervene in situations of oppression.

1. *Notice a critical situation.* It is important to be ready, to expect to see or hear something. It may be someone doing physical harm to a member of an oppressed group. It may be a microaggression, a hurtful or dismissive comment made by a member of the socially dominant group without conscious intention or rational awareness. It may be a situation in which bias, discrimination, and violence are not only committed by one perpetrator but are also facilitated by otherwise well-intentioned bystanders who fail to act or intercede when the incident occurs. Whatever type of harm you observe, it is natural to freeze or go into shock when seeing someone being physically, emotionally, or psychologically attacked or harmed in some way. Freezing is usually a response to fear that we won't know how to help, that we might be misunderstanding the context and seeing a threat where there is none, or that intervening will make things worse. Being prepared to notice harm is a way to counteract such responses.

2. *Construe the situation as serious.* It is important to recognize and respond to the feelings of the person being harmed; in other words, to see the situation from the perspective of the victim. Research

shows that it is often difficult to empathize with those we perceive as different from us (Fischer et al., 2011). Sager (2016) pointed out that there is a particularly acute empathy gap for white people when they try to imagine the feelings of Black people, and that inhibits them from recognizing, acknowledging, and understanding when harm is being done.

3. *Develop a perspective of personal responsibility.* We are all susceptible to diffusion of responsibility, which is thinking we don't need to help when there's someone else who could or should. Diffusion of responsibility may be more likely if we perceive that the responsibility for some harm or failed action lies with others, not ourselves; we didn't cause the problem, so it isn't our responsibility to intervene to fix it. Other reasons we may be reluctant to take responsibility include apprehension about being judged by others, a fear that we'll make mistakes or act inadequately, and a lack of any reaction or sense of concern from others (Latané & Darley, 1970). Murrell (2020) points to situations of racial bias or discrimination in which a desire on the part of white people to appear and perceive themselves in a positive and nonracist manner creates significant obstacles to doing something. They may fail to intervene and yet maintain a self-perception of being egalitarian, nonracist, and unbiased by denying facts, incidents, or examples (e.g., "it was just a few bad actors"), by reinforcing beliefs about meritocracy or deservedness (e.g., "they were likely guilty of something"), or by claiming color-blindness (e.g., "race isn't an issue here"). Such strategies make it possible for them to keep their sense of egalitarian values and anti-bias self-perceptions intact while, at the same time, denying any personal responsibility to intervene in situations involving racial bias and discrimination. Such inaction among well-intentioned bystanders provides a silent acceptance or validation of racial bias and signals silent agreement with racism and its consequences.

4. *Believe we have the skills necessary to succeed.* To move from passive to active bystander, we need to train ourselves or get training in how to identify and point out harmful behaviors, how to appeal to the perpetrator's higher principles, how to be an ally, and how to draw on different intervention strategies (Sue, et al., 2019).

5. *Reach a conscious decision to help.* This involves worrying less about the consequences of helping and more about the consequences of not helping. It involves an assessment of risk to oneself and weighing the alternative of violating one's own principles and beliefs or having to wonder if taking action might have helped someone. It involves courage, an ability to set limits, and a commitment to learn and grow from whatever happens.

Classroom Exercise 4.3, a social worker's true story, provides an opportunity for you imagine yourself in a bystander situation in the workplace and to brainstorm intervention strategies.

CLASSROOM EXERCISE 4.3

From Passive to Active Bystander: What Is My Assignment?

Break into small discussion groups and read the story out loud together. Then discuss the questions that follow.

The Sore of Racial Injustice—Working While Black by Deseria Galloway (2020)

I was a child protective investigator for almost 24 years. During the course of conducting an investigation, the person I was at the home to investigate, unbeknownst to me, called the police and reported that I was trying to break into her home and tore the screen door off its hinges. As a result, the police came four cars deep, with guns drawn, one demanding that I put my hands on the steering wheel, while the other officer was demanding my I.D. I was completely confused and caught off guard, shaking in my boots. I heard one officer on the radio say we have one Black female suspect in the car and in search of the second suspect, which they never located. I was so messed up, I found two I.D.s: one was my University of MN I.D. and the other was my driver's license and business card. I threw them out of the crack of the window while the officer kept using his baton to hit my windshield as he was yelling at me. He never really permitted me to speak. It was not until one of the female officers said, "Something is not right here. I do not believe that this was a burglary in progress." Only after 25 minutes did the officers put the guns back into their holsters. They started leaving one by one, but the officer who kept hitting my windshield with the baton pulled his car around and parked in front of me and sat there an additional 15 minutes after he told me I was free to go. He never gave an apology or anything. I was so messed up crying. I returned back to the client's door, and she answered and said, "Oh, I thought you were going to hurt me." My reply to the client was, "Let's just get through this investigation."

The next day, I reported the incident to my supervisor. Nothing ever happened as a result. I did nothing wrong "working while Black," but I was treated like a criminal and demeaned by both the client, a white woman, and six officers, all of whom were white. There is nothing worse than being viewed as a threat just because of the color of your skin. The officers were successful at demeaning and devaluing who I was as a human being.

Go-Around Process

Right after reading the story, take turns sharing your initial response, reaction, and feelings. When it's your turn to speak, share your truth. When it's not your turn to speak, listen deeply to understand the person speaking. Do not comment or respond to anything that is said. Once everyone has shared, move on to discuss the following questions.

Discussion and Questions

1. Imagine you are Deseria's supervisor. What actions might you take to change the outcome from "nothing ever happened" to an antiracist intervention?

2. Imagine you are Deseria's co-workers, and when she tells her story during a staff meeting, no one says anything.

   a. What are all the things you see in the situation?

   b. How serious is what happened, to whom, and in what ways?

   c. What personal responsibility do you feel to do something?

   d. What do you need to know or what skills do you need to intervene?

   e. In what ways might you intervene? How feasible are they? What are the implications of taking action?

Summary

In this chapter we presented the concepts of cultural diversity and multi-culturalism within an anti-oppression practice framework. We illustrated, in both text and exercises, how social identities are granted either privilege status/advantage or target status/disadvantage. We scrutinized the common elements that create and maintain all oppressive systems, regardless of positionality. Discussion about multiple identities and multiple oppressions illustrated the complex dynamics related to issues of power and privilege. Oppression is characterized by social rather than individual power, is maintained politically and socially by the institutionalization of norms, practices, and laws; and is held in place by ideology and violence, both in physical expressions and threatened. The concepts of moral exclusion and bystander intervention were presented as tools to help us explore our beliefs about who is deemed worthy of being treated fairly and to help us develop strategies for challenging and dismantling oppressive systems.

In the next chapter, we focus on the development of racial and social identity as a way to encourage you to think critically about your life experiences and how you may have both internalized and discarded dominant societal beliefs as well as your privileged or targeted status. Such reflection and processing is the basis for anti-oppression social work practice.

References

Adams, P., & Adams, M. (Eds.). (2007). *Teaching for diversity and social justice*, 2nd ed. Taylor & Francis.

Abrams, L. S., & Moio, J. A. (2009). Critical race theory and the cultural competence dilemma in social work education. *Journal of Social Work Education, 45*(2), 245–261.

Brenden, M. A., & Van Soest, D. (1987, March). *An integrative model of social work practice.* Paper presented at APM, Council on Social Work Education, St. Louis, MO.

Bulhan, H. A. (1985). *Frantz Fanon and the psychology of oppression.* Plenum Press.

Bult, L. (2020, June 30). A timeline of 1,944 Black Americans killed by police. Vox.com. https://www.vox.com/2020/6/30/21306843/black-police-killings

Cho, S., Crenshaw, K. W., & McCall, L. (2013). Towards a field of intersectionality studies: Theory, applications, and praxis. *Signs, 38*(4), 785–810.

Collins, P. H., & Bilge, S. (2016). *Intersectionality.* Polity.

Crenshaw, K. W. (1991). Mapping the margins: Identity politics and violence against women of color. *Stanford Law Review, 43*(6), 1241–1299.

Cudd, A. E. (2005). How to explain oppression. *Philosophy of the Social Sciences, 35,* 20–49. https://doi.org/10.1177%2F0048393104271923

Cudd, A. E. (2006). *Analyzing oppression.* Oxford University Press.

DeRosa, P. (1988). *The four ism's* [Unpublished manuscript]. ChangeWorks Consulting. www.changeworksconsulting.org

Deutsch, M. (1990). Psychological roots of moral exclusion. *Journal of Social Issues, 46*(1), 21–26.

Fischer, P., Krueger, J. I., Greitemeyer, T., Vogrincic, C., Kastenmuller, A., Frey, D., Heene, M., Wicher, M., & Kainbacher, M. (2011). The bystander-effect: A meta-analytic review on bystander intervention in dangerous and non-dangerous emergencies. *Psychological Bulletin, 137*(4), 517–537.

Galloway, D. (2020). The sore of racial injustice—Working while black. *CEHD Connect.* https://connect.cehd.umn.edu/lived-experiences/

Garcia, B., & Van Soest, D. (2019). Oppression. *Encyclopedia of Social Work.* https://oxfordre.com/socialwork/view/10.1093/acrefore/9780199975839.001.0001/acrefore-9780199975839-e-271

Gil, D. (1990). *Unraveling social policy.* Schenkman.

Gil, D. (1998). *Confronting injustice and oppression.* Columbia University Press.

Giroux, H. A. (2000). Racial politics, pedagogy, and the crisis of representation in academic multiculturalism. *Social Identities, 6*(4), 493–510.

Goldberg, D. T. (1993). *Racist culture.* Basil Blackwell.

Gorski, P. (2009). What we're teaching teachers: An analysis of multicultural teacher education course syllabi. *Teaching and Teacher Education, 25,* 309–318.

hooks, b. (1996), *Killing rage: Ending racism* (reprint ed.). Holt Paperbacks.

Keefe, T., & Roberts, R. E. (1991). *Realizing peace: An introduction to peace studies.* Iowa State University Press.

Kendi, I. X. (2019). *How to be an antiracist.* One World.

Latané, B., & Darley, J. M. (1970). *The unresponsive bystander: Why doesn't he help?* Appleton-Century-Croft.

Mullaly, R. (2002). *Challenging oppression: A critical social work approach.* Oxford University Press.

Murrell, A. J. (2020, August). Why someone did not stop them? Aversive racism and the responsibility of bystanders. *Equality, Diversity and Inclusion, 40*(1), 60–73. https://doi.org/10.1108/EDI-07-2020-0191

National Museum of African American History and Culture. (2017). *#APeoplesJourney: African American women and the struggle for equality.* [Video]. https://www.youtube.com/watch?v=X5H80Nhmn20

Opotow, S. (1990). Moral exclusion and injustice: An introduction. *Journal of Social Issues, 46*(1), 1–20.

Pharr, S. (1988). *Homophobia: A weapon of sexism.* Chardon Press.

Pinderhughes, E. (1989). *Understanding race, ethnicity, and power.* Free Press.

Sager, Jessica (2016, October 4). The Empathy Gap and How to Fill It. *Education Week, 36*(7), 26–27.

Salmi, J. (1993). *Violence and democratic society.* Zed Books.

Stevenson, B. (2003). Keynote address: Race to execution symposium. Presented at DePaul University College of Law, Chicago, IL.

Sue, D. W., Alsaidi, S., Awad, M. N., Glaeser, E., Zalle, C. Z., & Mendez, N. (2019). Disarming racial microaggressions: Microintervention strategies for targets, white allies and bystanders. *American Psychologist, 74*(1), 128–142.

Van Soest, D., & Bryant, S. (1995). Violence reconceptualized for social work: The urban dilemma. *Social Work, 40*(4), 549–557.

Van Soest, D. (1997). *The global crisis of violence: Common problems, universal causes, shared solutions.* NASW Press.

Walters, K. L. (2020). *History through a native lens.* Indigenous Wellness Research Institute, University of Washington. https://nativephilanthropy .candid.org/timeline/

Wiesel, E. (1986, 10 December). *Acceptance, Nobel Peace Prize.* [Speech]. https://www.nobelprize.org/prizes/peace/1986/wiesel/26054-elie-wiesel -acceptance-speech-1986/

Wilkerson, I. (2020). *Caste: The origins of our discontents.* Random House.

Young, I. M. (2000). Five faces of oppression. In M. Adams, W. J. Blumenfeld, R. Castenada, H. W. Hackman, M. L. Peters, & X. Zuniga (Eds.), *Readings for diversity and social justice* (pp. 35–49). Routledge.

CHAPTER 5

Social and Racial Identity Development in the Context of Oppression

I n Chapter 4 we analyzed how oppressive systems operate and illustrated, in text and exercises, how social identities are granted either privilege status/advantage or target status/disadvantage. Now we turn to the process of social and racial identity development, which is about how people come to understand who they are within a society that is characterized by structural inequities, white supremacy, and systemic oppression. In this chapter we ask you to use racial identity development models to examine your own identity and ascertain how it affects your responsibility and ability to confront oppressive systems.

Thinking critically about your life experiences—and how you may have internalized and discarded dominant societal beliefs and your privileged or targeted status—is an essential component of cultural competence and the foundation of anti-oppression work. The development of racial identity is premised on ongoing reflection of your experiences as you encounter social and political events that contradict your fundamental beliefs in a just world. Becoming aware of your responses to the multiple dimensions of oppression—where it occurs, your awareness of it, and its manifestations (Hardiman et al., 2007)—at different stages of your development may activate uncomfortable thoughts, feelings, and behaviors for reasons made clear by Tatum (2017):

The concept of identity is a complex one, shaped by individual characteristics, family dynamics, historical factors, and social and political contexts. Who am I? The answer depends in large part on who the world around me says I am. Who do my parents say I am? Who do my peers say I am? What message is reflected back to me in the faces and voices of my teachers, my neighbors, store clerks? What do I learn from the media about myself? How am I represented in the cultural images around me? Or am I missing from the picture altogether? (p. 99)

Our self-concept comprises several identities that involve an "awareness and understanding of oppression in the social environment, and also within every person, as part of the developmental process" (Adams, 2007, p. 17). Consistent with the major premise of this book—that racism is the foundational oppressive system in the United States—we highlight in this chapter the necessity of understanding your own racial identity as a bridge or a lens through which to connect with others' social identities. The way that we experience our racial identities is mediated by other intersecting dimensions of who we are such as "male, female, or transgender; young or old; wealthy, middle-class or poor; gay, lesbian, bisexual, or heterosexual; able-bodied or with disabilities; Christian, Muslim, Jewish, Buddhist, Hindu, or atheist" (Tatum, 2017, p. 99).

With the multidimensionality of social identity in mind, Reflection/ Journaling Exercise 5.1 provides an opportunity for you to explore the question "who am I?"

REFLECTION/JOURNALING EXERCISE 5.1

Social and Racial Identity

Respond to each of the following questions by writing your responses so you can refer to them later and/or consider sharing them with others in class.

1. When did you first become aware of your family's economic status? What aspects of your family's living situation stand out in relation to you class status?

2. What memories stand out regarding the effects of your family's socioeconomic status on your family life?

3. When did you first become aware of your ethnicity as white, African American, Latinx, Asian, Native American, or other ethnicity? What experience brought that awareness to your attention? What positive or negative associations do you have with that memory?

4. What memories do you have about learning about diverse others and difference, meaning groups different from your family? What was the message in your family about "others"?

5. When you look back on when you began to talk about sensitive issues around difference, what do you think made it so difficult to talk about diversity and difference? For yourself? For others?

6. What expectations do you recall that you felt were based on your social identity? How was the group(s) you identified with "supposed to be" or to "act?"

The Learning Process: Exploring Your Racial Identity

We begin this discussion about racial identity development by presenting Hardiman et al.'s (2007) perspective of oppression, which focuses on awareness of the manifestations of racism in relation to the contexts in which they occur, and a determination of the intentionality that drives the behavior and/or practice. This perspective highlights how racism is manifested at multiple, interactive dimensions. Similar to DiAngelo (2018), it is a perspective that focuses on building awareness and learning the varied manifestations of oppression and racism rather than focusing on whether individual behavior is racist. Hardiman et al.'s (2007) dimensional perspective serves as a guide for anti-oppression practice in several ways. It provides a framework for increasing one's awareness of oppression. It focuses on the manifestations of oppression as a way to develop awareness, insight, and critical thinking. It emphasizes that naming what we see is essential to managing what is aroused in us so that we can act. It builds in us the personal, intellectual, and political knowledge that is essential for developing a social justice perspective.

It can be eye opening to explore what we may have considered to be an individual choice and examine it instead in relation to contextual factors and then come to realize the role those factors played in our judgment and decision making. Hardiman et al.'s (2007) framework shines a spotlight on the ways in which oppression is manifested at three contextual levels:

- *The individual/behavioral* context refers to the thoughts, feelings, and behaviors that are elicited in interactions with others and in the varying contexts through which we move. How you see yourself is complicated by contextual factors, such as who others think you are. To draw from a wellness perspective, this dimension emphasizes the importance of being mindful of our responses; that is, paying attention to how you feel, physically and psychologically, in different settings. Do you experience privilege or disadvantage? Are you treated in ways that you expect?

- *The institutional* context refers to the policies, practices, and norms—both formal and informal—that support and/or promote discrimination, segregation, exclusion, disadvantage, privilege, and other oppression-related phenomenon. For example, redlining in banks, glass ceilings for female employees, disproportionality in mental health diagnoses across racial groups, discrepancies in K–12 schools in different communities, and segregated neighborhoods are some examples of how oppression is demonstrated in the institutional dimension. How we see ourselves—in other words, how we identify ourselves—is influenced and affected by how we are treated by society's institutions.

- The *societal/cultural* context refers to values, beliefs, and customs. This dimension manifests itself in how we are represented in the media; the promulgation of some values over others (e.g., Christianity); the judgment of difference as negative; and the societally imposed, reductionist view of difference as one-dimensional (i.e., complexity is invisible). The invisibility of identities and experiences of marginalized populations in the media has a particularly significant impact on how we see ourselves and how others see us.

- To the three dimensions above, we add the *interpersonal context.* Although oppression is a structural systemic phenomenon, it is carried out through relational dynamics. Ultimately, policies and regulations are put into practice in relational contexts, between people. Privilege and target statuses are associated with complex dynamics related to contextual factors (e.g., interpersonal, structural, societal) as well as psychosocial and cognitive development (Adams, 2007).

Inherent in Hardiman et al.'s (2007) perspective is the concept of consciousness, our recognition and understanding of the intentionality of the behaviors or practices. Although the oppression may not be intentional, the consequences of the behavior or practice speak volumes when we examine the effects on people's lived experiences. The contextual dimensions that go into one's sense of racial identity are further complicated and affected by the intersection of various dimensions of one's identity (i.e., intersectionality) as illustrated in the following vignette.

Dr. Elise Camacho is a divorced, Mexican American, first-generation professor (i.e., the first to go to college) who grew up in a working-class multicultural left coast (i.e., West Coast) community.

- *Intrapsychological/behavioral:* As the first born in a Mexican American family, Dr. Camacho's mother was clear about wanting to raise her children "to fit in and become independent." As the child with the darkest skin in the family, Dr. Camacho grew up dealing with racism in the family. She remembers her neighborhood as multicultural. At a young age, due to her high academic performance, she experienced school as a refuge; (e.g., she was chosen to represent students at a press conference when her newly built elementary school was inaugurated). Her focus on performing well in school and teachers' recognition of her academic potential blunted the perceptions of discrimination that she may have otherwise experienced, for instance, in the form of patronizing.

- *Interpersonal:* Later in her life as a young MSW professional, Dr. Camacho enjoyed recognition of her skills and perspective from colleagues. As a practitioner, she was about to be involved in social justice advocacy efforts within the context of a supportive husband and home life. Her social network was increasingly composed of relationships with friends of diverse backgrounds.
- *Institutional:* As an MSW-level social worker in a clinical practice setting, Dr. Camacho was perplexed by the response of a senior clinician at a staff lunch when she asked for clarification about social work education, and he said, "Where do you start with, Elise?"
- *Cultural/societal:* In her teens and young adult years, Dr. Camacho was very aware that she didn't have societal role models with whom she could identify. Although she was in the college prep track in high school and had a Mexican American male teacher, she had no mentors and was never encouraged to consider higher education. She graduated from high school with plans to enter a local community college to learn to be a secretary. Fortunately, a chance encounter with a classmate that summer encouraged her to apply to a local university.
- Later in her teaching career, Dr. Camacho went up for early tenure with a white colleague who had acknowledged that the two of them had equal publishing records. Her white colleague became a full professor, but Dr. Camacho did not; due to her unrelenting perseverance, she became a full professor the following year.

As illustrated by Dr. Camacho's life, the context of macro-level institutional and cultural/societal dynamics and their interaction with personal and interpersonal dynamics are powerful influencers on identity.

Racial-Ethnic-Cultural Identity Development

In this section we present three racial identity models that illuminate the powerful role of context, situational factors, and social environment on the development of racial identity, both as hurdles and as initiators of change. Helms (1990) defined racial identity as "a sense of group or collective identity based on one's perception that he or she shares a common racial heritage with a particular racial group" and racial identity development theory as concerning "the psychological implications of racial-group membership, that is, belief systems that evolve in reaction to perceived differential racial-group membership" (p. 3). According to Cross and Cross (2008), racial identity development models are best considered as racial-cultural identity or racial-ethnic-cultural identity models. They emphasize that "racial, ethnic and cultural identity overlap at the level of lived experience to the point that there is little reason to discuss them separately" (p. 156).

Racial identity development models focus on the process that we go through as we come to terms with and reject oppression throughout our lifetime. Both people of color and white people must deal with the task of recognizing the internalization of racism and undoing its effects. No one remains untouched by dominant, mainstream society's distorted view of individuals and populations based on dominant ideology. Given the dominant/subordinate and privileged/oppressed relationship of white people and people of color in society, however, it is not surprising that the developmental change process unfolds in different ways depending on one's positionality.

Developing one's racial identity involves a process of recognizing racism and oppression in one's immediate and global social environment, and in oneself. The assumption is that everyone's identity, regardless of background, is affected as a consequence of growing up in a racist systemic context. An awareness of our multiple identities helps us realize that most of us have characteristics related to being both privileged and disadvantaged. For example, the ability to walk into a classroom reflects ableist privilege. Each of our identifications is associated with some degree of high or low social power, and the constellation of these in any one person produces an overall identification as privileged or marginalized. Although we limit our discussion to models of racial identity development, we encourage you to explore the extensive literature on other social identities related to gender, sexual, religious, and ethnic identity as well. Current developments of disability identity models addressing the complexities posed by the vast range of types of disabilities, their inception, and age-related factors of onset will greatly expand the knowledge base of social workers committed to anti-oppression practice.

In the following vignette about some of the experiences of social work student Caterina, we focus on how the contextual factors and the change process in which she is engaged affects her racial identity.

Caterina is a Latinx student living in a new city in the Southwest. She is working on her master's degree in social work. Through curriculum and field education experiences, she is exposed to learning about diversity. As part of her education she has the opportunity to observe community people engaged in advocacy efforts. Much of what she witnesses in community and town hall meetings involves citizen complaints about city or county practices. Experiencing the passion of community people from all walks of life and socioeconomic classes as they express concerns and hold public officials accountable is new to her. One night she is particularly impressed when white upper-middle-class citizens, some of them professors from the university, participate in a meeting about an incident in which an African American school principal was stopped in traffic and required to lie spread-eagle on the street while police checked her documents. The next day, as Caterina is shopping for a new sweater in the upscale mall that she enjoys going to occasionally, she notices—for the first time and in a different way—that the few Latinx there, apart from herself, are menial workers. All the shoppers are White, and most are middle and upper class. She feels like a door of new awareness is opening for her.

Caterina's experiences introduce several important concepts about racial and social identity that are discussed in this chapter. Her account demonstrates that we respond, as meaning-making beings, to others based on meanings we attach to their behavior (Berger & Luckman, 1966). When you consider the vignette, keep in perspective assumptions that you bring about Latinx regarding homogeneity and heterogeneity regarding that population and about acculturation. We tend to create a sense of self that, in part, is based on what significant others expect of us. The sociopolitical context in which this process occurs is enormously instrumental in shaping the direction in which identity develops. Caterina's experiences illustrate that all individuals internalize oppression and racism merely by virtue of exposure to socialization in an oppressive and racist environment. Exposure to socialization isn't good or bad; we don't choose to be exposed to it.

What is important is what we choose to do with our learning and awareness about socialization. Again, as Caterina's story shows, exposure to new experiences and socialization processes provides the foundation for developing a socially conscious and responsible self. The personal work in which she is engaged through her social work education complements the social advocacy work she is observing at the organizational and institutional levels. Her learning process involves changing how she views society, how she views herself, and how she sees herself as an agent of change. It is an emotional and intellectual change process that engages her in reflecting on how oppression has influenced her life and her relationships. The process is complex and involves making connections between social, political, and institutional factors and her personal experience.

There are certain dynamics and tasks that you too can expect to experience as you explore and learn about your racial identity development process. Your main task is to engage in cognitive learning about oppression and its relationship to your beliefs, and to recognize your feelings about those beliefs as you go through different life experiences. This effort involves identifying, naming, and processing one's feelings—work that can and often does involve dealing with conflicts, tensions, or discomfort related to coming to terms with what these experiences mean in your life. The growing awareness of these psychosocial effects on ourselves and others is bound to arouse strong feelings, which we see as a positive indication of personal growth and change.

There are several ways in which the following racial identity development models can be useful and valuable to you. By using them as a tool to think critically and reflect on your own racial development, you will be able to do the following:

- Examine aspects of your identity associated with various factors such as sociocultural backgrounds, family, and national origin.
- Explore and think critically about your relationship, as it evolves over time, with the values you hold and your identification with dominant societal ideological beliefs about race. This includes the "shoulds" and values related to what is considered normative and good and how you should act.
- Gain insight about factors that contribute to the expectations others hold of you and how you feel about those expectations.
- Make new connections between life events, societal and institutional factors, and your subjective experiences, which will make you less intimidated by strong reactions from others to sensitive topics regarding racism.
- Gain a new perspective that helps you address fears or anxieties in the face of microaggressions or when you are subjected to derisive labeling associated with your racial identity based on either privilege or disadvantage.
- Gain insight into your life experiences and the effects of oppression on your identity that, in turn, can increase your ability to view the world from the perspective of others.
- Increase your ability to empathize with others based on your ability to accept yourself.
- Discern racism and analyze the ambiguities associated with both its implicit and explicit manifestations.
- Avoid the risk of perpetuating oppression, which often results from a lack of understanding of your own racial identity.
- Better analyze your own and others' behaviors, which is an essential aspect of the use of self-concept in social work practice.

As you engage in exploring the complexity of your racial identity, we suggest that you keep a journal of your process. Reflection/Journaling Exercise 5.2 provides a format for journaling that promotes reflection on the above points.

REFLECTION/JOURNALING EXERCISE 5.2

Rediscovering My Feelings About Being a Person of Color, White, or Biracial/Multiracial*

Think back to when you first became truly aware that you were a person of color or white or biracial/multiracial. Close your eyes and imagine yourself back in the situation. Try to feel what you felt at the time. Focus on yourself rather than on other people. Write about your experience in your journal.

1. Who was involved in the situation, and what were their races?

2. What happened to you? What was your experience?

3. When that happened, describe how you felt.

4. Describe your bodily sensations at the time.

5. What did you do in response to your feelings or bodily sensations?

6. How did you feel about being a person of color/white/biracial/multiracial when this particular situation was over?

7. What did you learn about being a person of color/white/biracial/multiracial?

You may want to try this exercise several times, using experiences from different times in your life for analysis.

Refer back to your analyses of yourself. We hope they provided some ideas about how you react daily to being a person of color/white/biracial/multicultural person. Consider keeping a daily diary in which you record your conscious experiences.

*Adapted from Helms (1992, pp. 69–72).

What follows are descriptions of three racial identity development models for Blacks, ethnic whites, and biracial/multicultural individuals. All three models identify the tasks involved in personally confronting racism and undoing its effects on identity. All models, as well as current evidence, support the perspective that a positive sense of oneself as a member of a group is important for the health of both individuals and communities. The models highlight the tasks involved in confronting your experiences as either privileged and/or oppressed. This can mean dealing with multiple identities that embody both privilege and target status, depending on inter-sectional factors.

The models address how one becomes aware of the internalization of dominant ideological belief systems, realization of an identity based on privilege or marginalization, and movement toward an identity based on self-definition. When you have a integrated identity, you have the capacity to own characteristics that had been projected onto you and others in the form of negative stereotypes. You are free of the distortion that comes from privileged or targeted status. The distortions to be undone for those in a dominant position involve undoing the overestimations of self that come from a status of privilege and entitlement. The distortions to be undone for those in a subordinate position involve undoing the underestimations of self and giving up the devaluation of their group that was projected on them by the dominant ideology and internalized by its members.

Each racial identity development model offers a framework for under-standing the personal journey that begins with a lack of awareness of dominant societal oppression and progresses toward development of an integrated wholesome identity. This identity is free of being defined in rela-tion to the "other." It is an identity that is defined on its own terms rather than being defined by a context imbued by a biased distribution of power and privilege.

As you study the three racial identity development models, it is import-ant to keep in mind the following caveats:

- Although racial identity models are premised on stage concepts, life does not unfold in a sequential way that can be identified by rigid stages, but rather unfolds in ways where stages may be skipped, and/or recycled even though one has progressed to an advanced stage. Tatum (2017) suggested that identity development models are similar to "moving up a spiral staircase: as you proceed up each level, you have a sense that you have passed this way before, but you are not in exactly the same spot" (p. 174).
- Helms (1995) suggested that you move and transition through a series of points or statuses, rather than stages, that represent

attitudinal (i.e., behavior, affect, cognition) factors that regulate how you interpret racial information. Individuals may not go through all of the statuses, nor are they age related.

- Movement from one status or state or stage to another may be initiated when existing perceptions are too limited to help you cope with a personally meaningful racial event. Most often, the new perspective is triggered by an event or several events that focus the individual on a manifestation of racism (Tatum, 2017).

- Movement from one status to another is also influenced by how people cope in relation to what information processing strategies they use (Helms, 1995).

Black Racial Identity Development

As a social construct, race is a relational and political concept that fulfills economic and social functions and plays a formative role in one's psychosocial development. Black racial identity models focus on the consequences of racism on a person's awareness related to his or her identification as being Black. The Cross (1995) Black identity development model (Cross, 1995) identifies movement through points on a continuum. One end of the continuum represents the internalization of negative stereotypes and devaluation of oneself and one's group. The other end represents self-confidence based on internalization of a new racist-free identity. Racial identity development ultimately involves a renunciation of internalized racism and the emergence of a positive racial identity as a Black person.

The change process is initiated either by an event that devastates one's identity or worldview or by a "series of smaller, eye-opening episodes" that elicit anger and guilt. These events lead to less engagement with dominant society and more immersion into one's own group, followed by the development of an identity that meets new personal needs (Cross, 1995, p. 105). Personal and social changes are conceptualized as passages through the following five "ego statuses": preencounter, encounter, immersion/emersion, internalization, and internalization/commitment.

1. The *preencounter* stage is characterized by an out-of-awareness devaluation of oneself and one's group, along with efforts to fit into dominant cultural life. In this stage, the person has absorbed many of the beliefs and values of the dominant white culture, including the notion that white is right and Black is wrong. Although internalization of Black stereotypes may be outside conscious awareness, the person seeks to assimilate and be accepted by whites and actively or passively distances themself from other Blacks. This deemphasis on the person's racial-group membership may allow them to think that race has not been or will not be a relevant factor in their own achievement, which may contribute to a belief in a U.S. meritocracy that is often a part of the preencounter worldview.

2. The *encounter* stage is a two-part process that involves the person experiencing an event that challenges their current worldview and precipitates an interpretation of the event from a new perspective. Sue et al. (2019) suggested that an event, such as the death of Martin Luther King Jr., can stimulate a shift in worldview because one's prior worldview cannot explain his death. On a personal level, instances of social rejection by white friends or colleagues may lead the person to conclude that many whites will not view them as an equal. Faced with the reality that they cannot truly be white, the person is compelled to focus on their identity as a member of a group targeted by racism. Such a shift can be accompanied by feelings of anger and guilt as the person is forced to acknowledge the impact of racism on their life.

3. The *immersion/emersion* stage is characterized by a person's full attention being focused on their own culture. An increasing sense of cultural pride develops. This stage is characterized by the simultaneous desire to be surrounded with visible symbols of the person's racial identity and active avoidance of symbols of whiteness. As persons transition through this stage, anger may be experienced against whites. This anger typically dissipates, as much of the person's energy is directed toward their own group and self-

exploration. The result of this exploration is an emerging security in a newly defined and affirmed sense of self.

4. The *internalization* stage is characterized by the person being secure in their own sense of racial identity. Pro-Black attitudes in general become more expansive, open, and less defensive. While still maintaining their connections with Black peers, the internalized person is willing to establish meaningful relationships with Whites who acknowledge and are respectful of their self-definition. The person is also ready to build coalitions with members of other oppressed groups.

5. The final stage, *internalization/commitment*, is psychologically similar to the internalization stage. However, the person at this stage has found ways to translate their personal sense of being Black into action for or commitment to the concerns of Black people as a group. With a positive sense of racial identity, the person is able to perceive proactively and transcend race. This new racist-free identity is one that meets their new personal needs and is reflected in a commitment over time to Black community concerns (Cross, 1995).

White Racial Identity Development

White racial identity development models point to racism as a significant aspect of being a white ethnic. They highlight how whites are socialized into perceiving themselves as entitled to privilege and maintaining their privileged status through mechanisms such as denial, distortion, and aggression (Hardiman, 1982; Sue & Sue, 1999). The models also illuminate how movement through the development points or statuses involves recognition of how, by exercising privilege, a person has participated in oppressive practices. The person then moves on to confront their biases and prejudices and, ultimately, to take responsibility for personal and social change. The development process involves both the abandonment of racism and the development of an antiracist perspective. Sue et al. (2019) presented a model developed by Helms (1992) that includes two phases, each with three levels, called statuses.

Phase I: Abandonment of Racism

1. *Contact*: The person is color-blind about difference and accepts white supremacy. They lack awareness of cultural and institutional racism and of their own white privilege. They believe that white is not a color. This status often includes naïve curiosity about or fear of people of color based on stereotypes learned from friends, family, institutions, and the media. These stereotypes represent the framework in use when a person at this status makes a comment such as, "You don't act like a Black person." Whites whose lives are structured with limited interaction with people of color may remain at this stage indefinitely.

2. *Disintegration*: The person begins to see the consequences of racism and feels conflicted, and this breakdown of denial can mean anxiety and psychological pain. They begin to think that maybe being white does matter, and they begin to move from the bliss of ignorance or lack of awareness to the discomfort of guilt, shame, and sometimes anger at the recognition of their own advantage and acknowledgment of the role of whites in a racist system. Attempts to reduce discomfort may include denial, withdrawal, and attempts to change other white folks' attitudes toward people of color. For example, a person may begin to notice the racist content of jokes or comments of friends and relatives and try to confront them.

3. *Reintegration*: The person regresses into the dominant ideology as a retreat from the discomfort and adopts a "bootstrap" perspective about poverty with an "I did it, so can they" attitude. While the person recognizes their whiteness, this status is characterized by a defensive attitude: "So what if I'm white?!" Societal pressure to accept the status quo and a desire to be accepted by one's own racial group may lead the person at this stage to reshape their beliefs to be more congruent with an acceptance of racism. The person's guilt and anxiety may be redirected as fear and anger against people of color, who are now blamed as the source

of discomfort. It is relatively easy for whites to become stuck at this stage, particularly if they can avoid interactions with people of color. However, if there is a catalyst for continued self-examination, the person begins to question their previous definition of whiteness and the justifiability of racism in any form. Because the person's worldview at the reintegration status tends to be rigid and firmly held, movement out of this stage usually necessitates a personally jarring event, such as a drastic change in racial climate, a racist incident that cannot be simply justified, or a significant relationship with a person who succeeds in breaking through to challenge the person's assumptions.

Phase II: Defining a Nonracist Identity

1. *Pseudo-independence*: The person experiences events that trigger insight into racism and induces more understanding of diversity differences while still valuing solutions that support the status quo. The person is abandoning beliefs in white superiority but may still behave in ways that unintentionally perpetuate the system. They look to people of color to help them understand racism and often try to disavow their own whiteness through active affiliation with people of color. The person feels alienated from other whites who have not yet begun to examine their own racism, yet also feels rejected by people of color who are suspicious of their motives.

2. *Immersion/emersion*: The person moves into dealing with their whiteness, privilege, biases, and oppression; this involves undoing distortion and denial. This is a major shift away from focusing on people of color to focusing on understanding racism and on changing oneself. The person seeks to replace racially related myths and stereotypes with accurate information about what it means and has meant to be white in U.S. society. Learning about whites who have been antiracist allies is a very important part of this process of getting to know that others have found ways to resist racism.

3. *Autonomy:* The person's increased awareness of their own whiteness involves less guilt, recognition of their role in maintaining racism, and commitment to giving up their white privilege (Sue et al., 2019). The person has internalized a newly defined sense of self as white. The positive feelings associated with this redefinition energize their efforts to confront racism and oppression. Alliances with people of color can be forged more easily at this stage because the person's antiracist behaviors and attitudes are expressed more consistently.

Biracial and Multiracial Identity Development

In our racist society, people who identify as biracial, multiracial, or multicultural face societal pressure to identify as belonging to one racial group. They are often categorized as having one overriding, monolithic racial identity; in fact, before 2000, respondents to the U.S. Census only had the option of selecting one race. Based on the concept of "white purity" and concerns in the deeply segregated South that those "tainted" with Black ancestry might try to "pass" as white, the "one drop rule" (Wright, 1994) was used by the dominant society to classify people as Black when their parents were European American and African American. The one drop rule is based on the *hypodescent* concept, which is the automatic assignment of children of a mixed union between different socioeconomic or ethnic groups to the lowest social group—in other words, the lowest social power status (Root 1996, Sue & Sue, 1999).

As a result of society's difficulty to appreciate and accept an identity based on not one but multiple ethnic and racial heritages (Root, 1990, 1992, 1996, 2001), biracial and multiracial people experience considerable marginalization, prejudice, and discrimination. Being told to identify differently (i.e., deny parts of self) due to negative stereotyping denies people the option of identifying as they see themselves or processing the meaning of their multiple identities, that is, intersectionality (Rockquemore & Brunsma,1999). Denying and questioning one's identity and being denied membership by a group with which one does identify have been found to be associated with "integration conflict and lower social belonging" (Albuja et al., 2020, p. 398). Exclusion and mental health concerns have been found to be associated with biracial individuals who experience being challenged and questioned about their background and whose identity is invalidated (Albuja et al., 2019, 2020; Franco & O'Brien, 2018).

Within the context of the dominant values of a racist society that is characterized by systemic oppression, it takes considerable work to integrate the complexities of multiple racial and social heritages. It falls on the shoulders of each biracial, multiracial, and multiethnic person to work through the conflicts and validate their own background and to do so in ways that may not be supported within their immediate support network. Biracial/multiracial identity development models can be a tool to help people process experiences such as the possibility of feeling marginalized in their primary groups (Stonequist, as cited in Kerwin & Ponterotto, 1995), self-esteem and feelings of disloyalty in the face of society's uncertainty regarding race, and finding support for functioning in more than one culture (Jacobs, 1992; Kerwin & Ponterotto, 1995; Kich, 1992; LaFromboise et al., 1993; Poston, 1990). Rockquemore and Brunsma (1999) proposed that individuals with biracial identities have several options from which to choose, including a single racial identity, biracial identity, a changing identity depending on context, and a transcendent identity that focuses on being human.

Poston's Biracial Identity Development Model

Poston (1990), who recognized that existing models of minority identity development did not reflect the experiences of biracial and multiracial individuals, proposed the first model for the development of a healthy biracial and multiracial identity. His five-stage model suggests that biracial people will experience conflict and periods of maladjustment as part of their own identity development. This model also divides the biracial and multiracial identity development process.

1. *Personal identity.* At this stage a person's sense of self and personal identity is based on personality constructs that are developed within

the family. Personal identity occurs during childhood when the child is not aware of their mixed heritage.

2. *Choice of group characterization.* This stage is based on personal factors (such as physical appearance and cultural knowledge) and environmental factors (such as perceived group status and social support). During this stage, the person feels pressured to choose one racial or ethnic group identity over another due to peer, societal, or physical appearance factors and may choose a multicultural identity that includes both parents' heritage groups or one parent's racial heritage.

3. *Enmeshment/denial.* This stage is characterized by confusion and guilt over not being able to identify with all aspects of one's heritage. The person may feel disloyalty and self-hatred about choosing one group over another, subsequently denying the differences between the racial groups and identifying with both racial groups. Resolving guilt is important to move past this stage.

4. *Appreciation.* This stage is characterized by exploring and increasing knowledge about multiple heritages and broadening one's racial-group membership. A person may largely identify with one group more than others and yet also explore the other group(s) and grow to appreciate them during this stage.

5. *Integration.* This stage is characterized by a sense of wholeness that comes with recognizing and appreciating all of one's racial and ethnic identities. The person may still identify with one group but appreciates the integration of their multiple racial identities.

Root's "Resolving 'Other' Status" Multiracial Identity Development Model

Root (1990, 1992) maintained that mixed-race people are their own racial category and that they thus undergo their own unique racial identity development process. She proposed a model that integrates multiracial identities in a fluid, nonlinear way and includes assessment of sociocultural, political, and familial influences on the identity formation process.

Root's model suggests that biracial and multiracial people may self-identify in more than one way at the same time and/or move fluidity among a number of identities. These alternatives for resolving the "otherness" imposed by dominant society are not mutually exclusive; no one resolution is better than another. On the one hand, any combination of mixed-race identity can reflect a person's positive racial identity. On the other hand, the person may appear to have an integrated identity, when in reality they may not identify with any social group (Renn, 2008). This model includes four resolutions that biracial and multiracial individuals can use to positively cope with the otherness imposed on them by a dominant racist society.

1. *Acceptance of the identity society assigns.* The person identifies with the group that others assume they belong to the most. Family ties and personal allegiance to the racial group (typically the minority group) to which others have assigned them are often determining factors. The resolution may be a positive identity, but it is often tenuous.

2. *Identification with more than one racial group.* The person may be able to identify with both (or all) heritage groups. This is largely affected by societal support and one's ability to retain resistance to the influence of others. This active resolution of identity status may be idealistic and may not be possible in certain contexts (i.e., communities and contexts).

3. *Identification with a single racial group.* The person chooses one racial group independently of external forces. This is also an active resolution of identity status that may not be possible in certain contexts.

4. *Identification as a new racial group.* The person may choose to move fluidly throughout racial groups, but overall identifies with other biracial or multiracial people. This resolution is characterized by a strong kinship with other biracial/multiracial people. It is a positive resolution of identity status as long the person is not trying to hide or reject any aspect of their heritage.

REFLECTION/JOURNALING EXERCISE 5.3

Applying a Development Model to My Racial Identity Journey

This exercise is an opportunity for you to reflect on your unique experiences with events and experiences that were instrumental in moving you from one point to another in your racial identity process. Look at the stages of the racial identity developmental model that applies to you. Review the stages and look at the trajectory of your life. You might consider some formative points related to chronology or your age. Reflect and take notes on the following questions in preparation for possibly sharing these in class with another student.

1. How would you compare where you are now in your racial identity development compared to when you were 10 years old, an adolescent, and a young adult?

2. What stage of development in the model is the most familiar to you?

3. If you are a person of color, do you recall a period where you ever wanted to be different from yourself in terms of your phenotype or racial identity? If you are white, do you recall any impressions you had of others, in your youth, who were not white?

4. Think of an event or series of events that caused you to begin to question not only what you know about race, but also who you are. Think about how you felt (e.g., discomfort, anger, guilt) and what you did.

5. Think of a life experience or a context that you associate with a specific stage (e.g., coming of age in the 1960s or 2000s and being influenced by the social movements of those times and identifying with social movements). Why was it significant? How did it stimulate change in you and how you felt about your racial identity?

6. What leads you, today, to think that you are at a particular stage of development? What are the indicators and what experiences do you have that support your identifying with that stage?

Additional Social Identity Development Models

Identity development models have been created to explain the developmental trajectory of several other social identities such as gender (Downing & Roush, 1985), sexual orientation (Cass, 1979), and others.

A particularly useful model for anti-oppression practice developed by Worell and Remer (2003) defines four levels or stages that both privileged and oppressed group members may traverse within any given social identity (e.g., race, gender, sexual orientation, social class, ability):

1. *Preawareness.* Both privileged (e.g., white people, men) and oppressed (e.g., people of color, women) group members support values and beliefs that are often created by privileged group members with no recognition of the disparate nature of the impact of privilege and oppression.

2. *Encounter.* The worldview of privileged and oppressed group members starts to diverge as they begin to understand the nature and impact of social advantages (e.g., they can access the benefits of white privilege) or disadvantages (e.g., they experience acts of racism) that are associated with privilege or oppression. This newfound understanding of privilege and oppression leads to negative emotions for both privileged (e.g., shame, guilt) and oppressed (e.g., anger) group members.

3. *Immersion.* Privileged group members seek to initiate contact with, become more open to engaging, and begin to empathize with the experience of oppressed group members. On the contrary, oppressed group members prefer contact with other oppressed group members and seek to learn more about their own unique cultural heritage. The divergent needs of people from privileged and disadvantaged groups at this stage can create conflict and engender criticism from those who are privileged.

4. *Integration and activism.* Both privileged and oppressed group members become more comfortable being around members of the other group, better understand their own social identities, and are more prepared to recognize social inequities around them. Also, members of both groups are willing to equitably distribute valued societal resources and actively participate in social advocacy work.

Summary: Racial Identity Development and Anti-Oppression

In this chapter we emphasized that understanding racial identity development is essential to cultural competence and developing a commitment to social justice. Three distinct racial identity models were presented, addressing the dynamics of coming to terms with racism and oppression in society as well as the internalization of their effects as they work for or against members of different racial groups. The models focused on the movement from internalizing dominant ideological belief systems to realizing that one's identity is grounded in privilege or marginalization to the formulation of an identity that is no longer defined or contingent on oppressive beliefs, practices, or behaviors.

It is essential that social workers who strive to be culturally competent and committed to dismantling systems of oppression are aware of their own racial and social identity. They must be willing to confront the issues in their own personal and professional lives as a prerequisite for attending to their clients' racial and social identity needs. That means taking time to do the emotional and intellectual work required to address the complex concerns that arise from their own racial and social identity development processes. It means working toward a holistic identity with the capacity to own characteristics that may have in the past been projected onto others through negative stereotyping. It means being free of the distortion that comes from privilege or target status and to appraise and reject overestimations of self premised on entitlement and privilege, or underestimation of self based on one's target status.

The old adage of starting where the client is offers a particularly useful guide as you engage in learning about diversity, oppression, and social justice. It is essential to validate your own struggles and intentions. Throughout the process, suspend negative self-judgment and remember that integrating the political into the personal is a lifelong process. As you explore and analyze your own racial identity development, you are engaging in work that most people do not have the courage to do. The work is uncomfortable, so be gentle with yourself and your peers through the process. That is how social justice is created, person by person.

References

Adams, M. (2007). Pedagogical frameworks for social justice education. In M. Adams, L. A. Bell, & P. Griffin (Eds.), *Teaching for diversity and social justice* (2nd ed., pp. 15–34. Routledge.

Albuja, A. F., Sanchez, D. T., & Gaither, S. E. (2019). Identity denied: Comparing American or white identity denial and psychological health outcomes among bicultural and biracial people. *Personality and Social Psychology Bulletin, 45*(3), 416–430.

Albuja, A. F., Sanchez, D. T., & Gaither, S. E. (2020). Intra-race intersectionality: Identity denial among dual minority biracial people. *Translational issues in Psychological Science, 6*(4), 392–403.

Berger, P., & Luckman, T. (1966). *The social construction of reality*. Doubleday.

Cass, V. C. (1979). Homosexuality identity formation: A theoretical model. *Journal of Homosexuality, 4*, 219–235.

Cross, W. E. (1995). The psychology of nigrescence: Revising the Cross model. In J. G. Ponterotto, J. M. Casas, L. A. Suzuki, & C. M. Alexander (Eds.), *Handbook of multicultural counseling* (pp. 181–191). SAGE.

Cross, W. E., & Cross, T. B. (2008). Theory, research, and models. In S. M. Quintana & C. McKown (Eds.), *Handbook of race, racism, and the developing child* (pp.154–180). Wiley.

DiAngelo, R. (2018). *White fragility: Why it's so hard for White people to talk about racism*. Beacon Press.

Downing, N. E., & Roush, K. L. (1985). From passive acceptance to active commitment: A model of feminist identity development for women. *Counseling Psychologist, 13*, 695–709.

Franco, M. G., & O'Brien, K. M. (2018). Racial identity invalidation with multiracial individuals: An instrument development study. *Cultural Diversity and Ethnic Minority Psychology, 24*(1), 112–125.

Hardiman, R. (1982). White identity development: A process oriented model for describing the racial consciousness of White Americans. *Dissertations Abstracts International, 43*, 104A (University Microfilms No. 82-10330).

Hardiman, R. Jackson, B., & Griffin, P. (2007). Conceptual foundations for social justice education. In M. Adams, L. A. Bell, & P. Griffin (Eds)., *Teaching for diversity and social justice* (2nd ed., pp. 35–66). Routledge.

Helms, J. (Ed.). (1990). *Black and White racial identity: Theory, research and practice*. Greenwood Press.

Helms, J. E. (1992). *A race is a nice thing to have*. Content Communications.

Helms, J. (1995). An update of Helms's White and people of color racial identity models. In J. G. Ponterotto, J. M. Casas, L. A. Suzuki, & C. M. Alexander (Eds.), *Handbook of multicultural counseling* (pp. 181–191). SAGE.

Jacobs, J. H. (1992). Identity development in biracial children. In M. P. P. Root (Ed.), *Racially mixed people in America* (pp. 190–206). SAGE.

Kerwin, C., & Ponterotto, J. G. (1995). Biracial identity development: Theory and research. In J. G. Ponterotto, J. M. Casas, L. A. Suzuki, & C. M. Alexander (Eds.), *Handbook of multicultural counseling* (pp. 199–217). SAGE.

Kich, G. K. (1992). The developmental process of asserting a biracial, bicultural identity. In M. P. P. Root (Ed.), *Racially mixed people in America* (pp. 304–317). SAGE.

LaFromboise, T., Coleman, H. L. K., & Gerton, J. (1993). Psychological impact of biculturalism: Evidence and theory. *Psychological Bulletin, 114,* 395–412.

Poston, W. S. (1990). The biracial identity development model: A needed addition. *Journal of Counseling and Development, 67*(2), 152–155.

Renn, K. A. (2008). Research on biracial and multiracial identity development: Overview and synthesis. *New Directions for Student Services, 123,* 13–21.

Root, M. P. P. (1990). Resolving "other" status: Identity development of biracial individuals. In L. S. Brown & M. P. P. Root (Eds.), *Diversity and complexity in feminist therapy* (pp. 185–205). Haworth.

Root, M. P. P. (1992). *Racially mixed people in America.* SAGE.

Root, M. P. P. (Ed.). (1996). *The multiracial experience.* SAGE.

Root, M. P. P. (2001). Negotiating the margins. In J. G. Ponterotto, J. M. Casas, L. A. Suzuki, & C. M. Alexander (Eds.). *Handbook of multicultural counseling* (pp. 113–121). SAGE.

Rockquemore, K. A., & Brunsma, D. L. (1999). Between black and white: Exploring the biracial experience. *Race and Society, 1,* 197–212.

Sue, D., & Sue, D. (1999). Counseling the culturally different (3rd ed.). Wiley.

Sue, D., Sue, D., Neville, H. A., & Smith, L. (2019). *Counseling the culturally diverse: Theory and practice* (8th ed.). Wiley.

Tatum, B. D. (2017). *Why are all the Black kids sitting together in the cafeteria?* (20th anniversary ed.). Basic Books.

Worell, J., & Remer, P. (2003). *Feminist perspectives in therapy: Empowering diverse women.* Wiley.

Wright, L. (1994, July 25). One drop of blood. *The New Yorker,* 46–55.

PART III

Pulling It All Together

CHAPTER 6

Anti-Oppression Practice in Action

When I first came to know social workers half a century ago,
they had a mission that was, to me, appealing and significant:
to help poor people, to improve community life. ...
Certainly many professional social workers are still committed
to the public social services, to helping poor people, and dealing
with social problems like homelessness and child neglect,
but a large part of the profession is adrift in the
psychotherapeutic seas. (Specht & Courtney, 1995, pp. ix–x)

The concern, expressed in the preface of *Unfaithful Angels* (Specht & Courtney, 1995), about the social work profession's drift away from social justice is not new. The case or cause debate over what is the "true" social work goes back to the profession's origins with the differing perspectives of social work pioneers such as Jane Addams, whose focus was on social reform and political action, and Mary Richmond, whose focus was on individual casework. While neither perspective has eclipsed the other, the influence of each waxes and wanes depending on societal, cultural, and political changes. For example, progressive reform took a beating during the age of McCarthyism in the 1950s, reemerged in the tumult of the late 1960s, and once again retreated during the conservative leadership of President Ronald Reagan during the 1980s (Abramovitz, 1998).

In the 21st century, political and social movements once again influenced the push and pull away from direct practice toward the social change arm of the profession. 2020 was an exceptional year in which many social issues—food, housing, and job insecurity; police violence; and the disproportionate suffering of Black, brown, and Indigenous people from the COVID-19 pandemic—were thrust to the forefront by a president who refused to address the pandemic or denounce white supremacy. Individuals and communities were suffering, institutions were stretched, and our country was divided along systemic racism and poverty lines.

In the wake of fervent demands for change—stemming from persistent racial disparities in key welfare institutions and the growing wealth gap in our economic system—we have another opportunity to reimagine and recommit to an antiracism, anti-oppression future for social work. Never before have social workers been more needed at all levels of practice. Never before has there been a greater opportunity to merge our clinical and macro skills to help individuals, communities, our country, and even the world. And never before have the challenges been greater in the face of the reality that our profession practices within racist and other oppressive systems that it, at the same time, works to dismantle.

In this era, anti-oppression social work practice must reach across all areas of professional practice, from clinical to policy to administration to community organization to advocacy to social action. Anti-oppression social workers, regardless of their practice specialty, must assess and make clear connections. These connections include client circumstances at the micro-individual level of practice, policies and practices at the meso-institutional level of practice, and the social environment at the macro-structural level of practice. Those who work primarily as clinicians or case managers (e.g., in mental health settings) need to be aware of various social policies and community services so they can advocate with and on behalf of their clients at organizational, community, and state levels. And those who use their skills in policymaking and advocacy (e.g., in community organizing or political settings) need to be informed by the experience and expertise of direct practice social workers so that they can effectively introduce and implement just policies and practices. Reardon (2012) quoted a social worker's concern:

Clinical social workers, through their direct practice with individuals, may become aware of previously undetected social issues that negatively impact clients … it is not possible to fulfill the mission of social work to combat social injustices and end societal oppression without incorporating macro work into clinical practice. (p. 20)

In this chapter we start with a framework for anti-oppression practice that serves as both a summary of the concepts already presented throughout the text and an introduction to strengths-based and empowerment-based principles of practice. This is followed by opportunities for you to apply an anti-oppression consciousness to two case studies and consider interventions on individual, interpersonal, institutional, and structural levels of practice.

Framework for Anti-Oppression Practice

Cultural Competence and Humility

The scope of this text does not include learning about diverse cultures per se. However, that does not minimize the critical importance of *cultural humility*, a practice that includes acknowledgment of "not knowing," self-awareness, openness to learning about diverse cultures, and a willingness to learn from mistakes while developing skills in working with others whose culture is different from your own. It is essential that we know the history and context of diverse others' experiences in order to effectively communicate with them. It is essential that we facilitate and listen to how they perceive their experience and what is important to them. Process skills used to engage with others and initiate dialogue are quintessential cultural competency skills. The following are proposed as cornerstones of such practice:

- *Personal risk.* Willingness to put effort into learning about your own background, history, and influences on your life; willingness to examine how you have been affected by these factors; willingness to develop curiosity, take initiative, and "stretch" to connect with others different from yourself.

- *Process/interaction; interpersonal skills.* Individualizing instead of generalizing about people different from you; awareness of how you affect others and a willingness to adapt your style in the interest of communicating effectively.
- *Content/knowledge base for developing hypotheses that are tested and modified through practice.* Seeing people, families, and communities as they see themselves; resisting our natural tendency to fit our perceptions into what you have always believed, refusing to cling tenaciously to long-held beliefs even in the face of information to the contrary; setting aside your own beliefs in new environments to avoid missing important details.
- *Contextual supports.* Sustaining your practice with diverse others by promoting institutional support and validation of difference. Cross et al. (1989) proposed a continuum of an organizational commitment to cultural competence that ranges from harm to proficiency and highlights the significance of the institutional context and support for practitioner cultural competence.

From Cultural Competence to Anti-Oppression

The main premise of this text is that anti-oppression practice includes and goes beyond effective interaction with people across cultures. It requires an understanding of how difference and labeling people as the "other" is used to produce structural inequities. A quick review of the concepts that were identified in prior chapters provides a roadmap for anti-oppression practice.

- Under the umbrella of diversity, many groups are targeted by oppressive systems as other or different from the norm, such as people who are Black, Indigenous, Latinx, of other color or ethnicity, female, with disabilities, noncisgendered, nonheterosexual, non-English-speaking or U.S. born, or non-Christian.
- Basic to anti-oppression social work practice is understanding the ways in which people from targeted groups are excluded from power and advantage and the inequitable structure of our society.

- Racism is centered as the core system of oppression on which our nation was founded. A deep-seated and intractable belief in white supremacy that is woven into the very fabric of American culture, society, and laws is an essential framework for understanding all other systems of oppression.
- Anti-oppression practice requires learning about and comprehending the patterns, dynamics, and consequences of oppression at all levels of intervention and in all practice arenas.
- Two social justice perspectives—the racial contract and human rights—provide the grounding for anti-oppression social work practice.
- Anti-oppression strategies and interventions at all social work practice levels (i.e., micro-individual, meso-institutional, macro-structural) are informed by awareness of and knowledge about structural inequities.
- The concept of intersectionality clarifies the complicated ways in which oppressive systems affect all of us. We all have multiple identities, which, regardless of positionality, confer or deny social power that plays out in our lives.
- Anti-oppression practice requires an understanding of the common elements of all systems of oppression (i.e., power and advantage, invisibility, institutional nature, ideology, and violence).
- A broadened conceptualization of violence, both in relation to how it is defined and its different types, reveals how oppression is maintained at individual, institutional, and structural-cultural levels of practice.
- Anti-oppression social workers are committed to exploring their own social identity, particularly as it relates to race and ethnicity. Social and psychological racial identity development models provide tools for us to analyze our own struggles and intentions as we face the challenges of anti-oppression practice.

Empowerment and Strengths-Based Practice

Anti-oppression social work practice is empowerment-based (Dubois & Miley, 2005; Gutierrez, 1995; Gutierrez et al., 1995; Gutierrez et al., 1998; Simon, 1994; Solomon, 1976), supporting self-determination and recognizing the multiple levels and dynamics of oppression and racism. Traditional definitions of empowerment include phrases such as "to give power or authority," "to authorize," "to enable or permit," "to license." Within an anti-oppression framework, the concepts of empowerment and liberation are strongly influenced by Paulo Freire's (2018) process of conscientization; that is, the ways in which individuals and communities develop a critical understanding of their everyday social experience through reflecting and acting on the root causes of oppression. To be empowered is to be able to recognize and seek alternatives to oppression and injustice at community, organizational, national, and global levels.

To facilitate the empowerment of diverse clients, we need to start with ourselves. Solomon (1976) emphasized the need for professionals to be empowered in order to facilitate the movement of others toward empowerment. Simon (1994) pointed out that a prerequisite for empowerment practice is the professional's fundamental belief that individuals and environments can indeed change. Gutierrez et al. (1998) distinguished three forms of power that underlie empowerment practice: personal power, the ability to be effective in change efforts as well as aware of the power one has; interpersonal power, the ability to influence others and develop skills to use power; and political power, the ability to influence the allocation of resources and use varied strategies to attain goals.

Empowerment is a social process that occurs in a context of interactions, and it is also an individual process that occurs when we accept personal responsibility to act to bring about change in ourselves and in our environments. This social process is not an event where we endow another with empowerment. As power is realized, we become free to transform ourselves and to discover untapped strengths. When we are empowered to advocate for social justice, the authority that already belongs to us as human beings and as citizens is affirmed. Our individual actions of protest, resistance, and creativity create a ripple effect that empowers others. At the heart of the empowerment process is the phenomenon of facilitating in others an ability to see something that they haven't seen before and, subsequently, to act on that insight.

Although there can be tremendous satisfaction in seeing individuals and families transform their lives, it can also feel overwhelming to consider the daunting task of dismantling oppressive systems. It is helpful to view empowerment as a process that begins with the smallest of individual actions. Those actions, when joined with the actions of others, create a chain reaction that releases human energy. Over time this energy, with a focus on social change, can build to a critical mass that results in social justice. Each person's awareness and actions, no matter how small or insignificant they may seem, increase the likelihood that a critical mass will develop and lead to change.

Creating a just society and world is a global issue of overwhelming proportions. A transformation from injustice and oppression to just alternatives will not come about easily or quickly. Giving birth to social justice is a long and sometimes painful process that requires personal commitment and social transformation on a massive scale. Despite the magnitude of the problem, however, if social change for social justice is to take place, it will grow from the grassroots, at the level of individuals, small groups, local organizations, and communities. By starting at this level, the empowerment process becomes a bridge that connects the person and the smaller group with larger social change movements. This bridge becomes a vehicle for change as we join with others in crossing over to yet uncharted terrain. If we trust the process, empowerment will provide the energy needed for creating a just society. Social movement actions, such as the sample of historical events in Chart 6.1, illustrate the potential power of strengths-based empowerment practice at multiple levels with individuals, families, groups, communities, and organizations.

Chart 6.1   Sample of Key Empowerment Events and Actions in the United States, 1827–2020

1827	*Freedom's Journal*, first African American newspaper, is published.
1859	John Brown raids Harper's Ferry.
1863	Emancipation Proclamation; African American soldiers join Union Army.
1864	13th Amendment to the Constitution abolishes slavery.
1866	Congress passes Civil Rights Act of 1866.
1876	Battle of Little Big Horn; Lakota and allies annihilate Gen. Custer's white troops.
1880	Helen Hunt Jackson's *A Century of Dishonor* influences public conscience about poor government treatment of Indians.
1895	Booker T. Washington gives Atlanta Compromise speech
1905.	Niagara Falls Convention promotes more militant pursuit of African American rights.
1909	NAACP is founded.
1934	Wheeler Howard Act restores lands to tribal ownership.
1939	Marian Anderson performs at Lincoln Memorial in Washington, DC.
1941	Fair Employment Practices Committee prohibits discrimination in war and government industries.
1943	Ban on Chinese immigration is lifted.
1946	Court ends *de jure* segregation in California.
1948	Truman appoints Presidential Committee on Equality of Treatment and Opportunity in the Armed Services.
1952	McCarran-Walter Act relaxes some immigration restrictions.
1954	*Brown v. Board of Education* rules "separate but equal" illegal.
1955	Rosa Parks arrested; Montgomery bus boycott begins.
1956	Congress passes Civil Rights Act; Martin Luther King Jr. founds Southern Christian Leadership Conference.
1960	Black student sit-in Greensboro, North Carolina; Student Nonviolent Coordinating Committee is formed.
1961	Freedom Rides protest; National Indian Youth Council is formed.

1962	James Meredith is the first Black student to enter University of Mississippi.
1964	Economic Opportunity Act is passed to fight poverty; Civil Rights Act of 1964.
1965	Mexican American labor leader, Cesar Chavez, organizes the United Farm Workers.
1966	Black Panther Party is founded in Oakland, CA.
1967	Voting Rights Act of 1965 is passed.
1968	*Loving v. Virginia* rules prohibiting interracial marriage is unconstitutional.
1970	President Johnson signs Civil Rights Act of 1968, outlaws discrimination in housing.
1978	*Bakke v. University of California* upholds affirmative action in university admissions; American Indian Religious Freedom Act; Indian Child Welfare Act.
1982	*Plyer v. Doe:* children of undocumented immigrants have right to free public education.
1990	Americans with Disabilities Act (ADA) is enacted.
1991	Civil Rights Act of 1991 strengthens existing civil rights law.
2008	Barack Obama is the first Black person elected president.
2012	Indigenous social movement Idle No More is established.
2018	First American Indian woman is elected to Congress.
2020	Standing Rock Sioux Nation court victory halts Dakota Access Oil Pipeline; Kamala Harris is the first woman and woman of color elected vice president.

Timeline adapted in part from Adams and Adams (2007) and Walters (2020).

Empowerment in Action: Allies and Accomplices

If you have come here to help me, you are wasting your time.
But if you have come because your liberation is bound up
with mine, then let us work together.
—LILLA WATSON, INDIGENOUS AUSTRALIAN ACTIVIST

Even though oppression is systemic, it is reproduced by each of us, personally and interactionally, on a daily basis. That is why the empowerment process begins with investigating those parts of our identity that are privileged and how that privilege operates in our lives. The next step is determining the ways in which we can use our privilege in the service of social change as allies and/or accomplices. The difference between the two is a matter of degree and risk. An ally is a member of a privileged group engaged in actions that are carried out in solidarity and partnership with members of a marginalized group and that are aimed at dismantling the system of oppression. An accomplice takes a higher level of risk by acting in a more direct and overt way at the risk of losing their own privilege and comfort, reputation, and livelihood—even their own safety and freedom in order to support marginalized groups of people. For example, in solidarity with Black people, white accomplices risked physical assault when they protested segregation by riding in buses across the South in the Freedom Rides of 1961 (Jackson, et al., 2020).

According to Jackson et al. (2020), the amount of personal risk you want and are willing to take will determine whether you are acting as an ally or an accomplice. This decision is based on the situation and the particular context, as well as where we are at in the empowerment process. Consider that you are a social worker in a high school where a group of students of color, as well as a few white students in solidarity with them, are planning to kneel during the national anthem at the homecoming football game to protest racism in the school and are circulating a petition demanding that the school district create a new diversity and equity leader position. As an ally, you may support their right to act at the football game and sign their position; as an accomplice, you may kneel with them at the football game and take the greater personal risk of angering other teachers and the administration and/or damaging your reputation.

Anyone who has privilege has the potential to act as an ally and accomplice (Jackson et al., 2020; Kendall, 2006) as long as they do the following:

- Engage in critical reflection about the societal advantages they are afforded and that are denied to historically marginalized groups.
- Do their own research about the concerns of the people with whom they are aligned.

- Use their privilege to leverage the concerns of historically marginalized groups without speaking for them.
- Recognize mistakes as learning opportunities and discomfort as a sign that they are learning.
- Listen to, respect, and support the leadership, perspectives, and experiences of members of the oppressed group.
- De-center themselves and their feelings, and instead center the concerns of, be accountable to, and work in solidarity with the marginalized group.

Pulling It All Together: A Reflection/Journaling Exercise

In this section, a case study gives you an opportunity to apply, in a step-by-step reflection/journaling process, the anti-oppression concepts discussed throughout this text. Information about Jason and his family in Reflection/Journaling Exercise 6.1 is followed by a series of seven sets of questions that ask you to reflect in writing about your beliefs, values, life experiences and behavior related to issues of power and privilege and how they might affect your work with the family. The idea is to increase your awareness and understanding by writing down your thoughts about the questions as they arise without evaluating them or worrying about the words you use. Before you begin, we suggest that you review the freewriting techniques in Chapter 1.

REFLECTION/JOURNALING EXERCISE 6.1

Case Study: Jason and His Family

Read the case study below. Then stop to reflect in your written journal about the questions listed in each section before moving on to the next instructions.

Jason and His Family

Jason is a 13-year-old African American boy who sleeps a lot and spends most of his time at home watching television. He is unable to keep up in school and talks about dropping out as soon as he can. Outbursts between him and other students often result in his being singled out and penalized by the teacher, with lesser consequences for the other students. He has begun experimenting with alcohol and other drugs.

Jason lives with his mother, Mary, and her partner of 10 years, Claire. Mary, who is Black, is a licensed independent beautician and works in a local shop. Claire, who is white, is a schoolteacher. They consider themselves to be middle class. While Jason's mother and Claire and their circle of friends provide Jason with strong support and a loving home, his struggles are causing them considerable concern at this critical stage in his life.

Jason's father Desmond was arrested for armed robbery and brutally beaten by the police who justified it on the grounds that he acted bizarrely and reached for a weapon. Even though he denied both being armed and committing a robbery, he accepted a plea bargain on the advice of his court-appointed attorney and is currently serving a prison sentence. Jason is very angry about what happened to his father. His mother is concerned that the sporadic contact Jason has with him is an extra stress on him that will only further exacerbate his problems.

Jason's troubles began in the first grade when, as an active and personable child bursting with kinetic energy, he got failing marks in school. When he was passed on to second grade anyway and his mother asked how he could be promoted if he hadn't learned first grade work, she was told that his public school was overcrowded and needed the room for new first graders. His mother's partner Claire complained to the school about the situation, telling them she was a schoolteacher herself and that she had been a significant mother figure for Jason since he was 3 years old. But they would not talk to her, saying that the school had a policy to deal only with family members.

This past fall, when Jason was ready to start eighth grade, Claire got him enrolled in the religiously related charter school where she teaches, hoping he would get the help he needed there. The school social worker established a good relationship with Jason and had him tested. He was diagnosed with depression, attention-deficit/hyperactivity disorder (ADHD), and dyslexia, among other learning disabilities, and was referred to a private psychiatrist and other special services. The expenses for Jason's health (mental and physical) needs were prohibitive but would be covered by Claire's employment-related medical plan if she and Mary were married. Gay marriage had just become legal in their state, so they married but kept it a secret out of fear that if the administration found out, it could jeopardize Claire's employment and Jason's enrollment in the charter school. As the end of the school year now nears, Claire has just received notice that her contract will not be renewed due to budget cuts, which she and the school social worker both suspect is not the real reason.

Reflection/Journaling Questions

Dynamics of Difference: Understanding Issues of Power and Privilege in the Situation

To start, do some free writing about your thoughts and feelings about the case situation. Do not censor yourself; just write whatever comes to mind and let the words come out without judging or evaluating them. They are for your eyes only. Remind yourself that you are in charge and can keep your freewriting strictly private.

Now imagine that you are the school social worker and that Claire has confided in you about what happened and asked for your help. Examine your own thoughts and feelings related to issues of diversity by journaling about the following reflection questions:

1. Focus your writing now on the issues of diversity in the case study. List all the elements related to "difference" and/or cultural diversity that are represented.

2. Write about all the ways Jason and his family are similar to you and your family. For each point of similarity, write down all your thoughts and feelings about those similarities.

3. Write about all the ways Jason and his family are different from you and your family. For each point of difference, write down all your thoughts and feelings about those differences.

4. Now look at your two lists of thoughts and feelings, those related to similarities and those related to differences. Which of them do you think represent possible strengths in your ability to help the family? Which of them do you think represent possible obstacles or barriers?

5. How can you build on the strengths? What do you need to do to address the potential obstacles?

6. Whom and what could you turn to for help in addressing the obstacles? Develop a plan for building on the strengths and overcoming the obstacles.

7. Now loop back to the free writing you did at the beginning. Take notes on anything that strikes you as surprising, interesting, or confusing. Has anything changed for you since you focused your thinking on responding to Questions 1–7?

Unpacking Your Privileges

While exploring your thoughts and feelings in the above exercise, you may have identified points of discomfort. It is particularly important to stay with that discomfort and explore it further. As we maintained in Chapter 3, an obstacle to learning about diversity is often fear and anger rooted in the secret of unmerited privilege that comes with being a member of a dominant group. Unearned privileges are granted by a system that advantages some people due to race, gender, sexual orientation, and ability, while it disadvantages others. Unearned privileges include the daily ways in which privilege makes some people comfortable or powerful and provides supports, assets, approval, and rewards to those who are members of the privileged group (McIntosh, 1995).

The case of Jason illustrates how the concept of privilege works. Jason, who is African American and has disabilities, is denied privileges that are conferred on those who are white and have no disabilities and perhaps whites who have disabilities. Mary, Jason's mother, is denied privileges that are conferred on those who are white, male, and heterosexual. Jason's father, who is imprisoned, is denied privileges that are conferred on those who are white. Claire, Mary's partner, is denied privileges that are conferred on those who are male and heterosexual, while she is granted privileges that are conferred on those who are white. It is important that social workers understand the role of privilege and power in the lives of Jason, Mary, and Claire. Further, to deeply understand the role of privilege in their lives, social workers must first look at their own privilege or lack of privilege related to race, gender, sexual orientation, ability, and other relevant social identities. To that end, you are encouraged to journal about following reflection questions.

1. List the characteristics associated with your identity related to race, gender, sexual orientation, ability, and religion. In other words, are you white or a person of color? Biracial? Multiethnic? Male or female? Heterosexual or LGBTQ? A person with or without a disability? Christian, Jewish, Muslim, atheist, agnostic, or other?

2. Go back to Chapter 3 and review the work you did in Reflection/ Journaling Exercises 3.2, 3.3, 3.4, and 3.5 related to race privilege, gender privilege, heterosexual privilege, and other identity-related privileges. If you did not do those exercises, you are encouraged to do so now.

3. How do you feel about having and benefiting from the privileges that have been conferred on you? How do you feel about not having privileges when they have been denied?

4. .How is your having or not having privilege based on race, gender, sexual orientation, ability, and religion similar to or different from Jason and his family? What are your thoughts and feelings about the similarities and differences in your privileges compared to theirs?

5. What are the points of discomfort about privilege that you might experience if you were to work with this family?

6. What can you do to address any points of discomfort or other potential obstacles that could interfere with your being of help to Jason and his family?

7. Review what you wrote in Reflection/Journaling Exercise 3.6. How might you, as Claire's colleague working in the same charter school, use your privileges to be her ally and accomplice?

Understanding Oppression: Distinguishing Among Prejudice, Discrimination, and Racism

As a member of a middle-income, African American family, with a mother and her partner in a lesbian relationship, and a father with a history of addiction and incarceration, Jason is vulnerable to prejudice, discrimination, and institutional racism. Racism is unique in that it represents societal belief patterns that are seen as normal. Unlike prejudice and discrimination, which assume malintent, racism's institutional characteristics allow its practice even among the "well intentioned" (Gaertner & Dovidio, 1981). Earlier exercises explored how the intersectionality of a person's social identities and dominant cultural values results in either societal validation and affirmation or invisibility and denial, or both. Societal validation or denial is based on one's membership in a group that is the target of oppression (e.g., racism, classism, sexism, heterosexism).

Although behavioral and institutional phenomena may, and often do, overlap, the decisively powerful element that compromises and complicates people's lives is when prejudice and discrimination occur in a context of institutional racism. More important, the intersection of racism and classism and other social identities determine the extent and ways that racism affects one's life. The following questions first ask you to examine individual behavioral dynamics such as prejudice and discrimination, and then shift to institutional dynamics, specifically racism.

1. Identify negative stereotypes that come to mind about Jason and his family. Address these stereotypes based on each of the following identity groups: race, class, gender, sexual orientation, ability, and religion/spirituality.

2. Now draw a map or picture of individuals, groups, and organizations that are in your own life space. The picture should show those with whom you are most intimate, those who are closest to you.

3. On your map, circle in color those individuals, groups, and organizations that have articulated or might openly articulate prejudices based on those stereotypes identified in the first question. Provide examples.

4. Circle in a different color those individuals, groups, and organizations in your life space that have engaged in or could engage in discriminatory actions based on the stereotypes identified in Question 1 (e.g., through exclusion, name-calling, harassment, physical assault). Give some examples.

5. Consider how institutional racism has affected Jason and his family. What examples come to mind of business-as-usual policies or organizational practices that create limits on the family based on race, without intentionally singling out Jason and his family. How are these examples different from the discriminatory actions you identified in Question 4?

6. Describe policy or program directives that could create obstacles that would interfere with the well-being and healthy functioning of this family.

7. How might Jason's experiences have been different if his mother had a graduate degree and achieved some level of recognition for her competence? If she were White? If she were heterosexual? Give specific examples and write about your rationale for each.

Elements of Oppression: Invisibility, Moral Exclusion, Intersectionality; Psychological Versus Social Power

The next set of questions give you an opportunity to focus more deeply on the specific dimensions of institutionalized oppression associated with multiple identities. A common element of oppression is the invisibility endured by the individuals in groups that are oppressed. When society devalues and renders invisible certain aspects of a person's identity, this inevitably leads to individuals undervaluing and making invisible to themselves substantive parts of their own origins and history. An example of this can be a lack of role models who share one's identity.

The concept of moral exclusion explains how exclusionary behavior is promoted and maintained on an interpersonal level through moral exclusion. This type of exclusion places those who are different from oneself or one's group outside the boundaries of fair treatment by invoking assumptions about who deserves just treatment and who should enjoy society's benefits. For example, Jason's mother Mary and her wife Claire represent LGBTQ persons, who have been and are excluded from the norms and values of social justice. The following questions will help you work with the concepts of invisibility, moral exclusion, and the notion of individual and social power as they relate to you and your family and to Jason and his family.

Jason and His Family

1. Given the impressions that you have of Jason and his family's culture and life experiences, what images come to mind regarding the media characters, heroes, and contemporary and historical role models whom Jason would admire? What images are visible? What images are invisible? Consider both genders and all ethnic/racial groups.

2. In relation to moral exclusion, where morality is invoked for the purpose of exclusion, what negative judgments could be made about Jason and his family based on so-called moral judgments?

3. What strengths do you see in Jason and his family that might be invisible to others? What type of individual power do you see Jason and his family having? Describe some examples of how they have or could exercise their individual power.

4. Describe the social power (i.e., low, high) that Jason and his family have. What are some examples and settings where social power is exemplified in their lives?

You and Your Family

5. Identify the media characters, heroes, and contemporary and historical role models who currently have a place of prominence in your life. Consider all genders and ethnic/racial groups.

6. What assumptions do you and your family make about the values that are held by the dominant cultural group? Are the values you hold the same as those held by individuals and families such as Jason's? Be specific.

7. What aspects of your background and life experiences do you see as strengths that you identify with and enjoy having people know about you? Describe the individual power that you feel you have and the people (e.g., family, friends, intimates, co-workers/colleagues) with whom you exercise that power.

8. Describe the social power (low, high) that you have. Be specific regarding the basis (source) of that power and where you exercise it (e.g., as a family member, with your church group, as a college student, in your community, etc.).

Dimensions of Oppression and Jason's Social and Racial Identity Development

As the school social worker, consider that you have been trying to help Jason with the challenges and the problems he faces. To understand Jason and his situation, you need to assess how he identifies (sees himself) socially and racially. Review the Black racial identity development model in Chapter 5, and then consider the next set of questions.

1. Make four lists of the dimensions that you think may have influenced and are presently influencing how Jason identifies himself racially: personal, interpersonal, institutional, and societal factors. Be specific.

2. Look at each list and identify the resources that Jason has or may have developed for himself up to this point in his life and that he might seek in the future. If you think he doesn't have an image of the future, say that, too.

3. What further information do you need to gather to understand more about how Jason sees himself as a Black adolescent?

4. What are some events in the sociopolitical context of Jason's life so far that might influence how he sees himself, his present options, and his future? What further information do you need to gather to be able to answer the question more completely?

5. Given what you know about Jason, what are your general thoughts about his racial identity development? How might you go about assessing that?

Social Identity Dimensions and Stereotypes

Now that you have considered Jason in relation to his racial identity development, the following questions give you an opportunity to develop consciousness of the influence of your own racial identity on your work with him.

1. Step back and assess yourself in relation to the similarities and differences between yourself racially and Jason. Make four lists of the dimensions that have influenced how you identify yourself racially: the personal, interpersonal, institutional, and societal factors. Write them out in detail as you did with the lists for Jason.

2. Look at each list and identify the resources that you have developed for yourself up to this point in your life and that you hope to seek in the future. How are your resources similar or different from those of Jason?

3. What are some events in the sociopolitical context of your life so far that influence how you see yourself, your present options, and your future? How are they similar to and/or different from the sociopolitical context that influences Jason's life and options?

4. What do you and Jason have in common in relation to life experiences? How are your life experiences different?

5. In thinking about establishing a helping relationship with Jason and reflecting on the similarities and differences in your life experiences and racial identities, make a list of things you need to learn about Jason in order to understand life from his identity experience as much as possible. What issues within yourself related to your own racial identity do you need to attend to when working with him?

Anti-Oppression Practice Concepts and Interventions

When writing about the following questions, imagine yourself as both Jason's social worker and as Claire's colleague. She has confided in you about Jason and her family, her marriage, and her fears about the future. She is angry and suspicious about why her contract is not being renewed.

1. Given the presence of various levels of oppression (prejudice, discrimination, institutional racism) in the situation, what dynamics might arise in relation to Claire's perceptions of you as a representative of the social work profession? As an employee of the charter school? In light of your ethnicity/race, class profile, sexual orientation, and/or religion?

2. Consider the historical events that have relevance for you personally and that may have relevance for Claire and Mary, Jason, and his father. It may help to refer to Chart 4.1 in Chapter 4. Do free-association writing about your thoughts and feelings, any resulting concerns or ambivalence you have vis-à-vis your relationship with Claire when historical context is considered.

3. What empowerment-based actions that support self-determination might you discuss with Claire on a micro, meso, and macro (i.e., individual, institutional, structural-cultural) level? Give examples and discuss how they embody your professional social work values.

4. Consider different social change/anti-oppression interventions that might be taken at the community and organizational levels. What are some examples of social change efforts that Claire and you might consider taking?

5. What are some examples of social change or social justice efforts that you could engage in as a professional and an ally at community, organizational, and institutional levels? What worries might you have about taking action?

Empowerment Practice

Promoting social justice requires practice that is empowerment-based. It is critical that anti-oppression social workers feel empowered to advocate for social justice if they want to be able to facilitate the empowerment of diverse clients to advocate for themselves. The following questions address your own sense of empowerment in your relationship and work with Claire.

1. Empowerment concepts suggest that you, as the school social worker, must first feel empowered to facilitate the empowerment of Claire and Jason's mother. How do you see yourself as an empowered person? Describe qualities about yourself that reflect empowerment. Where you feel ambivalence in relation to Claire and the charter school in which you both work, describe what you think you need to do to feel more empowered. Address your experiences on all three levels of personal, interpersonal, and political power as you reflect on how you see yourself as empowered or disempowered in the situation.

2. Based on your reflections above, what goals might you set for yourself to move toward a stronger sense of empowerment? Be specific and realistic in setting your goals.

3. Empowerment practice is founded on your belief in the capacity of individuals and environments to change. Consider the issues that might interfere with bringing about change in relation to the three levels of empowerment (personal, interpersonal, political). What might Claire need to feel empowered on all three levels? Do the same for Jason's mother.

4. In what ways might you be an ally for Claire and Mary? An accomplice? What might interfere with you being empowered to act on different levels (personal, interpersonal, political, institutional)?

Pulling It All Together: A Classroom Exercise

The Case of Maryam Henderson-Uloho

Now that you have reflected through private journaling about your thoughts and feelings and how you might apply the anti-oppression concepts in this text to a case situation, here is an opportunity for you to take the next step and engage in a similar process with others. Maryam Henderson-Uloho's story is interspersed with questions to provide a structure for you, in consultation with three to four of your peers, to analyze the systems of oppression inherent in her situation.

CLASSROOM EXERCISE 6.1

The Story of Maryam Henderson-Uloho (adapted from Pendergrass & Hoke, 2018)

Following is the story of Maryam (Ms. Mary) Henderson-Uloho, age 61, from Arabi, Louisiana. In a small group, take turns reading the excerpts in each part of Maryam Henderson-Uloho's story below out loud. After each of the three parts of her story, stop reading and discuss the questions before going on to the next part. For Part III you will need a computer or an iPad so you can watch Maryam's video together during that part of this exercise.

PART I: MARYAM'S PREINCARCERATION STORY

In Maryam's own words (to be read aloud):

> *You know, sometimes I say to myself, I have all the ingredients to be a failure. I was born in 1957. When I was 15 months old, my mother moved us to Fort Worth, Texas, where I grew up. My father passed when I was 3. He was in prison for robbery ... he was a serious gangster ... never went anywhere without his .45. People always told me I look just like him .... My mother worked all the time. So I didn't have anybody, I felt like I was just so alone.*

> *When I was younger I didn't socialize with people. I didn't like to be touched. ...Intellectually, I was very advanced. But ... I had no friends.*

> *There were eight of us kids ... . We all had different fathers ... . My mother has a third-grade education. My sister Rosemary was very mean. She had short, thin hair. I have very long, thick, coarse hair ... . kids would make fun of me*

and call me "Little Nappy Head." ... they laughed at me because they said I was ugly.

When I was 11, my mother married my oldest brother's father and we moved to Dayton, Ohio... he was mean to my mother, and they fought a lot ... when I was 12e ... my mother tried to shoot him with her .38.

When I was about 14, my mom left my stepdad, and we moved into the projects ... the projects were violence, abuse, more violence, more abuse. You had to mind your own business.

When I was 16 I went to my first party ... there were a lot of Nigerians at the party—grown men. This man came walking down the steps ... he had zits all over his face and he was so ugly! ... . But he acted like he was the handsomest thing in the room.... I didn't know that his father was like a king, and people actually bowed down to him ... he wasn't all that bad, you know, he was a lot of fun. We had sex for the first time when I was 16. ... He figured out I was pregnant, and he told my mother, and together they made all the arrangements for me to get married. He picked me up from high school one day and took me to the justice of the peace, and that's where we got married. I cried like a baby.

Summary Account (read aloud):

After her marriage, Maryam gave birth to three boys. She developed a sense of love for her husband, enough so that she moved to Nigeria with him, where she spent the next 9 years with wealth and status beyond her imagination. In 1984, however, after severe abuse and threats from her husband, she moved back to Dayton alone. When her children joined her, they lived in a car briefly until she was able to get on her feet. She got a community college degree in property management and real estate, and then worked on developing programs for the housing project. In less than 8 years, she'd bought dozens of properties and had a major real estate investing business. But then things went downhill.

What happened, in Maryam's own words (read aloud):

Unfortunately, I became public enemy number one with some detectives in Dayton . . . [who] wanted to use some of my properties for sting operations ... (but) some of my clients wanted to help women and children get into their own homes or help senior citizens. I felt like that was a good thing, and I was in support of it. The police wanted me to help raid these guys, and I wouldn't go along with it. So I became a problem.

In 2000, my business was raided. The police didn't find anything because I wasn't involved with drugs. But when they raided the office, they left the building open. The property was robbed and vandalized. Everything was gone ... it caused sort of a nervous breakdown for me ... I ended up in the hospital. They put me on medication that had me not thinking straight. On TV I saw that Mardi Gras was coming up and I just booked a bus ticket ... and went on a vacation to Louisiana.

Summary Account (read aloud)

In Louisiana, Maryam met a man that she lived with. In 2001 they were pulled over by the police. The man was suspected of armed robbery and was arrested. Maryam was also arrested and charged. She pleaded innocent, and no witnesses put her at the scene of the crime, so the charges were dismissed. But she was convicted of obstruction of justice for refusing to turn state's evidence and was sentenced to 25 years.

Discussion Questions

1. What problems did Maryam experience on an individual level during her formative years? What institutions were implicated in what happened to her and in what ways?

2. Make a list of the social and racial identity groups to which Maryam belongs. In what ways is she labeled as "the other" by the dominant society based on her membership in different marginalized groups?

3. If you are a member of a privileged group in relation to any of the marginalized groups to which Maryam belongs, discuss the ways in which you benefit and she doesn't. How do you perceive yourself, and how do you think you might be perceived by her? Similarly, if you are a member of one of the same marginalized groups as Maryam, discuss the ways in which that might affect your perceptions of her.

4. Based on what you know about Maryam's multiple identities, discuss her situation through the lens of intersectionality (i.e., the overlapping and interdependent systems of discrimination or disadvantage based on race, gender, class, religion, and other factors).

PART II: MARYAM'S INCARCERATION

In her own words (to be read aloud):

When I was first arrested and taken to Jefferson Parish Jail, it was a really scary experience for me. Now, here I am, this professional woman, never in my life have I been in a holding tank ... I was held in jail for 18 months while I was waiting for a trial. ... Inmates and guards would find ways to mess with me. One time the guards sent three women to fight me, and they stood on the other side of a window and watched. Another time six or seven guards kicked a mentally ill woman until I saw blood coming out of every hole in her head. They beat her unconscious, then took her to a room and strapped her down and kept her there. And these were supposedly Christian people. I was a die-hard Christian, but I actually turned to Islam partly because the guards and inmates who were Christians could be so cruel. ... So I converted there in jail. I needed peace, and I found it in Islam.

I was convicted and sentenced in February 2003 ... a few months later, I was moved from jail to prison . . . and I have on my hijab and the officers tell me to take the rag off my head. I said, "No, I can't do that. I'm Muslim. I don't know where I am. I don't know if there's men around here, and I'm not taking my scarf off." As Muslim women, we keep our heads covered, especially in the presence of men, because we're taught that you don't expose your beauty to strange men, you just don't do that ... so ... they put me in a cell by myself. I was in the hole.

I was the only woman in the prison who was Muslim, the only one who wore a headscarf. When I got out of solitary after those first 2 days, I took my scarf off to let them see I wasn't hiding anything. I didn't want confrontation. ... A week later, the prison deacon was handing out prayer books . . . he asked me if I was Christian or Muslim. I said I was Muslim, and he refused to give me a book. He said, "they're only for Christians, and you can't be both. You'll have to choose." So I walked down the hall, put my scarf back on and from that day forward it was war.

A chaplain there . . . told me, "Before I allow you to infest this compound with Islam, you will do your entire time in the hole on lockdown." . . . the guards would see me with my scarf and just say, "take that rag off your head, fool! Are you crazy? Are you stupid? You can't wear that rag here." I'd say, "No ma'am, I won't. Can't do that." And then they'd lock me up, put me in the hole. I'd be in for 90 days at a time. Then eventually they'd let me out, but it would happen again. The longest I'd stay out was 2 weeks or so.

Summary Account (read aloud)

The solitary cell was a little bigger than a bathroom, about 9 feet long and 6 feet wide, with cinderblock walls, a 6-inch square window with metal mesh on it, door of metal bars, a steel bed with a mattress and pillow wrapped in heavy plastic. In the corner was a steel sink and toilet and a step or two from that a steel desk fixed to the wall. The fluorescent lights were always on. The hole consists of a hallway with 20 cells so prisoners could pass things from cell to cell through little openings. Once Maryam realized the guards were trying to tear her down, she strengthened her mind and developed a mentality of survival.

In Maryam's Own Words (read aloud)

You had the hole ... but then you had the hole inside of the hole ... at the end of the hallway with two cells that are separate and even smaller, and they're under 24-hour surveillance ... a lot of women didn't make it out of the hole. I remember one young girl, she was 26 ... she ended up in the hole within the hole ... I knew she was getting to a breaking point. So I asked a guard, "Could you let me go back there and take her cell and she can come in mine?" ... And the guard said, "you don't tell me what to do, you don't run nothing around here. You think you're runnin' shit, but you don't tell me what to do. I'll check on her when I'm ready to check on her." So to spite me, she didn't even look in on her. And the girl hanged herself.

I was angry. I was beyond the point of being able to respect any of the guards. I way saying things like, "Y'all murdered her, and you know you did." ... Because of that, they put me in the tank. The tank is worse than the hole inside the hole. In the tank, they strip you buck naked. They take all your clothes, put you in a smock, take your mattress and pillow, and give you a blanket/mattress thing and a roll of toilet paper ... you know if you go in the tank, you might not come out alive. I went in not expecting to come out. I was in there 2 weeks. I kept my mind busy making flowers out of the toilet paper. My whole cell was filled with flowers ... there were flowers all over the head and foot of my bed, the sink, the floor. That's how I made it through 2 weeks.

Summary Account (read aloud)

For the first 3 years Maryam was in prison, the rule was that women couldn't cover their hair at all, so she spent a lot of time in the hole. Around 2010, it got to the point where she got a medical order from a hospital that the hole was detrimental to her health so they could no longer put her in the hole. When she was in the general population, she became very close to her cellmates and found solace inside her own form of solitary with her Quran, her prayer rug, and Islamic books. She was finally released from prison on April 21, 2013.

Discussion Questions:

1. Review the following five elements of oppression in Chapter 4 and discuss all the ways they operated in Maryam's life: power and advantage, institutionalization, invisibility, ideology, and violence.

2. Identify and discuss the strengths you see Maryam having.

PART III: POSTINCARCERATION

In Maryam's Own Words (read aloud)

I honestly think they let me out because I was so much trouble. I made it so they had to let people observe their religions, even the Wiccans. And let me tell you, the prison did not want no witches having a service. ... They brought me to this place called the Exodus House ... for people in substance abuse recovery and with mental disabilities ... as a dorm mother ... I was supposed to look out for the women in one of the buildings ... it smelled like a dump and it was just as filthy ... I cleaned the place up, started cooking for everyone. I worked for my room and board. I was there 3 or 4 months. I would have stayed longer, but my supervisor started making advances on me, and when I turned him down, he told me it was time for me to go....

I went to this apartment ... where I'd seen a "for rent" sign, but it was filthy. Roaches were everywhere, falling down in my hair when I opened the door. It smelled horrible. The window was broken ... I became a squatter ... I started cleaning and fixing up the place. When the owner found me there a month later, he was so impressed with how I'd fixed the place up, he let me stay. And he paid me to fix up other apartments.

During that time ... some Muslim brothers from my mosque used to ... take me to a flea market ... I would go to thrift stores and buy stuff and I'd put it in a suitcase that had wheels and I'd roll it up and down the street, you know, how bag women do with the grocery cart ... would get my profit ... and flip that money and flip that money. And that's how eventually I built my business, Sister Hearts. . . .

All the employees here are ex-offenders. If someone out of prison comes in and says, "I need a job," I'll do an interview on the spot. But if you just want a job, this is not the place for you. ... This is more of a program than a store. ... The name "Sister Hearts" comes from the way I felt about some of the other women in prison ... the women who held me when I cried. When I was hungry, the women who stole food out of the kitchen for me to eat. When I was sick, the women who went to the medicine line and hid pills under their tongues to bring back to me. The women who sometimes lied for me and stole for me and fought for me and stood beside me, Black and white. . . . Every time the words "sister heart" ring off someone's lips in this free world, they're remembering my sister hearts in prison.

Summary Account (read aloud)

Maryam runs her Sister Hearts Thrift Store "like a marine captain." She hires formerly incarcerated people, and if they have nowhere else to go, houses them in a separate area above the 17,000 square foot store. Louisiana is often called the incarceration capital of the world, with Black people more than four times as likely to go to prison as white people. Maryam spent nearly 13 years in a Louisiana prison, 7 of them in segregation. When she went in, she was a successful real estate investor. She says she was targeted in prison and sent to isolation because she's Muslim and refused to take off her hijab.

Instructions

Before discussing the last set of questions below, watch the Square video on Maryam Henderson-Uloho and Sister Hearts together: https://squareup.com/us/en/dreams/sister-hearts.

Discussion Questions

1. Share your emotional reactions to the video with each other. What stood out for you and why?

2. Thinking back to the discussion about intersectionality, what different kinds of identities of Maryam stood out for you?

3. What other identities did you observe among the other people in the video? What did you see as their physical and emotional needs? What role do you think their different identities played in meeting those needs?

4. What empowerment and/or strengths-based practices did you observe taking place in the video?

5. Imagine interviewing some of the women in the video. Conduct a cultural humility self-assessment by discussing the following kinds of questions: What do you **not** know about them? What would you want to know in order to understand what life is like for them? What makes you anxious or holds you back from asking them questions (e.g., concern about asking the wrong thing or probing too much, worry about making mistakes, feeling that you should know)? How might you begin the interview?

6. If you could ask Maryam three questions, what would they be?

Maryam Henderson-Uloho's case study was adapted from Pendergrass (2018, pp. 17–32).

Pulling It All Together: From Case to Cause

The treatment of prisoners who endure indefinite or many
years of solitary segregation amounts to torture.
—UN CONVENTION AGAINST TORTURE AND OTHER CRUEL,
INHUMANE OR DEGRADING TREATMENT OR PUNISHMENT

Tucked away and out of public sight, an estimated 80,000 to 100,000 people are being held in solitary confinement cells in our nation's jails, prisons, and immigration detention centers, many for years on end. Through the stories of Maryam Henderson-Uloho in Assignment Exercise 6.1 and others like her, light is being shed on the practice of solitary confinement and the impact of mass incarceration on individual lives (Casella et al., 2016; Pendergrass & Hoke, 2018).

When anti-oppression social workers hear such stories, either secondhand or directly in their practice, they make a micro-to-macro or case-to-cause connection. Take, for example, social worker Mary Buser. She began her career in the Mental Health Department at New York's notorious Rikers Island prison as a social work intern brimming with ideas and eager to help incarcerated women find a better path. Her reassignment later to a men's jail coincided with the dawn of the city's stop-and-frisk policy, a flood of unprecedented arrests, and the biggest jailhouse buildup in New York City history. At the men's jail, she was faced with black eyes, punched-out teeth, and frantic whispers from inmates about being beaten by officers, and at the dreaded solitary confinement unit, she saw individual horrors she'd never imagined. Moving from case to cause, Buser became an outspoken advocate against the inhumane treatment of the incarcerated, especially the mentally ill. She wrote a book, *Lockdown on Rikers: Shocking Stories of Abuse and Injustice at New York's Notorious Jail* (Buser, 2015), that shines a light into the deepest and most horrific recesses of the criminal justice system and founded an organization called Social Workers Against Solitary Confinement (https://socialworkersasc.org/) that combats the use of solitary confinement and seeks the support of other social workers in the fight against this social injustice.

Assignment Exercise 6.1 provides an opportunity for you to follow a similar micro-to-macro, case-to-cause process. You will construct a structural analysis of an issue related to Maryam's story that explores the histories, social forces, institutions, and policies on a macro/structural level, then link your analysis to the lived experiences and everyday realities of individuals, their families, and their communities.

ASSIGNMENT 6.1

Writing a Case-to-Cause Op-Ed: Critical Analysis and Practical Application of Social Issue

After reading and discussing Maryam's Henderson-Uloho's story in Classroom Exercise 6.1, this assignment is an opportunity for you to do something about it by moving from micro to macro and macro to micro; in other words, to make a case-to-cause connection.

Step 1: Select an issue prompted by Maryam's situation that you have a particular interest in exploring and researching further. Some suggestions:

- The challenges of reentry into society from prison with suggestions for four improvements that would mitigate those challenges

- Solitary confinement and the Eighth Amendment of the Constitution that bans "cruel and unusual punishment" of people who are incarcerated

- The ways in which we should consider intersectionality (in relation to social identity) in our criminal justice system, laws, and institutions

- Why freedom of religion in the Bill of Rights should apply to incarcerated citizens

- Topics related to Maryam's experience or one that her story may have triggered your interest in:
  - The psychological effects of solitary confinement
  - The use of solitary confinement in immigrant detention
  - Short- and long-term effects of solitary confinement
  - How already marginalized people (women, people of color, transgender people, people with disabilities, etc.) are further marginalized by the prison system and the disproportionate use of solitary confinement

- Other (with approval of your instructor)

Step 2: Research and gather information about your chosen issue that will help you to construct a structural analysis that links the history, social forces, institutional policies, and structural/cultural ideologies to the lived experiences and everyday realities of people affected by the issue. Use resources that demonstrate a thoughtful understanding of the various elements and their interconnections. Sources may include news articles, blogs, policy briefs, Web pages, periodicals, and any other informational source that will help you to complete a critical analysis of your chosen topic. Some resources are included below.

Step 3: Write a 500- to 700-word op-ed (i.e., an opinion-based editorial-type article about your topic) that is backed with credible facts, figures, and statistics from your research. Your op-ed should include the following:

- Opening paragraph: What is the issue you are addressing? Offer your argument about the issue in a single sentence, and state or suggest the importance of considering your view. It's a good idea to introduce the issue along with a story that personalizes it and makes it relatable for the reader.

- Middle paragraphs: Opinions need evidence and support, such as data and statistics to reinforce the argument being made. Based on your research, offer supporting points to back up your argument and provide appropriate evidence for each point. Put your argument forward in a persuasive, authoritative manner. Don't be afraid to be passionate in arguing your point. Write as if you are debating with a friend. Use simple, everyday language that is easy to understand. Keep in mind that you are writing for a general audience who may not be as familiar with the subject as you are.

- Take-away paragraph: Offer a message that directs readers to rethink their previous assumptions or to act in a particular way based on the argument you've presented. Don't leave your readers wondering what comes next, or what they can do about a particular issue. Leave them with a call to take some action(s).

Step 4: This is a useful step to take before you turn in your paper, so you have a chance to revise it and to consider where you might submit it for publication. In a small learning group, take turns sharing your op-ed essays with each other. Give and receive feedback based on questions such as: Does it make sense? (If not, consider revising.) Does it have a timely lead? Does it have a good title? Is it convincing? What might make it more convincing? What is the best audience for it; where might it be published?

Resources

A Council on Social Work Education (CSWE) database of more than 300 resources (https://docs.google.com/spreadsheets/d/1WBrxqwiFmpDipnIZux uQihU1vFSrMYoh5eay1beydo/edit#gid=1648978831) offers a comprehensive overview of solitary confinement that includes voices of those who have been affected by it, the ethical dilemma of health and social service providers who work in criminal justice facilities, policy issues, and humane alternatives. The resources are grouped in four general categories:

1. The prison system, practices, and conditions

2. Mental and physical health effects of solitary confinement on prison inmates

3. Issues for social work and healthcare professionals in correctional settings

4. Advocacy, legislative, and policy practice in criminal justice

Other Resources

- Dual Loyalty in Solitary Confinement (the role of professionals)
  https://www.cswe.org/CSWE/media/Diversity-Center/7-SWASC
  -Toolkit-3-Ethics.pdf

- Alternative Policy to Solitary Confinement
  https://www.cswe.org/CSWE/media/Diversity-Center/8-SWASC
  -Toolkit-4-Alternatives.pdf

- Do We Have a Right to Torture Prisoners and Violate their Human Rights?
  https://www.cswe.org/CSWE/media/Diversity-Center/9-SWASC
  -Toolkit-5-Human-Rights.pdf

- Psychological, Physical and Societal Consequences of Solitary Confinement
  https://www.cswe.org/CSWE/media/Diversity-Center/6-SWASC
  -Toolkit-2-Consequences.pdf

Summary and Conclusion

In this chapter we reviewed and applied the key concepts and understandings that were presented in the first five chapters to two case studies. The goal of the exercises was twofold: (1) to apply your understanding of and role in relation to the patterns, dynamics, and consequences of oppression on diverse clients and (2) to increase your knowledge and skills to effectively assess, intervene, and promote social and economic justice as a basic element of anti-oppression practice.

To achieve that goal, these concepts and principles were directly applied in a step-by-step personal, reflective process to both Jason and his family and to you as the hypothetical school social worker. Focusing on both sides of the helping relationship, the client and the social worker, emphasizes the impact of the personal experiences, values, beliefs, and feelings of all parties in the helping relationship. Through reflection and journaling, you were given the opportunity to increase your consciousness of personal obstacles and issues, particularly those related to feelings of fear and anger related to diversity and social justice issues, and face any barriers with openness, and honesty.

A second case example, the story of Maryam Henderson-Uloho, provided an opportunity for you to take another step out of your comfort zone by sharing your thoughts, feelings, and assessment about yourself and the case situation with your peers.

Finally, the chapter ended with an assignment that provided an opportunity for you to take yet another step by moving from case to cause, from being concerned about individual troubles to being concerned about social conditions and advocating for social justice on a structural level as an ally and/or accomplice for change.

The goal of the exercises in this chapter has been to help you develop knowledge, understanding, awareness, and skills that facilitate your facing the double challenges of understanding societal oppression and translating that understanding into actions designed to facilitate social change for social justice. The concepts addressed in the exercises may have raised challenging and difficult issues for you. This is to be expected. Learning about diversity and oppression is a lifelong endeavor that involves humility, questioning of assumptions, and exploring alternative ideas, a process that can be not only difficult but also emotionally explosive at times. The journey to anti-oppression social work practice requires patience and gentleness—both with yourself and with others.

In the next chapter we examine some of the ways in which the journey changes how we experience the world and our roles and responsibilities in it.

References

Abramovitz, M. (1998). Social work and social reform: An arena of struggle. *Social Work, 43*, 512–526.

Adams, P., & Adams, M. (Eds.). (2007). *Teaching for diversity and social justice* (2nd ed.). Taylor & Francis.

Buser, M. (2015). *Lockdown on Rikers: Shocking stories of abuse and injustice at New York's notorious jail.* St. Martin's Press.

Casella, J., Ridgeway, J., & Shourd, S. (Eds.). (2016). *Hell is a very small place: Voices from solitary confinement.* The New Press.

Cross, T., Bazron, B., Dennis, K., & Isaacs, M. (1989). *Towards a culturally competent system of care* (Vol. 1). CASSP Technical Assistance Center, Georgetown University Child Development Center.

Dubois, B., & Miley, K. (2005). *Social work: An* empowering *profession.* Allyn and Bacon/Longman.

Freire, P. (2018). *Pedagogy of the oppressed: 50th anniversary* (4th ed.). Bloomsbury Academic.

Gaertner, S. L., & Dovidio, J. F. (1981). Racism among the well-intentioned. In E. Clausen & J. Bermingham (Eds.), *Pluralism, racism and public policy: The search for equality* (pp. 145–159). Macmillan.

Gutierrez, L. M. (1995). Understanding the empowerment process: Does consciousness make a difference? *Social Work Research, 19*(4), 229–237.

Gutierrez, L. M., DeLois, K. A., & GlenMaye, L. (1995). Understanding empowerment practice: Building on practitioner-based knowledge. *Families in Society, 76*, 534–542.

Gutierrez, L., Parsons, R. J., & Cox, E. J. (1998). *Empowerment in social work practice.* Brooks/Cole.

Jackson, R. G., Huskins, K., Skelton, S. M., & Thorius, K. A. K. (2020). Ally and accomplice: Two sides of the same coin. *Equity Dispatch.* Midwest & Plains Equity Assistance Center. https://greatlakesequity.org/sites/default/files/202003022136_newsletter.pdf

Kendall, F. (2006). *Understanding white privilege: Creating pathways to authentic relationships across race.* Routledge.

McIntosh, P. (1995). White privilege and male privilege: A personal account of coming to see correspondences through work in women's studies. In M. L.

Anderson & P. H. Collins (Eds.), *Race, class, and gender: An Anthology* (pp. 76–87). Wadsworth.

Pendergrass, T., & Hoke, M. (2018). *Six by ten: Stories from solitary.* Haymarket Books.

Reardon, C. (2012) "Case" and "cause" in social work education—a balancing act. *Social Work Today, 12*(2), 20.

Simon, B. (1994). *The empowerment tradition in American social work.* Columbia University Press.

Solomon, B. (1976). *Black empowerment.* Columbia University Press.

Specht, H., & Courtney, M. (1995). *Unfaithful angels: How social work has abandoned its mission.* Free Press.

Walters, K. L. (2020). *History through a native lens.* Indigenous Wellness Research Institute, University of Washington. https://nativephilanthropy .candid.org/timeline/

CHAPTER 7

Commitment to Social Justice
Beyond Nine to Five

The motivating force of anti-oppression social work practice is, in essence, the act of challenging structural inequities, including the oppressive dynamics of the service institutions in which we are employed and with which we interact. In this final chapter, we examine our moral, ethical, and legal responsibilities as members of a profession committed to social justice to challenge inequality both on and off the clock. As witnesses to the complex nature of oppression in the lives of people who are targeted, current events and evidence of societal injustice take on new meaning. We bring something unique to the struggle for social justice beyond our professional practice. The question is: What responsibility do we have to incorporate the enormous amount of knowledge we have into efforts to promote justice in our profession, in society, and in the world in terms of health care, poverty, employment, neighborhood development, the environment, and so forth? Because we know that social justice is not possible without social change, the question before us now is this: How can we embrace and apply anti-oppression principles and behaviors both to our professional work and to our lives as citizens?

Self-reflection and critical analysis are essential for shaping an anti-oppression political identity as both citizens and professionals. And when our notions about professionalism hinder our ability as citizens to challenge structural oppression, they need to be confronted. One of those notions, according to Dudziak (2002), is a fear of conflict that reinforces a dominant self-image of professional social workers as positive and caring helpers, peacemakers, and problem solvers. Because we know that anger spurs people to social justice activism, such as the civil rights and women's movements, we need to deconstruct any professional notions about confrontation and anger that prevent us from acting as citizen social workers in the world. We suggest that this means applying critical thinking to your perspective on what it means to be a responsible and principled professional. Just as the journey to being an anti-oppression social worker is a transformative one, so too is the path to citizen social worker that Smith (1996) called us to be:

> Let social workers, supported by schools of social work, attend to the civil society without which the economy will be neither just nor inclusive and without which democracy will be shallow and monotonous. There is a future to politics. There is a future to social work. These futures converge in efforts to support the civil sector locally and internationally. (p. 265)

Defining our role as citizen social workers in the world involves several tasks and challenges. It requires sorting through conflicting responsibilities—to the agencies with which we work, to our clients, to our colleagues, to our profession, to society, and to ourselves. It requires learning how to personally connect the political with the social, to integrate our roles as citizens with our roles as professionals, and to create bridges and work in solidarity with the community and people who are most affected by oppression. By engaging in the process one step at a time, we can learn how to be effective allies and accomplices and to move more freely from the social to the political. In essence, we will find ways to incorporate notions of citizenship into the very fabric of what it means to be a professional social worker.

Responsibility to the Social Work Profession

Like our nation, the history of social work is complicated. Just as colonization, racism, white supremacy, and other systems of oppression are engrained within American institutions and systems, so too have they shaped social work ideology and practice for generations. We cannot ignore the history of how social workers have colluded in perpetuating systems of oppression, such as the harms inflicted on Black, Brown, and Indigenous families by the child welfare system, mass incarceration, the war on drugs, and systems of economic and health disparities. While social workers have played a role in working to create an antiracist society—such as in the fight for civil rights, access to health care, the War on Poverty, and marriage equality—we have an ethical responsibility to build on the positive aspects of our history.

Regardless of practice setting, the NASW (2017) Code of Ethics requires us, as both citizens and professionals, to promote social justice and the general welfare of society from local to global levels. However, our professional social justice mandates are not prescriptive, nor do they define the social action we should take to confront social injustice, racism, and inequality. The operative word is "action." We are charged to do something, with our ethical mandates serving as a roadmap, but leaving it up to us to make our own decisions about the actions we will take to meet the current historical moment. We have a responsibility to make the mandates more specific and to hold our profession and ourselves accountable for the injustices that social workers have perpetuated, both past and present. Reflection/Journaling Exercise 7.1 provides an opportunity for you to learn how Indigenous social workers are holding the profession accountable for harms that the profession perpetuates and to make a personal commitment to act to heal, repair, and right those wrongs.

REFLECTION/JOURNALING EXERCISE 7.1

Accountability and Reconciliation for Harms Done to Indigenous and Tribal Peoples

In 2019, inspired by the accountability statements of Canadian social workers,* the Indigenous and Tribal Social Work Educators' Association (ITSWEA) launched a project to use a similar mechanism to hold social workers in our country accountable for harms done to Indigenous and Tribal Peoples and obtain a professional commitment to take action to right those wrongs. A volunteer group charged with the task was composed of Indigenous educators, students, and allies from various backgrounds who consulted as needed with members of other specific populations.

On June 25, 2021, the ITSWEA Statement of Accountability and Reconciliation for Harms Done to Indigenous and Tribal Peoples was adopted by the Board of Directors of the Council on Social Work Education (CSWE). The complete document is available on the CSWE website (https://cswe.org/getattachment/ Education-Resources/Indigenous-and-Tribal-Content/CSWE-Statement-of-Accountability-and-Reconciliation-for-Harms-Done-to-Indigenous-and-Tribal-Peoples.pdf.aspx). Following is the executive summary:

> Social workers promote social justice and focus on empowerment of people who are vulnerable and oppressed (NASW, 2017), yet there is no doubt that social workers have also functioned as agents of social control, upholding the norms of a colonial, racist society, and encouraging clients to assimilate to the larger American culture. As social work educators, CSWE and its members are responsible for educating future generations of social workers. Understanding our history informs our efforts to move forward. This statement is one mechanism for holding our profession accountable for ways social workers have harmed Indigenous and Tribal Peoples.

> Despite colonization, dispossession of land, and denial of inherent rights of self-determination and sovereignty, Indigenous and Tribal Peoples continue to demonstrate strengths and resilience. We recognize that Indigenous and Tribal individuals and Peoples are competent, capable, and engaged in directing their own lives and futures. In no way should this acknowledgement of past and current injustices inadvertently contribute to dismissing Indigenous and Tribal strengths and agency.

> The United States exists on the colonized lands of Indigenous and Tribal Peoples, and its colonial reach extends beyond national boundaries. We provide an overview of Indigenous and Tribal Peoples within the boundaries of the US, its territories, and commonwealths including Native Americans (American Indians), Alaska Native Peoples, Taino, Kanaka Maoli (Native Hawaiians), CHamorus, Peoples of Nations Affiliated with the United States through Compact of Free Association (COFA), and American Samoans.

> This statement documents specific examples, past and present, of harms done by social workers through commission or omission, accompanied by a call to action for our profession to recognize these wrongs and commit to just and equitable practices, now and in the future. Recommendations include but are not limited to the following:

> * commit actively to engagement across policy and practice levels to repair past harm, stop current harm, and prevent future harm to Indigenous children, families, and communities;

- advocate for the federal government to fulfill its treaty and public policy obligations to Indigenous and Tribal Peoples including provision of adequate funding and support for social, health, cultural, and educational programs;

- ensure research funding, research design, data collection and analysis, oral or printed interpretations, and education about Indigenous and Tribal Peoples is driven by Indigenous and Tribal People and their protocols;

- prioritize decolonization in social work education in concert with Indigenous partners, recognizing that Western paradigms continue to be privileged across practice levels and that they may result in practices that are often unhelpful and even harmful for Indigenous and Tribal Peoples;

- support self-determination of communities to build culturally congruent systems of economic, social, and spiritual supports and promote Indigenous and Tribal Peoples to heal and thrive; and

- recruit and support Indigenous and Tribal People into the social work profession at every level, including social work education.

Colonization is both the foundation and an expression of racism and bigotry. Oppression of any people threatens all people. We are not yet aware of all the harms that social work and social work education have done; thus, we offer this statement as a partial account of social work and social work education's role in harms committed against Indigenous and Tribal Peoples. Recognizing the harms done by social workers and social work educators is a step in disrupting racism and fulfilling our commitment to social justice.

Statement of Apology and Commitment to Reconciliation, adopted by the Canadian Association of Social Workers (CASW), October 2017. https://www.casw-acts.ca/en/statement-apology-and -committment-reconciliation; *Statement of Complicity and Commitment to Change*, adopted by the Canadian Association of Social Work Education (CASWE) Board of Directors, May 31, 2017. https://caswe-acfts.ca/about-us/our-commitment-to-change/

Exercise Instructions

Step 1: Free Writing

After reading each paragraph of the CSWE Executive Summary of the accountability statement (shown after these instructions), stop and write for 5 to 10 minutes. Allow yourself to write whatever you want without judgment or evaluation. The words are for your eyes only. If you get stuck and can't think of what to write next, you can repeat the last word or type nonsense until an idea pops into your mind. Or you might ask questions about what happened—What am I experiencing right now? Where did my mind go?—and see what thoughts come. When you pose questions without searching for answers, often ideas are sparked.

Step 2: Focused Writing

Take in the full Executive Summary in one reading and then go back and read what you wrote after each paragraph. Now use the following prompts to focus your writing:

- What are some of the ways I have been affected by the harms social workers have done to Indigenous and Tribal Peoples, ways I have been negatively affected, ways I have benefited?

- What are some of the ways I have colluded or participated, either through commission or omission, in inflicting harm?

- What can do to acknowledge the wrongs done?

- What are some things I can do to hold myself responsible, to repair, and to bring about healing?

- What are some actions I can take to create just and equitable practices?

- To avoid upholding colonialist, racist, assimilationist, paternalistic norms, I will ...

- I will hold myself accountable to the above by ...

- I will be an ally and/or accomplice by ...

Step 3: Research and Loop Writing

After doing focused writing for 10–15 minutes, take a step back and do this research: Check with your local, state, and national social work organizations to see what positions they have taken related to acknowledging our harmful actions to Indigenous and Tribal peoples. What steps has CSWE taken in regard to the statement of accountability? Have any implementation steps been taken?

- Do some writing about your research: What did you learn? What is your reaction to what you learned?

- Now go back and read everything you have written starting with the first step. Mark up the passages that ring the most true for you. Then select one action you will take and rewrite it in a sentence that starts with "I make a commitment to ..."

Step 4: Go-Around Sharing and Listening

The goal of this step is to ensure that everyone has an opportunity to share their truth and make a public commitment without interruption or comment from others and to ensure that everyone has the opportunity to listen deeply to others.

Follow this process:

a. Go around the classroom or small group.

b. When it's your turn to speak, share your own truth, starting with "I make a commitment to ..."

c. When it's not your turn to speak, listen deeply to understand the person who is speaking. Do not comment or respond, either verbally or nonverbally, to anything that is said.

d. After everyone has had a chance to speak, everyone agrees not to talk to anyone about anything that was said for 24 hours. Just hold each others' truths for that period of time.

Professional Social Justice Ethics

Social work, as the only human services profession with a code of ethics (e.g., psychology, counseling, psychiatry) that specifically identifies social justice as an ethical mandate, does so as follows.

- The pursuit of social justice is fundamental to ethical social work: The preamble of the NASW Code of Ethics embodies the profession's charge to actively pursue social justice. "Social workers pursue social change, particularly with and on behalf of vulnerable and oppressed individuals and groups of people. Social workers' social change efforts are focused primarily on issues of poverty, unemployment, discrimination, and other forms of social injustice" (NASW, 2017, p. 5).

- Engage in social and political action (Standard 6.04d): Social workers are required to engage in actions that promote fair and equitable policy, opportunities, and the expansion of knowledge and resources to advance social justice in the United States and globally. "Social workers should act to prevent and eliminate domination of, exploitation of, and discrimination against any person, group, or class on the basis of race, ethnicity, national origin, color, sex, sexual orientation, gender identity or expression, age, marital status, political belief, religion, immigration status, or mental or physical ability."

- Stay abreast of current affairs and of social issues (Standard 4.01, Competence): Social workers are required to critically examine and keep current with emerging knowledge relevant to social work, routinely review the professional literature, and participate in continuing education relevant to social work practice and social work ethics. Many publications, documentaries, and webinars that address the multifaceted nature of racism and other systems of oppression are available to help you make informed decisions about how to make change.

- Become knowledgeable and self-aware (Standard 1.05c, Cultural Awareness and Social Diversity): "Social workers should obtain education about and seek to understand the nature of social diversity and oppression with respect to race, ethnicity, national origin, color, sex, sexual orientation, gender identity or expression, age, marital status, political belief, religion, immigration status, and mental or physical ability." As emphasized throughout this text, self-reflection and examination about social justice and antiracism is a critical starting point for building the knowledge and expertise needed to partner with diverse people and communities in anti-oppression efforts.

- Respect colleagues (Standard 2.01b, Respect): Anti-oppression behavior and action starts with the way we treat our colleagues and professional peers. Social workers need to "treat colleagues with respect … avoid unwarranted negative criticism of colleagues … criticism may include demeaning comments that refer to colleagues' level of competence or to individuals' attributes such as race, ethnicity, national origin, color, sex, sexual orientation, gender identity or expression, age, marital status, political belief, religion, immigration status, and mental or physical ability." Social workers need to avoid microaggressions—those verbal, behavioral, or environmental indignities, whether intentional or unintentional, that communicate hostile, derogatory, or negative attitudes toward colleagues who are members of stigmatized or culturally marginalized groups. We need to be vigilant of our own biases and fears, seek out interactions with people who are different from us, be open and nondefensive about discussing how our biases may have hurt others or in some sense revealed bias on our part, and be an ally by standing personally against all forms of bias and discrimination.

- Do not condone, facilitate, or collaborate with any form of discrimination (Standard 4.02, Discrimination): Turning a blind eye to inequality, injustice, racism, and discriminatory practices is both unethical and it supports unethical behavior. Social workers should not practice, condone, facilitate, or collaborate with "any form of discrimination on the basis of race, ethnicity, national origin, color, sex, sexual orientation, gender identity or expression, age, marital status, political belief, religion, immigration status, or mental or physical ability."

- Prevent, expose, and address racism and discrimination and other unethical practices (Standard 2.10, Unethical Conduct of Colleagues): Calling out racism and other social injustices is an ethical responsibility. The Code provides guidance on how to do so ethically with colleagues, directly with the people involved but, if not feasible or likely to resolve the issue, by exploring channels for addressing the issue such as going to the employer, licensing board, or other bodies with oversight of the professional or practice setting.

Ethical Responsibility to Our Clients

Reamer (2018) suggests the following areas of responsibilities to clients.

- Commitment to clients: Keeping client need as a priority in the context of competing responsibilities and such as societal; for example, refusing to provide services to nondocumented clients.

- Self-determination and paternalism: Basing judgment on the practitioner's best interests "for the client," as opposed to the client's informed decision making, for example, withholding information on a client's diagnosis.

- Informed consent: Presenting thorough and understandable information regarding their rights and the risks involved in the intervention/treatment. This involves attention to the client's language dominance as well as other factors related to comprehension (e.g., level of education). Special attention is needed, for example, for clients with diminished capacity and regarding mental health concerns, age, technology, or mandated services.

- Practitioner competence: Practitioners have responsibility to lifelong learning as a means of maintaining competence in their scopes of practice. Moreover, it is important to be clear with clients regarding our expertise and make efforts not to misrepresent our scope of practice.

- Cultural awareness and social diversity: Responsible, competent practice with diverse populations is a specific area that requires life-long learning. Cultural humility recognizes our limitations and the significance of a lifelong commitment to learning via workshops, supervision, and other resources. It is important for practitioners to be aware of differences between personal and professional values and the implications of discrepancies.

- Conflicts of interest: These conflicts occur in many ways that can compromise the relationship with the client. For example, lives of the social worker and client might intersect in unexpected ways, or unintended practitioner personal information might be revealed. Boundary issues often arise, in relation to gift giving and social encounters.

- Privacy and confidentiality: The client trust in practitioner confidentiality as the foundation of a working alliance. It is essential to be clear about under what conditions and how confidential information is released. There are some conditions that must be explained to the client where consent is not required, for example, related to duty to protect. How to address circumstances related to potentially fatal infectious diseases "remains less clear" (p. 50).

Ethical Responsibility to Our Agency in Practice Setting

Reamer (2018) identified the following areas that bind practitioners to ethical responsibility in their practice settings and agencies:

- Supervision and consultation: These are indispensable functions that are a basis for ethical practice. Supervision takes place for all levels of practice that include direct services and administrative. Consultation can be arranged within an agency or external consultative resources. Boundary issues can arise in the supervisory or consultative relationship that could potentially harm the supervisee, as in dual-relationship situations between the supervisor or consultant. For example, an employer asked a licensed clinician to supervise his wife, at another agency, for the purpose of the wife's licensing hours.

- Education and training: Clients have a right to be informed about their practitioner's education and training, for example, when the practitioner is a student at an internship.

- Client records: Documentation is a cornerstone of ethical practice, which includes comprehensive client information and intervention planning that addresses identification of issues, goals, intervention planning, implementation, and outcomes of services. Effectiveness of services can only be determined via thorough, reflective documentation. Timeliness and precision are essential; falsification or alteration of records is unethical. This resource is especially important when clients are transferred from one caseload to another.

- Client transfer: In cases where a social worker is contacted by a client regarding changing their social worker, to avoid conflict of interest, the social worker needs to talk with the client about the "nature of the potential clients' current relationships with other clinicians and the possible benefits and risks of transferring to a new clinician" (Reamer (2018, p. 103).

- Administration: The administrative role encompasses a number of tasks, which can elicit ethical dilemmas. These include decisions on "agency resources, dual relationships, conflicts of interest, and ethical misconduct" (p. 105). Managing these decisions ethically involves transparency in communications with staff regarding bases for decision making on resource spending and creating a senior staff consultation group to assist in determining fair criteria for decision making.

- Commitments to employers: Practitioners' commitment to their organization builds trust among colleagues and enhances agency functioning. However, should practitioners find agency practices unethical, they have a responsibility to question those practices. Reamer (2018) stated that "whether to honor or violate one's commitment to employers in the face of seemingly unethical practices and policies is one of the most daunting ethical challenges social workers encounter" (p. 108).

- In instances of agency collusion with oppression, it is necessary to consider options in raising this concern, which might involve processing conflicts regarding agency loyalty. Consider conflicts you may experience regarding agency policy that serves organizational interests more than individual client needs. Consider what is involved in challenging whose voice is heard, the agency or the clients?

Ethical Responsibility to Our Colleagues

Reamer (2018) proposed the following areas of ethical responsibilities to our colleagues:

- Interdisciplinary collaboration: The interprofessional collaboration (IPC) approach is based on shared responsibility for client outcomes and team planning based on best practices and services within the team. All team members share in implementing the determined goals. The different perspectives that social workers bring from within an agency or across agencies to problem-solve client concerns support enriched and thoughtful intervention planning and treatment. IPC originated as a framework to work across professions, for example, social workers collaborating with probation, corrections, counseling, psychology, psychiatry, or medical professionals as a team in serving individual clients. "Social workers should be certain [in interprofessional teams] to share their professions perspectives and diplomatically assert their relevance" (p. 80). For example, social work ethics require that clients are fully informed.

- Consultation: An invaluable tool for gaining from colleagues' practice wisdom, consultation can support our developing areas of practice, especially in understanding client dynamics, behavior, and situations. Reamer suggested informing clients from the beginning that collegial consultation may be used, along with supervision, and stressed the importance of exercising judgment in how much information to divulge in consultation. Client confidentiality a primary concern in consultation.

- Sexual relationships: Boundary issues direct social workers to refrain from sexual relationships with clients and others with whom you may have "supervisory or administrative authority … because such relationships can be exploitive and damaging" (p. 85). Boundary issues can also be associated with sexual relationships between peers, in that their statuses within an agency can change.

- Impairment of colleagues: Ethical issues can arise when it appears that a colleagues struggles with personal issues, such as health (e.g., mental health, substance use), relationships, or legal problems. These kinds of issues may impinge on their professional functioning. Concern could also arise regarding boundaries in instances of a dual relationship with a client. Ideally, a social worker will first consult with a colleague about the worker's concerns. In instances where communication with the colleague in question is fraught with potential threat, the social worker may need to revert to communication with "employers, an agency board of directors, the NASW Office of Ethics and Professional Review, a licensing board, or another professional organization" (p. 88).

- Incompetence of colleagues: There may be times where social workers note a level of functioning in colleagues that is a concern in meeting professional standards of care. The basis of the malfunctioning could be educational background, lack of agency support, or "limited skill or aptitude" (p. 89). There is an ethical responsibility to act on a situation where it appears that there may be harm to a client.
- Unethical conduct of colleagues: Any number of ethical concerns can arise in relation to collegial behavior, which includes sexual misconduct, fraud, falsification of documentation, and confidentiality issues. Despite denial by the perpetrator or the discomfort of confronting a concern, it may be necessary to contact an individual or organizational representative to alert them to your concerns. Moreover, it may be necessary to contact the licensing board or NASW Office of Ethics and Professional Review if there the individual is unresponsive to the feedback.
- Difficult conversations about diversity and social justice: It is essential to deal with colleagues regarding differing understandings of social justice. We may find that some colleagues find some behavior acceptable that we perceive to be oppressive. Begin the dialogue; share perceptions and perspectives. Discuss shared perceptions with colleagues of microaggressions and explore perceptions of meaningful disruptions of microaggressions.

It is important to learn how to sort through the complexities inherent in our professional responsibilities. The more you learn, the more you change, and the more you change, the more complicated and difficult relationships can become. Perhaps affinity groups, talking circles, or critical incident debriefing processes can be used to address the multitude of levels in which ethical dilemmas arise. Be creative and find processes that work for you in the classroom and in your internship.

Responsibility to Society

*Washing one's hands of the conflict between the powerful and
the powerless means to side with the powerful, not to be neutral.*
—PAULO FREIRE (1985, P. 122)

When faced with the reality of oppressive societal systems, our response
ultimately comes down to two choices: We can determine that the world
is an unjust place, or we can determine that it is a just place and decide
that the folks that aren't doing so well must somehow be responsible for
their suffering. The belief in a just world, a theory discussed in Chapter
3, encourages support of political agendas that focus on individual effort
rather than structural change—such as blaming the poor and the unem-
ployed for having an insufficient work ethic. When we face that as fragile
human beings we are subject to indifferent and sometimes malevolent
forces more powerful than we are, then we can find responsible ways to
embrace the realities of vulnerability while working to address the impact
of injustice. The point is not to assert that the world is just but to help
make it so (Harris-Lacewell, 2010).

Social workers have a responsibility to manifest their humanity in a
democracy as participating citizens. As members of a profession that tackles
the many effects of racism, poverty, and marginalization, we have a unique
responsibility to contribute to solving society's problems. That includes a
responsibility to actively seek the full inclusion of members of society who
have historically been, and are currently, excluded from manifesting their
humanity as participating members of society and denied the agency and
ability to effect change in their worlds.

Social workers have indeed led the way in essential human rights movements and have attracted public attention to pressing issues facing vulnerable
populations. Despite the flaws and limitations that come with being a product
of their time, social workers have been instrumental in several areas of societal
progress such as civil rights for all people regardless of gender, race, faith, or

sexual orientation; workers' rights legislation and programs like unemployment insurance, disability pay, workers' compensation, and Social Security; humane treatment and destigmatization of individuals with mental illness, developmental disabilities, and substance abuse; and access to health care, Medicaid, and Medicare for poor, disabled, and elderly people. Our sense of responsibility to society can be strengthened and inspired by the positive contributions made by some notable social workers throughout history:

- Jane Addams, community organizer, founder of settlement houses for immigrants, peace activist, and one of the first women to receive a Nobel Peace Prize.
- Frances Perkins, the first woman to be appointed to the cabinet of a U.S. president, who as President Franklin D. Roosevelt's Secretary of Labor, was responsible for drafting much of the New Deal legislation in the 1940s.
- Whitney M. Young, Jr., civil rights activist and the executive director of the National Urban League while serving as dean for the Atlanta School of Social Work, president of NASW, a respected expert in American race relations, and an inspiration for President Johnson's War on Poverty.
- Dorothy Height, civil rights and women's rights activist and president of the National Council of Negro Women that tackled issues facing African American women including unemployment, illiteracy, and voter awareness.
- Jeanette Rankin, women's rights activist and the first woman elected to the U.S. Congress, who introduced legislation that eventually became the 19th Constitutional Amendment granting unrestricted voting rights to women across the nation.

Responsibility to Self

The 21st century promises to be a political period of increased organizing against racial and other forms of oppression. To sustain ourselves so that we can show up for the needed anti-oppression work as allies, accomplices, and activists, we must take care of ourselves.

Social work isn't a job for anyone who has trouble coping with stress. And for anti-oppression social workers, much of the stress can be expected to come from the tension between advocating for clients and meeting agency needs, the conflict between social justice philosophy and the organizational work environment (Lloyd et al., 2002). Because of the intimate and sometimes traumatic nature of our client's issues, our own trauma may be triggered by the wounds we have suffered as members of targeted groups or we may experience "secondary or vicarious" trauma. Whether we suffer from our own triggered trauma or from secondary/vicarious trauma, engaging in self-care practices is essential.

Self-care means taking care of yourself so that you can sustain your work as an activist. It is not an ongoing excuse to avoid uncomfortable growth. When realities of our unjust world are too heavy and painful to confront, we need to take time and space to heal or regroup. The ability to stop, rest, and recuperate is essential in order to keep going forward. Permanently distracting ourselves from the ways we are complicit in the oppression of others, however, is not self-care.

Create space for yourself—both physically and mentally. This is especially critical when unjust things happen that you cannot control. At those moments, self-care involves realizing that there are plenty of times when you don't need to be at it on your own. It involves getting to know yourself well enough to be aware of when you need external help. Self-care is an ongoing, shifting process that, among activists, is a political strategy born of the realization that activism without self-care is not sustainable.

Organizations and movements are finding ways to incorporate healing into their direct actions to sustain themselves and create new ways of being along the way. The Black Lives Matter movement has a Healing Justice Working Group, for example, that focuses on healing and wellness as essential to Black liberation from the institutions and systems that explicitly harm and undermine their capacity to live with full humanity, connection and purpose (Black Lives Matter, 2021).

Attending to individual and collective healing does not shift attention and responsibility from the work of dismantling systems of oppression.

Healing and working for social justice go hand in hand. Whether we're engaged in organizing, social service work, nonprofit work, or policy work, the healing process begins as soon as we realize that we are working with systems that have historically been and continue to be oppressive. It starts when we first become aware of the harmful impact of oppressive systems and find ourselves moved by our anger and hopelessness to take action. Although it feels good to channel our feelings by working to confront the power, it is not sustainable over the long haul unless healing justice is at the center of the work.

Taking time to remember and reaffirm our vision is key to centering healing justice. Anti-oppression work is grounded in our vision of creating a socially just world that is reflected in how we treat each other in our meetings, how we listen, and how we value and care for ourselves and others.

Healing justice is strongest if built into our everyday practices. Healing is about taking the time to notice what gets in the way of feeling connected to your life, your community, and your sense of possibility. Healing, at its core, is about slowing down so that we can better listen to ourselves and to others. Slowing down doesn't mean giving up. It means taking a breath so you can then go on.

Healing is about creating the conditions that allow transformation to happen. In addition to slowing down, it involves creating space for something to emerge, telling the truth about what is here and what we are experiencing, giving support to that space of truth, and waiting or listening for what happens next.

It also involves expecting that conflict and struggle will happen. The minute a body that has been under attack begins to rest, all of the pain it has been holding demands attention. That is true for individuals, and it is true for communities. Conflict and struggle are part of the work, a sign that something needs to shift for something new to emerge. Self-care in that moment means staying grounded in your vision, your greater purpose, and your sense of what is possible.

We invite you to use Reflection/Journaling Exercise 7.2 as an ongoing tool as you navigate the rocky terrain to social change.

REFLECTION/JOURNALING EXERCISE 7.2

Envisioning a World

This visioning exercise is a way for you to draw energy from naming and sourcing your visions, a way to take care of yourself by staying grounded in the hope of what's possible.

Begin by doing free writing in response to this prompt: I dream a world* ...

After you have written as much as comes to your mind, finish that part of your writing with the sentence: Such is the world I dream of!

Now read what you wrote after the "I dream a world" prompt and then do some free writing in response to the following questions:

- Why are you here, doing this work?

- Why are you on this planet to make change?

- What have your ancestors led you to?

- Looking at the world you wish to create for your descendants, what is your concrete part in making that happen?

Use this part of your journal as your ground to return to again and again. It is spiritual. It is political. It is about the way that your life connects into the past and the future, into all directions, and alongside all life. It is a way to sustain yourself.

I dream a world comes from a poem by Langston Hughes (https://allpoetry.com/I-Dream-A-World) that inspired Martin Luther King Jr.'s "I Have a Dream" speech.

Empowerment: The Key to Action

When we decide to navigate the complicated responsibilities involved in working for social justice as citizen social workers, we are embarking on a transformative journey. Taking even one small step outside our comfort zone changes our thoughts and feelings, just as new and different thoughts change behavior. When we engage in new and different actions, either to change our own personal situations or to change our communities, those actions change both our perspective on the landscape and our self-definition from that of victim to that of a person with power.

Actions are the steps on the empowerment journey, and the first ones are often the most difficult. Learning how to act in response to social injustice is an evolutionary process. What we are able to do today may be radically different from what we can do next month or next year. We learn that small steps lead to larger actions in a natural progression. As first steps on the journey, we usually think more about racism and other forms of oppression and begin to talk about it with families, friends, colleagues, and others in our immediate circles. Gradually, we're moved to read more about the subject, speak out at public gatherings, write letters, educate others, circulate and/or sign petitions, lobby political representatives, advocate for policy and practice changes in our field placements and agencies of employment, participate in peaceful demonstrations, and organize actions with others. It is important to acknowledge the significance of all efforts, including the smallest ones, and realize that social justice is accomplished by laying one brick at a time, taking one step at a time. It is equally important to know that we are not alone, that we take these steps with others. The power of individuals acting together cannot be overestimated. By taking action, in solidarity with and the support of others, our commitment to effecting change is strengthened, as are our chances for making social change possible. No matter how small each individual effort might seem, it is our combined efforts that produce change. "Small acts, when multiplied by millions of people, can transform the world" (Zinn, 2004, p. 71).

Barriers to Empowerment

In our professional practice we understand that there are barriers to empowerment that clients and other people from marginalized groups experience. It is just as essential to examine barriers that keep us as social workers from being advocates, allies, accomplices, and social change activists. A common block is a personal fear of taking risks, standing out by making a personal statement, being embarrassed in public, losing security or the respect of people who were thought to be friends, or being alienated from family. When we confront issues in a public way, we may be subjected to the ridicule, misunderstanding, and anger of others. For example, interrupting a racist joke or questioning a racist agency policy can be a terrifying and, thus, courageous action to take when it might evoke a negative response or prompt ostracism.

A fear of stepping outside our personal safety zones is another block that can deter us from taking action. We all have spheres of operation in which there is a sense of safety, and stepping outside this area can be risky. For example, wearing a Black Lives Matter button to work may be within my safety zone, but joining a protest may not be. The empowerment process, however, generates confidence and courage. As we become more involved with social justice actions, we discover support from others that sustains us, and we see our safety zones expand.

Another significant barrier can be a fear of creating communication gaps, tensions, and conflict within our own families and workplaces when prejudices within those systems are identified. In such situations it can be helpful to show sensitivity to each person's attitude about the issues and have realistic expectations about how others will respond and the pace of change—in other words, to communicate consideration for others' viewpoints while respecting our own.

For those of us who are members of the dominant culture, the potential of losing the privileges conferred on us based on our social identity in an oppressive system can deter us from taking action. As one social work student wrote in his journal:

> I feel terrible about the inequities I am learning about and I want to work to change the system. I must admit, though, that I am quite ambivalent about what I might have to give up in terms of the privileges and benefits I currently get from the system as it is, since I am a white, heterosexual male. It is easy to think theoretically about social justice, but when I think in practical terms—like maybe I wouldn't get preferential treatment in a job application situation if there were truly equal opportunity—I am ashamed to say that I have to think twice.

It is important to acknowledge the courage it takes to be honest about this obstacle and to face the cognitive dissonance rather than slip back into denial. Positive role models of people in the present and throughout history who were advocates for social justice can help in this regard.

A challenge, which is as much a psychological obstacle as it is a political problem, is figuring out what to do and believing that anything we do will make any difference. As Paul Loeb (1999) wrote in his book *Soul of a Citizen*,

> Society has systematically taught us to ignore the ills we see, and leave them to others to handle. Understandably, we find it unsettling even to think about the huge crises facing us. … We're led to believe that if we can't solve every one of the problems, we shouldn't bother to become socially active at all. … Whatever impulses toward involvement we might have, they're dampened by a culture that demeans idealism, enshrines cynicism, and makes us feel naïve for caring about our fellow human beings or the planet we inhabit. (p. 6)

Two additional barriers frequently impede progress in becoming social justice advocates: a fear of speaking out in public and a fear of not being sufficiently informed about the issues. By encouraging small steps, the empowerment process can be used to overcome these fears. Speaking out in public will seem less frightening if we first talk about ideas and perceptions with those with whom we feel most comfortable. Then, when we are ready, we can begin to speak to other people in small groups and at public meetings. It can be very rewarding to find that acquaintances and even strangers are willing to talk about racism, poverty, and other oppressive systems. Often the message on a pin or button (e.g., "Stop Racism" and "Another Student for Justice") will help begin a conversation. Speaking out is a natural outgrowth of increased commitment and involvement.

To reduce the fear of being uninformed, it is helpful to acknowledge that we can never have enough information or remember all the facts. Statistics change and one fact can counteract another. What is most important is to understand the underlying concepts. Once we develop an anti-oppression view as a framework for thinking, the facts will fall into place. A preponderance of information exists in books, articles, and other resources. To make sense out of the facts, it is helpful to absorb only small amounts of information at one time and take time to process it. We are soon surprised by how much we know.

Actions become the impetus for growth. The more we do, the greater our desire is to know more and to share what we have learned. Because we choose our actions, we set our own limits and control the rate of change. To get started, all that is needed is a strong commitment to work for an end to racism and other forms of oppression and injustice. And we can learn from the examples of others. When we begin to act, our actions join with the actions of others to provide us with energy for the journey.

Benefits of Empowerment

Throughout the empowerment process, we realize that actions are seeds that germinate best within a supportive environment. We become enriched and strengthened by the friendships we make with others who share common social justice goals. We get to know and appreciate and have authentic relationships with others whose backgrounds and lifestyles may be different from those we identify with, for example, people who are old and young, rich and poor, religious and nonreligious, heterosexual and homosexual and bisexual and transsexual, and come from a variety of cultural and racial and ethnic backgrounds. Our strength grows as we celebrate diversity, face our differences honestly, and learn to trust one another.

On the journey we begin to discover that we have developed previously untapped strengths and talents. We can see the same thing happening with others as they take actions they thought they could never take, when they become liberated. Like wildflowers, actions spread, affecting others. There is a ripple effect, and the circle of awareness continues to grow. As personal transformations become interwoven with social change, lives take on new meaning and deeper purpose.

A belief that actions make a difference sustains us. Although individual acts may seem insignificant, we see the tremendous power they have when joined with the efforts of countless others. Over time we can see how social and political changes—such as the abolition of slavery, the right to unionize, women's rights, and civil rights, to name a few—all came about as a result of grassroots efforts. If social justice is to become a reality, a collective commitment to change must be made at the local level. As more and more people unite, we gain the strength to change both the world and ourselves. Classroom Exercise 7.1 provides an opportunity for you to take seemingly small actions related to coded language that are in reality powerful and significant.

CLASSROOM EXERCISE 7.1 CODED LANGUAGE

Coded language is using words to subtly to describe and insult people based on their membership in a targeted group. It is a way that members of the public, media, and politicians talk about race, gender, ethnicity, sexual orientation, and religion that allows them to give voice to, and thus perpetuate, bigoted ideas while denying that's what they're doing. For example, consider the use of the words "thugs" and "looters" to describe peaceful protesters who are predominantly Black. Because "thug" has so often been used to describe Black men in particular, even when they're doing nothing wrong, and "looter" reinforces a desire by many white people to talk about economics instead of race, both terms carry racist connotations. Some other examples of coded language are "urban" and "inner city"; "Black on Black crime"; "radical Islam"; "sharia law"; "illegal immigrant" and "alien"; "bossy, sassy, and uppity"; and "angry Black women."

Because coded language obscures systemic causes of injustices, it impedes systemic solutions. And that is why, ultimately, the anti-oppressive response to coded language must be to call it out, explain what's really going on, and openly discuss how to work through bigoted fears and stereotypes. By not speaking out, we consciously or unconsciously maintain racist and other oppressive policies and practices. However, to speak out we need to know how coded language works and how to confront its use, which is the purpose of this exercise.

Small Group Instructions

1. Divide a piece of newsprint into three columns with these titles:

   • Racist code word or phrase (e.g., "looter")

   • Racist stereotype (e.g., "young Black male")

   • The real criminal (e.g., if the racist code word was "looter," then the real criminal might be "Wall Street" or "payday lenders").

2. Brainstorm several racist code words, such as "welfare recipient," "criminal," "gang member," "thug." Fill in the corresponding blanks under the other two columns.

3. Role play spontaneous dialogues:

   • Person 1: Make a comment using one of the racist coded words/phrases.

   • Person 2: Change the implicit color coding behind the racist stereotype and replace the code word with the "real criminal" reference.

   • Observers: Analyze and evaluate the effectiveness of making the change.

4. Discussion:

   • What insights did you gain from this exercise?

   • In what ways did the exercise empower you?

   • What are some ways you might intervene when you hear someone using coded language?

Moving Forward

In 1968, Rev. Dr. Martin Luther King Jr. and many others called for a revolution of values in America in a Poor People's Campaign, a broad fusion movement that brought poor and impacted people and activists from across the nation to Washington, DC, to bring the issue of poverty compellingly to the fore. Fifty years later, a revived Poor People's Campaign: A National Call for Moral Revival picked up the unfinished work of that campaign. In the spring of 2018, poor and affected people and activists launched the new campaign with 40 days of direct actions in almost all states across the country. The rallying cry of that campaign—"forward together, not one step back"—provides the inspiration for the final section of this book.

Finding Hope

> *What gives me hope is a simple truism. Once we lose hope,*
> *we are guaranteed to lose. But if we ignore the odds and fight*
> *to create an antiracist world, then we give humanity a chance*
> *to one day survive, a chance to be forever free.*
> — IBRAM X. KENDI (2019, p. 238)

As we keep moving forward together for social justice, the challenges and obstacles we face are great. The racism, white supremacy, and other forms of oppression that we seek to dismantle have, after all, been embedded in our country's institutions, including social work ideology and practice, for generations. In the face of the inevitable resistance to justice, we may sometimes feel despair and helplessness. Yet as social workers, we know that the antidote to helplessness and despair is hope: defiant, resilient, persistent hope. We can find hope by turning to history, to the stories that teach us how to find common solutions (see Figure 7.1). Our spirits are buoyed when we think about others who faced equal or greater challenges in the past and continued on to make a better world. We find hope in "seeing the world clear-eyed and yet acting with courage to make change, to believe in spite of the evidence, and then watch the evidence change" (Wallis, 2004, p. 203).

Figure 7.1

Sankofa, the mythical bird from the Akan tribe in Ghana, symbolizes the wisdom that the past serves as a guide for planning the future. With its feet firmly planted forward and its head turned backward, it reminds us that as the forward march for social justice proceeds, the knowledge of the past must never be forgotten.

When we turn to history, however, we need to avoid creating myths about our heroes that make it harder for us to act. For example, the Rosa Parks story, as popularly told, is that one day her feet were tired so she made a spur-of-the-moment decision not to move to the back of the bus, and as a result, she single-handedly gave birth to the civil rights movement and her action led to instant change. None of that is true. Rosa Parks acted as part of a community. She had been active in the NAACP for 12 years and was the secretary for the local chapter. She went to the Highlander School Civil Rights Center the summer before her arrest, where she strategized and brainstormed with people who had been active before. What she did on that bus was a very conscious action that was part of an existing movement for change in which many people were involved—often in seemingly insignificant ways—and it was taken strategically at a time when success was far from certain. In fact, even after the boycott was declared officially over and victory achieved, a dozen Black people were shot as they stood waiting for buses, whites went around Montgomery shooting Black people who dared to get on the buses, and for a while after the boycott, the city shut down bus service altogether.

The point is that it is the real stories of courage that give us hope, not a mythical magical courage like Superman, but the courage of ordinary people who acted despite all their uncertainties and doubts and in the face of real danger. Their stories illustrate how change is the product of deliberate, incremental action. They show us that sometimes our actions fail, other times they bear modest fruit, and at times they trigger a miraculous outpouring of courage and heart—as happened with the arrest of Rosa Parks and all that followed (Loeb, 2004).

With more opportunities than ever in the 21st century for groups to connect online, people step forward in huge numbers when given a real opportunity to make a difference. The story of one such group, MoveOn. org, illustrates how a small action, when combined with the small actions of many people, can turn into a roar (Hayes, 2008). In 2001, the 9/11 terrorist plane hijackings struck the World Trade Center, the Pentagon, and a Pennsylvania field, killing 2,977 people. The day after, a man named Eli Pariser, fearing that vengeance would bring even greater tragedies, created a small website that included a petition to President Bush and other world leaders asking them to use moderation and restraint in responding to the attacks rather than instruments of war, violence, or destruction. Eli was 20 years old and living in Boston. He emailed the petition to 30 friends, and within days his inbox was filled with thousands of emails from strangers. His server started to crash. Within 2 weeks, 515,000 people from 192 countries had signed the petition. In 2004 Eli became executive director of MoveOn.org, a major force for progressive change with a membership that grew from a few hundred thousand to over 7 million as of 2020.

Although such stories of astounding success give us hope, the reality is that the change we seek is slow. And when we get discouraged, it helps to remember the untold numbers of people who slogged through decades and even generations of boring and frustrating actions—no matter the odds, obstacles, or setbacks—to create a more just and equitable society. When we learn our history of persistence, faith, and resilience, we see how far we've come and how we got here. The common thread that weaves together all the stories is the struggle for social justice by incalculable numbers of people who joined together to take action and persevered against all odds. The story of creating a just and equitable society is far from over and the outcome is still uncertain. But social work, as the only profession with a mandate and commitment to social justice, is destined to play a part in shaping the story.

Forward Together, Not One Step Back

> *Do not get lost in a sea of despair. Be hopeful, be optimistic.*
> *Our struggle of a day, a week, a month, or a year, it is the*
> *struggle of a lifetime. Never, ever be afraid to make some noise*
> *and get in good trouble, necessary trouble.*
> —Representative John Lewis

What follows are suggestions intended to help you as citizen social workers play an effective role in efforts to create a just world, especially in hard times when your spirits may begin to flag (Van Soest, 2012).

Use Your Imagination

Allow yourself to imagine a better world and hold on to this imagination no matter what evidence there is to the contrary. Imagine all children being provided with what they need. Imagine the United States investing billions of dollars each year in federal funds to ensure that every child has enough to eat, access to better education and health care, and a place to call home. Imagine that our nation can afford this. Because it can. After the quick

2008 bailout of banks and the auto industry, there should be no doubt that the government can come up with billions, even trillions, of dollars to deal with a problem when it is deemed important enough. Think about this: An investment of $75 billion per year would equal less than what the 2001 tax breaks alone gave to the wealthiest one-in-a-hundred Americans each year (Edelman, 2004). Imagine the world you would like to inhabit and then believe it is possible to create such a world.

Be a Critical Analytical Thinker With a Heart

Don't unquestionably ingest what you see or hear or read in the news. Think about what you are being fed and ask uncomfortable questions. Strive for an enlightened perspective (Sirota, 2010). When someone uses the words "social change" or "social justice," don't assume they mean what you mean. Ask who is saying it and what they mean. Here's an example: Charles and David Koch have for years spent millions of dollars to bring about "social change" to advance what they called their "radical philosophy." Who are they? Billionaire oilmen. What social change platform are they working for? The abolition of Social Security, minimum wage laws, gun control, and all personal and corporate income taxes, for starters. And when you hear them talk about their strategy, listen to how much it sounds like social work strategies: They talk about education and grassroots organizing and lobbying and political action (Alterman, 2010). Think critically. Ask questions.

Change the Narrative

Don't buy into the dominant stories and beliefs at the structural or cultural level that undergird, give rise to, and perpetuate oppressive systems. Consider the narrative about lynchings in the South as an example. The dominant story is that they were carried out by the KKK (in other words, a fringe white supremacist group), which absolves mainstream white people of accountability. But the truth is that they were carried out, not by the KKK, but by bankers, lawyers, judges, businessmen, and the like, and not in isolated woods locations but on city hall lawns where crowds of good white church people, often numbering in the thousands, sat in chairs with their picnic lunches and cheered at the planned carnival-like lynching events. Knowing that Black people have been the victims of terrorism forever changes the narrative that they went north to find economic opportunity to the narrative that they were fleeing the violence of terrorism in the South of which they were targets (Equal Justice Initiative, 2017). Similarly, a broader understanding of how violence is used to oppress and terrorize targeted populations changes the narrative about why refugees come to our country; in other words, instead of simply seeking economic opportunity (which instills fear that they will steal our jobs), they are often fleeing in desperation from terrorism in their countries. Changing the narrative changes not only our understandings and beliefs but also the policies we support and the actions we take.

Know That No Action Is too Small, and That Every Action Counts

We know from the empowerment process that even one small step on the journey changes one's perspective on the landscape. Action, either practical or symbolic, overcomes the inertia and apathy connected with the absence of hope. Don't hold yourself up to the perfect standard. You don't have to do everything, be everything, be impossibly eloquent and confident and certain in a way that nobody is. That is a trap. It keeps us from taking action. Consider what you uniquely can offer, what kind of resources can you effectively put forth (e.g., time, skill, money). No matter how small each individual effort might seem, know that every single one of us can make a difference because it is our combined efforts that produce change.

Be Willing to Take Uncomfortable Steps

Acknowledge that it's human nature to stay in one's safe and familiar comfort zone, decide to do what's uncomfortable anyway, and then watch your comfort zone expand.

Don't Let "Those Who Have Power" Intimidate You (Zinn, 2004)

No matter how much power they have, they cannot prevent you from living your life, thinking independently, speaking your mind. Don't believe the messages you may have been told that what you feel doesn't matter or that what you believe is ridiculous or that what you envision is worthless or impossible. Follow the still small voice that whispers the truth to your heart.

Pair a Deep-Seated Sense of Social Justice With Pragmatism

Don't assume that people are either with you or against you. People are not arrayed along a simple ideological spectrum from right to left, nor do they occupy any given spot consistently. Many people who are not ideologically driven, but who may hold strong opinions on various issues, make up a vast center (Hardisty & Bhargava, 2010). Be willing to work with that center to enact reforms that are a beginning rather than an endpoint in the process of societal transformation. As American history consistently teaches us, this is pretty much the only way things change in our system. Over time, reforms like Social Security, Medicare, the voting rights act, and health care reform have added up to a kind of revolution, one that succeeded without bloodshed or widespread destruction of order, property, or necessary institutions (Alterman, 2010).

Reframe Issues to Effectively Reach More People

Our brains allow us to have contradictory worldviews and go back and forth between them. Many people have both conservative and progressive worldviews but on different issues. George Lakoff (2004), in his book *Don't Think of an Elephant,* calls such people "biconceptuals." To reach the millions of biconceptuals we need to reframe the issues to match the progressive part of their worldviews. Lakoff maintains that frames (or worldviews) take precedence over facts every time. Don't just negate the opposing position's claims, he urges, but instead tune in and reframe issues according to what's important to people.

Never Give Up

Creating an antiracist, anti-oppressive country and world that is fit for all our children and grandchildren is a task for marathoners—not sprinters. Keep coming back. Remember that there is no magic panacea that will solve all our social injustices and eliminate all oppressive systems at once. Change is a complex and long-term struggle that requires persistence.

Know When to Step Back

There are times when we feel our red-hot rage—no matter how justified—at the trampling of people's rights and their value as human beings. When that happens, it's time to take a breath and de-escalate, take a look at the spiraling anger of others, and make the choice not to ratchet it up. The theatrics of rage can easily backfire. Righteousness, when not rooted in humility and not focused on results and persuasive power, offends more than it attracts and falls victim to its own arrogance. As Cornel West (2004) said, "we need ... the courage to be impatient with evil and patient with people" (p. 296).

Hold Our Leaders Accountable

Hold yourself accountable for holding our leaders accountable. Some politicians at all levels will tell you that you shouldn't even bother to ask for anything that costs money—that deficits are terrible, our economy is sinking, we're at war, and it is just the wrong time to ask. Don't believe them. History proves otherwise. Consider this: The Social Security Act of 1935 was passed in the depths of a depression; disability coverage under Social Security and women being included in welfare (AFDC) were both passed during the Korean conflict; federal involvement in higher educa-tion started during the Cold War when millions of dollars were tied up in competition with the Soviet Union; and the Civil Rights Act, Medicaid and Medicare, the Elementary and Secondary Education Act, the WIC program, and the Economic Opportunity Act were all passed during the Vietnam War era. Each of these laws was lobbied for and passed during a time when our government was engaged in costly foreign wars or so-called bad budget years. Many of those laws took years to win but when people held their leaders accountable even during times of turmoil, the people made change happen (Amidei, 2010).

Believe That, in the Long Run, Justice Will Win Out

Cast your lot, as Adrienne Rich (2004) wrote, "with those who age after age, perversely, with no extraordinary power, reconstitute the world" (p. 274).

Resources and Organizations

Anti-oppression social work can be challenging and emotionally taxing. Although the issues are diverse and complex, the central tenets are the same. And we are not alone. More and more people and organizations are coming together to confront racism, poverty, and all other forms of inequality and injustice. The following sampler list of organizations and movements is an introduction and will also lead you to others.

- Center on Poverty and Policy (CPSC) (https://www.povertycenter .columbia.edu/) at the Columbia School of Social Work produces cutting-edge research to advance our understanding of poverty and the role of social policy in reducing poverty and promoting opportunity, economic security, and individual and family well-being.
- Movement for Black Lives (M4BL, https://m4bl.org/black-power -rising/) is a network of individuals and organizations creating a shared vision and policy agenda to win rights, recognition, and resources for Black people. The movement is based on five organizational pillars: mass engagement, local power, a multiracial strategy that builds across movements, leadership development, and electoral strategy.
- MoveOn (https://front.moveon.org/), with its millions of members, engages in rapid-response organizing and campaigning, communications interventions, digital innovation, and rigorous data science and testing. It promotes a culture of grassroots participation that has repeatedly produced real-world impact, changing outcomes and making our country better.
- Poor People's Campaign (https://www.poorpeoplescampaign.org/) is a broad, fusion movement that confronts the interlocking evils of systemic racism, poverty, ecological devastation, militarism and the war economy, and the distorted moral narrative of white religious nationalism. A state-based, national movement that works to shift the moral narrative, influence policies and elections at every level of government, and build lasting power for poor and impacted people.

- Race Forward (https://www.raceforward.org/) brings systemic analysis and an innovative approach to complex race issues to dismantle structural racial inequity and create equitable outcomes for all. Race Forward publishes the daily news site Colorlines and presents Facing Race, the country's largest multiracial conference on racial justice.

- Social Welfare Action Alliance (SWAA, https://www .socialwelfareactionalliance.org/) is a national organization of progressive workers in human services. Founded in 1985, the Alliance is based on key principles that reflect a concern for social justice, peace, and coalition building with progressive social movements. These principles articulate a need by social service workers for a practice and theory that responds to progressive concerns. SWAA was once named the Bertha Capen Reynolds Society. Reynolds was a pioneer American social worker, educator, writer, researcher, activist, outspoken trade unionist, and public speaker on issues of social justice, civil rights, and peace. Reynolds maintained the belief that "a diagnosis of an individual's unhappiness … cannot ignore a diagnosis of the sickness of society and what it is doing to the person's life."

- SocialWorkDegree.net. (https://www.socialworkdegree.net/social -justice-organizations/#civil) Social Justice in Action: A list of 100 websites and organizations dedicated to promoting equality and demolishing injustice (https://www.socialworkdegree.net /fair-housing-resources/). Organized by five areas: civil rights and community organizations, women's rights groups (https://www .socialworkdegree.net/social-justice-organizations/#women), health rights and advocacy (https://www.socialworkdegree.net /social-justice-organizations/#health-advocacy), elder and disabled advocacy, and other social justice themes.

- Social Workers & Allies Against Solitary Confinement (SWASC, https://socialworkersasc.org/) is a national task force of social workers and allies dedicated to confronting the issue of solitary confinement, both on a macro level as a core mechanism of our racist and classist system of mass incarceration, and on a micro level as a practice that social workers in correctional settings actively and passively participate in, while being simultaneously charged with upholding the human rights and dignity of all people.

Strategizing and Planning to Act for Social Change

Be the change you want to see in the world. As we learn more about the challenges that groups targeted by oppressive systems have faced—and continue to confront—in terms of prejudice, discrimination, violence, and inequality, remember that the changes that have been achieved throughout history came through people envisioning the possible and then strategizing and planning each step of the uphill climb to success. The goal of Assignment 7.1, the final exercise in this book, challenges you to manifest active citizenship through planning and strategizing thoughtful, cooperative, critically engaging, and responsible action aimed at bringing about social change.

ASSIGNMENT EXERCISE 7.1

Planning a Social Change Project

This assignment requires you to identify and analyze a social problem, formulate thoughtful strategies, question assumptions, and develop plans to act responsibly on your beliefs as a social work citizen.

The following steps and tasks, although presented in linear form, are not necessarily a lock-step progression. It may be necessary to return to tasks previously completed. Each step requires thoughtful action and the application of critical thinking to problems and issues.

Step 1: Pick a topic.

Choose a social issue or a targeted population in your local area about which you care deeply. It may be related to your social work internship or volunteer experience, your job, the neighborhood where you live, or something you've studied in the curriculum. Or you may use a social justice lens to generate a list of concerns and then choose the one you feel most passionate about for your project. Consider the following questions when making your decision:

- Is it something I care deeply about?

- Is it relevant to and will it manifest anti-oppressive principles and goals?

- Is it doable (feasible) and worth the effort? In what ways?

Step 2: Conduct research to learn all you can about your chosen issue.

Clarify the problem. Recognize its complexity and articulate a clear statement of the problem:

- What do I already know about the issue and what do I need to find out?

- Where can I get reliable information, such as written sources, organizations, online information, and interviews?

- Do the research to find out what I don't know.

- What factors contribute to the situation: What are the underlying causes of the situation (e.g., economic, personal, political, physical)? How are the causes interconnected?

Although you can do some of this work on the Internet, by searching research data, looking at activist websites, and reading the local newspaper, the best way to learn is actually to go to where the problem is or where the people are. Walk around the area, talk to people on the street, go to a meeting or other event addressing the problem, and visit local stores and restaurants. Really try to learn something about the community or the people most affected by the problem.

Step 3: State the problem.

Write a summary statement of the problem: What exactly is the problem—obstacle, difficulty, or shortcoming—that needs to be resolved? Your statement should be clear; that is, would people reading it understand it? Be specific; for example, does it include some of the key factors to work on? Include the interconnected causes.

Step 4: Brainstorm possible actions.

Based on what you learned about the issue and how it is being addressed, make a list of possible ways to confront the problem. Include the actions that people and organizations are already taking. Begin with some small-scale ideas and then build from there. Brainstorm potential actions under each of the following types of social actions:

- Educate (e.g., develop educational workshops, present at local organizations, churches).

- Advocate (e.g., organize a letter-writing or petition campaign to local or national representatives).

- Unite (e.g., organize an event that brings people together to raise money for or get people to join an organization working on the issue).

- Speak out (e.g., develop a public service announcement, work with local media to get it on the air).

- Engage (e.g., change your behavior in some way and start a campaign to encourage others to do so as well).

- Serve (e.g., raise money for or join a nonprofit or activist organization that is working on the issue).

Step 5: Choose an action and create a plan for carrying it out.

List the nuts and bolts of how you will carry out your plan of action, including time, cost, resources, and the people you need to call on. List the steps you will take. What are some obstacles you might face, and what are some possible methods for overcoming them?

Step 6: Carry out your action.

Monitor and evaluate your action as you go along. Keep a journal as you go along. Record what you did, how it went, the problems and challenges you encountered, and how you dealt with them and other significant experiences.

Step 7: Write a paper about your social action project that includes the following:

- Background: What is the issue and why is it an important problem that needs to be addressed? Include research evidence showing that this is a problem. State the problem clearly.

- Target population: Who, specifically, was your social change plan aimed at?

- Description of your plan of action: What type of action did you choose? What were the overall goals of your plan?

- Implementation: What methods/steps did you take? What challenges did you face and how did you deal with them? Did you accomplish your plan?

- Self-Evaluation: What were the two or three most important things you learned from this assignment? What would you do differently if you were able to do it again?

Conclusion

The reality of social injustice and the power of oppressive systems that we face, as social workers and citizens, is bleak and often desperate. But we are not alone. We are part of a larger community of "like-minded souls stretching across the globe and extending backward and forward in time" (Loeb, 2004, p. 3) to create a just world. Because we know that our common problems can only be solved through our common efforts, we end this book by sharing the optimism and hope we find in the words of historian Howard Zinn (2004):

> An optimist isn't necessarily a blithe, slightly sappy whistler in the dark of our time. To be hopeful in bad times is … based on the fact that human history is a history not only of cruelty but also of compassion, sacrifice, courage, kindness. What we choose to emphasize in this complex history will determine our lives. … If we remember those times and places—and there are so many—where people have behaved magnificently, this gives us the energy to act, and at least the possibility of sending this spinning top of a world in a different direction. And if we do act, in however small a way, we don't have to wait for some grand utopian future. The future is an infinite succession of presents, and to live now as we think human

beings should live, in defiance of all that is bad around us, is itself a marvelous victory. (p. 71–72)

References

Alterman, E. (2010). Money well spent, *The Nation, 291*(13), 10.

Amidei, N. (2010). *So you want to make a difference.* CreateSpace Independent Publishing Platform.

Black Lives Matter. (2021). Resources. https://blacklivesmatter.com/resources

Dudziak, S. (2002) Educating for social justice: Challenges and openings at the beginning of a new century. *Critical Social Work, 3*(1).

Edelman, M.W. (2004). Standing up for children. In P. R. Loeb (Ed.), *The impossible will take a little while: A citizen's guide to hope in a time of fear* (pp. 37–46). Basic Books.

Equal Justice Initiative. (2017). *Lynching in America: Confronting the legacy of racial terror* (3rd ed.).

Friere, P. (1985). *The politics of education.* Bergin & Garvey.

Hardisty, J., & Bhargava, D. (2010). Holding the center. *The Nation, 291*(3/4), 23–26.

Harris-Lacewell, M. (2010, May 31). Believing justice, blaming the victim, *The Nation,* 10.

Hayes, C. (2008, August 4/11). MoveOn @ Ten. *The Nation, 287*(4), 11–18.

Kendi, I. X. (2019). *How to be an antiracist.* One World.

Lakoff, G. (2004). *Don't think of an elephant: Know your values and frame the debate.* Chelsea Green.

Loeb, P. R. (2004). *The impossible will take a little while: A citizen's guide to hope in a time of fear.* Basic Books.

Loeb, P. R. (1999). *Soul of a citizen: Living with conviction in a cynical time.* St. Martin's Griffin.

Lloyd, C., King, R., & Chenowith, L. (2002). Social work, stress and burnout: A review. *Journal of Mental Health 11*(3), 255–265.

National Association of Social Workers. (2017). *Code of ethics of the National Association of Social Workers.*

Reamer, F. (2018). *The social work ethics casebook: Cases and commentary.* (2nd ed.). NASW Press.

Rich, A. (2004). From natural resources in the face of a doorframe: Selected poems.

Sirota, D. (2010, November 1). Paranoids of the world unite. *The Seattle Times, A11.*

Smith, R. (1996). The end of politics and the civil sector: The challenge to social work in the third millennium. In J. Ishmael (Ed.), *International Social Welfare in a Changing World* (pp. 255–268). Detselig.

Van Soest, D. (2012). Confronting our fears and finding hope in difficult times: Social work as a force for social justice. *Journal of Progressive Human Services, 23*(2), 95–109.

Wallis, J. (2004). Faith works. In P. R. Loeb (Ed.), *The impossible will take a little while* (pp. 203–206). Basic Books.

West, C. (2004). Prisoners of hope. In P. R. Loeb (Ed.), *The impossible will take a little while* (pp. 293–295). Basic Books.

Zinn, H. (2004). The optimism of uncertainty. In P. R. Loeb (Ed.), *The impossible will take a little while* (pp. 63–72). Basic Books.

Index